The Symbionese Liberation Army and Patricia Hearst, Queen of the Revolution

The Symbionese Liberation Army and Patricia Hearst, Queen of the Revolution

Gregory Cumming

Stephen Sayles

Great Oak Press, Pechanga, California

For information, contact Great Oak Press, P.O. Box 2183, Temecula, California 92593, www.greatoakpress.com.

Library of Congress Cataloging-in-Publication Data

Names: Cumming, Gregory, author. | Sayles, Stephen, author.
Title: The Symbionese Liberation Army and Patricia Hearst, Queen of the Revolution / Gregory Cumming, Stephen Sayles.
Description: Pechanga, California : Great Oak Press, 2019. | Includes bibliographical references and index.
Identifiers: LCCN 2018052377 (print) | LCCN 2018052653 (ebook) | ISBN 9781942279259 (E-Book) | ISBN 9781942279242 (pbk.)
Subjects: LCSH: Hearst, Patricia, 1954- | Symbionese Liberation Army.
Classification: LCC F866.4.H42 (ebook) | LCC F866.4.H42 C86 2019 (print) | DDC 322.4/2092--dc23
LC record available at https://lccn.loc.gov/2018052377

ISBN: 978-1-942279-24-2

Back Cover: Posters reading "We Love you Tania" with Patricia Hearst holding a machine gun appear on college campus bulletin boards. University of California, Berkeley, April 15, 1974. (Bettmann/Getty Images)

Published by: Great Oak Press, Pechanga, California

Printed in the United States of America

CONTENTS

LIST OF FIGURES

ACKNOWLEDGMENTS

I want to thank Wanita Terry from the United States Attorney's Office who granted access to files at the Federal Records Center (FRC) in San Bruno, along with the FRC staff David Drake and Patricia Bailey. They made accessing these extraordinary primary source materials very easy. The archival staff at the Hoover Building in Washington DC were very helpful as well and provided excellent service throughout my research visit. Lark Park proved to be an invaluable source early on in the process as she tracked down many hard to find articles and other news items when this project first began as my doctoral dissertation.

A number of individuals also took time to talk to me either on the record or off relating to this project. I want to thank the following individuals for their time and assistance in helping me better understand the events surrounding the SLA: David Bancroft, Robert Blackburn, James Browning, Tim Findley, Daryl Gates, Terence Hallinan, and William Harris.

I'd also like to thank Sabra Ladent for her meticulous work editing the manuscript and asking tough questions that needed to be asked. Dr. Thomas Long, has been an invaluable resource along the way as well. It has been my good fortune to have known Tom for over fifteen years as both editor and friend. Along with my Dissertation Chair from the University of California, Riverside, Dr. Clifford Trafzer, I have been extremely lucky to have two historians of the highest order to guide me from graduate school to publication. I want to thank you both for your friendship, counsel and assistance over these past few years.

Steve Sayles has been a mentor and friend since we both began our "tenure" at the University of La Verne in the Fall of 1982. Steve as Assistant Professor of History and yours truly as wide-eyed freshman. Steve has been a mentor, friend, confidant and sounding board. This book is your legacy as an educator and historian.

My family has had to take on a great deal of responsibility during the process of writing this book, beginning with my dissertation many years ago. My wife Lupe and my children Taylor and Jake have had to deal with constant references to Patty Hearst and the Symbionese Liberation Army for almost twenty years and served on the "frontlines" as I had deadlines to meet, chapters to write and constant edits to make. Thank you for providing the time to complete this journey. My parents and siblings also provided their insights, and like most siblings, their critiques. As I contemplate what everyone in my family gave up to make this happen, I can indeed look back and know that I am one of the luckiest men on the face of this earth.

Dr. Gregory Cumming

I want to express my thanks to my friend and collaborator, Greg Cumming, for his generosity, helpfulness, and collegiality in preparing this book, and I am very thankful that he invited me to be an equal partner in this project. I also wish to acknowledge the support of the Reference Desk at the University of La Verne's Wilson Library. Those who served at this post reaffirm novelist James Lee Burke's assessment that reference librarians are "the most valuable and unlauded investigative resource in the United States," that "their ability to find obscure information is remarkable and [that] they persevere like Spartans." I also want to thank Kristin Howland and my colleagues in the University of La Verne's History and Political Science Department for their sympathetic ear and helpful advice over the past several years. But, unquestionably, without the support of my wife, Barbara, and my son, Dan, this book would not have been written. Dan and his computer skills "saved the day" more than once. Thank you all for your help and encouragement.

Dr. Stephen Sayles

CAST OF CHARACTERS

Angela "Gelina" Atwood – The daughter of a labor leader in New Jersey and close friend of Kathleen Soliah. Known as "Angel" to her family, Atwood attended the University of Indiana, where she met her future husband, Gary Atwood, along with Bill and Emily Harris. She died in a shootout with police and FBI agents in Los Angeles on May 17, 1974.

Michael Bortin – Friend of James Kilgore and Kathleen Soliah. Bortin was involved in symbolic bombings prior to joining his friends in working with the Harrises and Patricia Hearst in 1974–75. He had a boisterous and angry relationship with Bill Harris.

Donald "Cinque" DeFreeze – A small-time thief and bomb maker who became radicalized while incarcerated in California from 1970 to 1973. His escape from Soledad Prison and arrival in the Bay Area led to the founding of the Symbionese Liberation Army (SLA). The unquestioned leader and catalyst for the SLA, De Freeze died in the shootout in Los Angeles on May 17, 1974.

Camilla "Gabi" Hall – From Minnesota where she attended Gustavus Adolphus College. Hall came to California to expand her horizons both artistically and sexually. She became embroiled in a sporadic relationship with Patricia Soltysik and gave Soltysik the nickname "Mizmoon." Hall died in the shootout in Los Angeles on May 17, 1974.

Bill "Teko" Harris – Born and raised in Indiana. He enlisted in the U.S. Marines Corps after high school and was sent to Vietnam, but he seriously injured his knee soon after his arrival in the country. He then attended the University of Indiana, where he met and married his first wife, Emily. Close friends with the Atwoods, the Harrises arrived in the Bay Area in 1972.

Emily Montague "Yolanda" Harris – Attended the University of Indiana where she met her future husband, Bill Harris. She spent a summer in the 1960s working at Disneyland in Anaheim, California.

Patricia Hearst – Granddaughter of William Randolph Hearst and daughter of Randolph Hearst, California newspaper moguls. Hearst was living with her fiancé, Steven Weed, when she was kidnapped at age nineteen.

James Kilgore – Onetime boyfriend of Kathleen Soliah. He joined the Harrises and Hearst following the May 17, 1974, shootout in Los Angeles. Kilgore escaped arrest in 1975; however, law enforcement caught up with him, and he was arrested in South Africa in 2001.

Russell "Osceola" Little – Attended the University of Florida where he first came into contact with the radical left. He moved to the Bay Area in the early 1970s with his girlfriend, Robyn Steiner. Little served as Donald DeFreeze's chief lieutenant and participated with Remiro and Defreeze in the assassination of Marcus Foster. He was arrested with Joe Remiro in Concord for the murder of Foster. Little was eventually released from jail when his conviction was overturned on a legal technicality.

Nancy "Fahizah" Ling Perry – Attended Whittier College, the alma mater of Richard Nixon, as a freshman and transferred to the University of California, Berkeley for her sophomore year. Perry became heavily involved in drugs and reportedly sold drugs to Patricia Hearst prior to Hearst's kidnapping. She died in the shootout in Los Angeles on May 17, 1974.

Joe "Bo" Remiro – A San Francisco native who served in the U.S. Army's Long Range Reconnaissance Patrol (LRRP) during the Vietnam War. Likely suffering from post-traumatic stress disorder (PTSD), he became heavily involved in drugs prior to joining the SLA. He was convicted of the 1973 murder of Oakland superintendent of schools Marcus Foster and is still incarcerated.

Jack Scott – Radical sports psychologist and later athletic director at Oberlin College. He was author of *The Athletic Revolution* and close friend of National Basketball Association standout Bill Walton. He met Bill and Emily Harris and Patricia Hearst after their return to the Bay Area in June 1974. He assisted in their move to the East Coast during the summer of 1974 and their return to California the following September. He hoped to write a book about the SLA.

Kathleen Soliah – Currently known as Sara Jane Olson. Soliah was the eldest sister of Josephine and Steven Soliah. A close friend of Angela Atwood, she delivered a stirring eulogy for Atwood and her SLA comrades following their death in the shootout in Los Angeles on May 17, 1974. She helped the surviving members of the SLA escape from California during the summer of 1974 and became involved with the group upon its return to California in September 1974.

Steven Soliah – Younger brother of Kathleen Soliah. He was a member of the group that assisted the Harrises and Patricia Hearst following the May 17, 1974, shootout in Los Angeles. Soliah was living with Patricia Hearst and was her boyfriend at the time of her arrest.

Patricia "Mizmoon" Soltysik – Also known as "Zoya." Soltysik arrived in Berkeley as a young freshman from Goleta, California. A feminist drawn to radical politics while a student, she provided a place for DeFreeze to live following his escape from prison. She died in the shootout in Los Angeles on May 17, 1974.

Steven Weed – Fiancé of Patricia Hearst at the time of her kidnapping. In the initial phase of their investigation, the FBI considered him a prime suspect, but he was eventually cleared of any involvement. Patricia Hearst never spoke to Weed following her abduction.

Thero Wheeler – A convict and associate of Donald DeFreeze while in prison. The SLA reportedly helped Wheeler escape from prison in 1973. Wheeler disagreed with DeFreeze's goals for the SLA and eventually split off from the group prior to the assassination of Marcus Foster.

Willie "Cujo" Wolfe – The son of a well-to-do doctor and the youngest member of the SLA. He became heavily involved in the prison reform movement upon his arrival in Berkeley, and reportedly he formed a strong bond with Patricia Hearst. Wolfe died in the shootout in Los Angeles on May 17, 1974.

TIMELINE

February 20, 1954 – Patricia Campbell Hearst is born in San Francisco.

March 5, 1973 – Donald DeFreeze escapes from Soledad Prison. Within days he moves in with Patricia "Mizmoon" Soltysik at her Parker Street residence in Berkeley, California.

March–November 1973 – The Symbionese Liberation Army (SLA) is formed. The initial group was composed of Donald DeFreeze, Patricia Soltysik, Russell Little, Joe Remiro, Nancy Ling Perry, Willie Wolfe, Angela Atwood, and Bill and Emily Harris. Camilla Hall would not go underground with the SLA until late February 1974.

August 2, 1973 – Thero Wheeler escapes from Vacaville Prison. DeFreeze tells Wheeler the SLA was involved with his escape. The exact nature of SLA involvement and what role it played is unknown.

November 3, 1973 – Oakland superintendent of schools Marcus Foster is shot and killed in an ambush by Donald DeFreeze, Russell Little, and Joe Remiro. Foster's deputy, Robert Blackburn, is also shot, but he survives.

November 6, 1973 – SLA issues communiqué about their decision to assassinate Marcus Foster in light of the outpouring of grief throughout the Bay Area for Foster.

January 10, 1974 – Russell Little and Joe Remiro arrested in Concord, California. Remiro is captured in possession of the Walther handgun used in the Foster assassination.

January 23, 1974 – Remainder of the SLA, except for Camilla Hall, goes underground and moves into a new safe house on Northridge Drive in Daly City, California.

February 4, 1974 – Patricia Hearst kidnapped from the Berkeley apartment she shared with her fiancé, Steven Weed.

February 7, 1974 – Radio station KPFA receives SLA "arrest warrant" for Patricia Hearst. To support their claim that it has Hearst, the SLA includes her Mobil Gas credit card in her father's name.

February 12, 1974 – The SLA sends its first audio communiqué. DeFreeze demands that Randolph Hearst establish a statewide food program for the poor. The program is estimated to cost over $400 million. The food program is to be only a good faith gesture for future negotiations. Randolph Hearst responds that the food program as outlined is beyond his financial means.

February 16, 1974 – Second audio communiqué received from the SLA goes into greater detail on the food program.

February 19, 1974 – Randolph Hearst responds to SLA's request by establishing the People-In-Need (PIN) food program with $2 million.

February 21, 1974 – In the third audio communiqué from the SLA, DeFreeze refers to PIN as "a few crumbs for the people" and demands that another $4 million be added to the food program.

February 22, 1974 – The first PIN food distribution is held. Violence breaks out at the Oakland distribution site, resulting in numerous injuries. Other distribution sites are peaceful.

March 6, 1974 – While in Washington, D.C., California governor Ronald Reagan responds to the PIN program by saying, "It's just too bad we can't have an outbreak of botulism."

March 9, 1974 – The fourth SLA audio communiqué is found in the restroom of Foster's Cafeteria in San Francisco.

March 20-21, 1974 – The SLA moves from its Daly City safe house to an apartment on Golden Gate Avenue in San Francisco.

April 3, 1974 – Patricia Hearst announces in the fifth SLA audio communiqué that she has decided to stay and fight with the SLA instead of being released.

April 15, 1974 – Patricia Hearst, along with other members of the SLA, is photographed robbing Hibernia Bank in San Francisco.

Late April 1974 – The SLA moves from its Golden Gate apartment to the Hunter's Point section of San Francisco. Within days, it will move to a safe house at 1808 Oakdale.

May 8, 1974 – The SLA leaves the Bay Area for Los Angeles.

May 16, 1974 – Bill Harris is seen shoplifting a pair of socks at Mel's Sporting Goods in Inglewood, California. As the staff attempts to handcuff and arrest Harris, Patricia Hearst opens fire with a submachine gun from across the street, thereby giving Bill and Emily Harris the opportunity to escape to the getaway van.

May 17, 1974 – A shootout unfolds at 1466 East Fifty-Fourth Street in South Central Los Angeles between the SLA and the Los Angeles Police Department and FBI. DeFreeze, Soltysik, Perry, Wolfe, Atwood, and Hall die in the gun battle and fire.

Memorial Day weekend, May 1974 – The surviving members of the SLA—Bill and Emily Harris and Patricia Hearst—return to the Bay Area by automobile.

June 2, 1974 – Kathleen Soliah speaks at a rally at Ho Chi Minh Park in Berkeley in response to SLA deaths during the May 17 shootout. Soliah had been a close friend of Angela Atwood.

June 8, 1974 – The last audio communiqué is received from the remnants of the SLA. Known as the "Eulogy Tape," it is left at radio station KPFK in Los Angeles.

June 1974 – Radical sports psychologist Jack Scott arranges for the transportation of Emily and Bill Harris and Patricia Hearst to the East Coast. They will spend the summer in rural New York and Pennsylvania.

September 1974 – Bill and Emily Harris and Patricia Hearst return to California from the East Coast and set up residence in Sacramento, California.

April 21, 1975 – Local resident Myrna Opsahl is killed during a bank robbery in Sacramento by Emily Harris.

May 1975 – The Harrises and Hearst return to San Francisco.

August 29, 1975 – The father of Kathy, Josephine, and Steven Soliah meets with his children in San Francisco at the request of the FBI.

September 18, 1975 – At 1:15 p.m., Bill and Emily Harris are arrested at the Precita Avenue safe house in the Bernal Heights section of San Francisco. Afterward, Patricia Hearst and Wendy Yoshimura were arrested at the Morse Street safe house in the Mission District of San Francisco that they shared with Steven Soliah.

January 15, 1976 – The trial of Patricia Hearst for her role in the Hibernia Bank robbery begins.

March 20, 1976 – Patricia Hearst is convicted for actions during the Hibernia Bank robbery and is ultimately sentenced to seven years in prison.

February 1, 1979 – Patricia Hearst is released from prison after President Jimmy Carter commutes her sentence to time served.

January 20, 2001 – On his last day in office, President Bill Clinton pardons Patricia Hearst.

INTRODUCTION
SETTING THE STAGE

The SLA was almost a cultural test tube, a specimen sample from a bitter side of the sixties that marched apace after virtually all their comrades veered aside. Yet they marked time oddly, retracing rather than resolving the past. Culturally rootless, out of their time, they leaped into the social void—and in an eerie half-life of their plunge, among themselves, if nowhere else, they recreated something of the pained and pimpled adolescence of the New Left.

Vin McLellan and Paul Avery, *The Voices of Guns*

THE SYMBIONESE LIBERATION ARMY (SLA), AS it existed originally, endured for a brief 192 days. It formed in the months leading up to November 1973 in Oakland, California, and saw its first major action with the assassination of the first African American superintendent of schools, Marcus Foster, on November 6. Its first phase ended on May 17, 1974, in Los Angeles, in a shootout that proved fatal to all but three of its members.

A year before the SLA took shape, the radical New Left splintered into many different factions, the most violent of which, the Weathermen, went underground. With the landslide reelection of President Richard Nixon in November 1972 and the announced end in January 1973 of U.S. involvement in the Vietnam War, the circumstances that had produced the antiwar movement began to fade away. As the war winded down, protest movements began to focus on civil rights issues, particularly through the lens of California prison reform. Berkeley, which remained a bastion of the counterculture atmosphere and lifestyle, was the epicenter of these movements. Indeed, Berkeley would give rise to the Symbionese Liberation Army, though the SLA would not remain there through its demise, less than a year after it formed

Not until the SLA assassinated Marcus Foster would it find itself isolated from other revolutionary groups within the New Left and treated as pariahs by stalwart figures such as Huey Newton, Angela Davis, and Jerry Rubin.[1] In fact, if a leftist revolution had ever truly erupted in the United States, it would have been from August 1973 through August 1974, when the revelation of a taping system in the White House led to a year-long constitutional crisis and ended with the resignation of President Nixon. Despite the national calamities that flared up during this time, the revolution that the SLA sought never started. Even though the group made nationwide headlines almost daily from February through mid-June 1974, droves of revolutionaries did not flock to join the SLA. Instead of leading a revolution, the SLA became a distraction—America's first reality television show disguised as news.

THE BERKELEY PROTEST MOVEMENTS

After 1964 and the launch of the Free Speech Movement (FSM), Berkeley served as a model of student dissent on college campuses nationwide. Students initially fought a stringent administration policy that restricted their rights to hand out political literature on the corner of Bancroft and Telegraph Avenues. Many FSM leaders had spent the previous summer involved in the civil rights movement, bravely facing down the Ku Klux Klan (KKK) in the Deep South as they worked to register black voters. As a result, the protests at Berkeley over students' right to hand out political literature expanded into a greater struggle for the right to free speech for all college students.

The arrest of Jack Weinberg on October 1, 1964, at Sather Gate, just outside the entrance to the University of California, Berkeley sparked a powerful student protest movement.[2] Berkeley student Mario Savio—most famous for his FSM speeches atop a police cruiser—exacerbated the student protest movement when he declared in the fall of 1964, "Last summer I went to Mississippi to join the struggle for civil rights. This fall I am engaged in another phase of the same struggle, this time in Berkeley."[3] Savio directly challenged the status quo often associated with the Eisenhower administration when he told the University of California Board of Regents and administrators in December, "There is a time when the operation of the machine becomes so odious, makes you so sick at heart that you can't take part, and you've got to put your bodies upon the gears and upon the wheels, upon the levers, upon the apparatus, and you've got to make it stop."[4] At that time, Savio probably did not realize that his words encapsulated the growing discontent of a generation of college students.

Although over 200 colleges and universities were represented during the Freedom Summer of 1964, nearly 60 percent came from Harvard, Yale, Stanford, Princeton, Berkeley, Michigan, and Wisconsin.[5] The growing counterculture elite, which would form the backbone of the student protest movements of the 1960s and 1970s, had established their credentials during the civil rights movement.

Figure 1: National Guard and protesters square off near Peoples Park on May 15, 1969 in Oakland/Berkeley, California. (Vincent Maggiora, San Francisco Chronicle/Polaris)

On March 3, 1965, John Thomson, a nonstudent radical from New York heavily influenced by the Free Speech Movement, undertook his own protest. Thomson wanted to make a statement: "F-U-C-K." These four letters, written on a piece of paper, led to the "Filthy Speech Movement." The students and the agitators who lived in and around Berkeley were increasingly viewing its professors and administrators as overbearing and conservative, and this movement was an attempt to push back. According to W. J. Rorabaugh, these campuses were protesting the notion of *in loco parentis*—that is, the concept that the "university should maintain parental supervision over the student."[6] The Berkeley students were going to fight autocratic power as they saw it, whether it was exerted in Mississippi or in their own backyard.

By August 1965, the Berkeley student protesters had shifted their focus to the U.S. involvement in Vietnam. The Gulf of Tonkin Resolution, which was approved by Congress with little debate in August 1964, led to America's longest war and provided student protesters with an issue to rally against. Meanwhile, the civil rights movement continued to be an important facet of the student protest movement, but not its only mission. Rather, students in northern California embraced the entire counterculture movement, and the many different movements within it.

The San Francisco Bay Area, in particular, would be forever linked with the student protest movements of the 1960s. The region

Figure 2: Third World Liberation (TWLF) student strike for the addition of a black studies department at the University of California Berkeley, 1970. (Stephen Shames/Polaris)

also served as home to 1967's Summer of Love and the development of the Black Panther Party. There, students at San Francisco State University held a 134-school-day strike over the issue of low minority student admissions, and it was there where one of the first African American Studies departments opened. The San Francisco Bay Area was also the scene of the People's Park riot, the closure of the University of California, Berkeley in response to the invasion of Cambodia, and hundreds of symbolic bombings aimed at the destruction of property.

At its 1969 national convention, the Students for a Democratic Society (SDS) split into various factions.[7] The battles over the future of the New Left included squabbles over "action versus political organization" and "Mao versus Lenin." As a result, the national organization that provided leadership to the New Left and direction to student protestors ceased to exist. In its place arose the Weathermen and the Progressive Labor Party. The action-oriented, violence-prone Weathermen served as a model for other organizations, such as Venceremos, which was founded in 1970 from a merger of the Chicano Brown Berets and a faction from the Revolutionary Union, which had split from SDS in 1969.[8]

Venceremos became a leader of New Left politics in the Bay Area through the spring of 1972. It was the largest and most radical group in northern California.[9] In 1971 the organization had been actively involved in the antiwar movement throughout the Bay Area. Like many of the other New Left groups in the post-SDS period, Venceremos unraveled over leadership and organizational issues. Out of this power vacuum within the New Left arose a new, more violent revolutionary group.

The Symbionese Liberation Army grew out of the Berkeley/ Oakland radical political culture, particularly in the streets surrounding the University of California, Berkeley campus. Future members of the SLA witnessed the collapse of the New Left because of disagreements about theory and action, along with the angry debate over the relevance of Marx, Lenin, Mao, and George Jackson. This new revolutionary group was enthralled by the film *State of Siege*, and hoped to be the vanguard of a violent revolution against the "fascist Amerikkkan state." In taking armed action, it sought to emulate the Tupamaro rebels of Uruguay. Many members of the SLA had served as members of the Maoist, direct action–oriented Venceremos organization, which has disintegrated entirely during the summer of 1973.[10] Venceremos should not be confused with the Venceremos Brigade, which had ties to Cuba and the SDS. The group that some future SLA members had been involved in functioned only in California.

THE SLA: ITS ORIGINS AND ACTS OF REVOLUTION

The story of the SLA is one of violence, tragedy, and failure. The founding members of the SLA—Bill and Emily Harris, Angela Atwood, Russell Little, Joe Remiro, Patricia Soltysik, Camilla Hall, Nancy Ling Perry, and William (Willie) Wolfe—can best be described as a small clique of young, self-absorbed, guilt-ridden, emotionally scarred white men and women who found their salvation in the ideas held by a black escaped convict, Donald DeFreeze. While an inmate, DeFreeze was befriended by Russell Little and Willie Wolfe, who were active in the prison reform movement. After his assisted break from prison, DeFreeze, the self-styled "Fifth Prophet," would serve as General Field Marshal Cinque Mtume of the SLA until taking his own life in May 1974.

The SLA grew as it absorbed members from the streets of Berkeley and Oakland, moving in and around the "Peking Man House," a commune on Chabot Road, where they were introduced to the Black Cultural Association and the prison reform movement. Others became involved as a result of the waning Vietnam War protests and the need to redirect their efforts. Later on, the lesbian communities of Channing Way in Berkeley became involved.[11] With the war coming to an end, protests at most of the nation's colleges had died down. However, for the radical movement Berkeley served as a ray of sunshine breaking through the clouds and despair arising from Richard Nixon's reelection. Members of the SLA found themselves drawn toward this unique community.

The SLA's first act of revolution was the assassination on November 6, 1973, of Oakland superintendent of schools Marcus Foster. The fact that Foster was an African American led many to believe that the assassination was a part of a Nazi or right-wing agenda.[12] However, the next day, the SLA issued its first communiqué to Berkeley radio station KPFA, announcing the death warrant from "The Court of the People" against Foster. Believing its actions to be just and revolutionary, the SLA was not prepared for the backlash: the radical communities of Oakland and Berkeley viewed the assassination with horror and grief. Although the mainstream media ignored this new radical leftist group, the New Left leadership viewed Foster's assassination and the SLA with contempt, not support. From this, the SLA learned that action itself would not generate the enthusiasm among the masses. In fact, Foster's death prompted widespread mourning and outrage—not the publicity, notoriety, and revolution SLA members had hoped for. Because the assassination changed the way in which the SLA was perceived, it could no longer claim to be a reform-minded organization in search of change. Instead of energizing the New Left throughout the Bay Area, the SLA emerged from the aftermath of Foster's murder isolated and alone.

The SLA's next act, the kidnapping of heiress Patricia Campbell Hearst, on February 4, 1974, brought the media attention the SLA craved. Unwittingly, perhaps, the kidnapping also sparked the attention of local, state, and federal law enforcement officials. However, despite the SLA's best efforts, the kidnapping did not conjure up respect from the New Left. Nor was the SLA suddenly perceived to be the vanguard of the revolution, as it had hoped.

Despite the national media attention, the SLA remained elusive as it moved around the San Francisco Bay Area from November 6, 1973, to May 16, 1974, when its members left for Los Angeles. Seven days later, the U.S. Federal Bureau of Investigation (FBI) and the Los Angeles Police Department (LAPD) received valuable information about the location of the SLA safe house. Law enforcement officials descended on it, and the largest shootout in California history ensued. All but three SLA members were killed, and those three, horrified, watched the shootout on a television set in a hotel room in Anaheim, California.

THE FBI'S INVOLVEMENT

The ability of the FBI to respond to the new domestic threat posed by the SLA had been severely curtailed in the years leading up to November 1973. On March 8, 1971, a group called the Citizens Committee to Investigate the FBI broke into a resident agency in Media, Pennsylvania, and absconded with numerous FBI documents. Shortly thereafter, these stolen documents found their way into the hands of various journalists and politicians.

When the *Washington Post* published a story on these stolen documents, the revelations led iconic FBI director J. Edgar Hoover to eventually cancel the FBI's secret counterintelligence program known as COINTELPRO. The FBI was able to maintain secrecy initially, but NBC reporter Carl Stern began investigating the meaning of these new documents, particularly those with the subject heading COINTELPRO. Meanwhile, U.S. Attorney General John Mitchell stonewalled Stern's requests for COINTELPRO documents. Stern countered by submitting a Freedom of Information Act (FOIA) request for all documents that related to COINTELPRO.

Stern's FOIA request began to bear fruit in December 1973, and the FBI released documents through March 1974.[13] In response to the public revelations of the FBI's involvement in domestic spying, the harassment of political dissidents and Hoover suspected of being disloyal to the United States, the agency came under greater scrutiny. An independent prosecutor took over its Watergate case in which members of the Committee to Re-Elect the President (CREEP) had been arrested for breaking into the headquarters of Democratic National Committee. This event continued to roil Washington and the Nixon administration and made it even more important for the FBI to solve the Hearst kidnapping case quickly. However, the resources that might have been available to the agency via COINTELPRO were suddenly not there. In the meantime, the SLA left few trails for the FBI to follow as it sequestered itself from society and the New Left. Not until after the Los Angeles shootout did the SLA receive any meaningful assistance from what remained of the New Left.

After the death of six of his SLA comrades in Los Angeles in May 1974, Bill Harris announced his leadership of the new SLA, or its second team. His first order was to return the SLA's base of operations to the Bay Area. He had the help of several new members and sympathizers, including Angela Atwood's close friend Kathleen (Kathy) Soliah. By now, Patricia Hearst, as described in the chapters that follow, had shifted from kidnap victim to SLA member. As one of only three survivors of recent events, Hearst had to take on a more active role in the development of the second team, all while establishing her own identity as a revolutionary feminist and helping to identify several safe houses in the Bay Area. For the next sixteen months, the remaining SLA members were able to stay a step ahead of law enforcement. On September 18, 1975, the FBI arrested the Harrises and Hearst. During booking, Hearst declared her occupation to be "urban guerilla."

THE OUTCOME

Patricia Hearst's trial, which began on January 15, 1976, was a futile attempt to understand the rebellion stirring among the nation's youth for the previous ten years. It was thought that if one could understand why Hearst had turned her back on her family, then perhaps the riddle of the cultural phenomena of rebellion could be solved. Unfortunately, the trial produced more questions than answers. Hearst was given the maximum sentence of up to thirty-five years, pending a reduction at her final sentencing trial, which resulted in a seven-year sentence. In 1979 President Jimmy Carter commuted her sentence to time served, and on January 20, 2001 (his last day in office), President Bill Clinton granted her a full pardon.

The narrative of the SLA, and Patricia Hearst's willing participation in the SLA after her kidnapping, in large part represents the last vestiges of the counterculture spirit in the United States. This small band of revolutionaries gained recognition from the national media in a way that no other domestic criminal or terrorist group had ever done, and in less than a month they coerced Randolph Hearst and the Hearst Corporation into funding and distributing food to the poor. Although the SLA made the national headlines almost daily from February through June 1974, society did not condone its violent nature. Its disregard for human life made it no different from the institutions it claimed to oppose. Though the SLA did capture the nation's attention by monopolizing the news industry, undermining the Watergate scandal, and raising other relevant social issues, it failed to lead the revolution it sought.

1

THE BERKELEY "PATRIOTS"

FROM THE 1960S THROUGH THE MID-1970S, Berkeley and the San Francisco Bay Area were a mecca for idealistic youth protesting their government, their university, and other distrustful establishments. As the scene of the Free Speech Movement, the Beats in the North Beach section of San Francisco, the protests against the Vietnam War in 1965, and the Summer of Love in 1967, Berkeley and the San Francisco Bay Area gained a reputation as the destination for New Left and antiestablishment activities. For future members of the Symbionese Liberation Army (SLA), who saw themselves as patriots, Berkeley and the San Francisco Bay Area symbolized an opportunity for education and greater involvement in radical New Left politics—and the possibility of real revolution.[1]

Except for SLA founder Donald DeFreeze, who was African American, the members of the SLA were white middle to upper-class Americans. Most had trouble maintaining their marriages and close relationships with loved ones. Some of those difficulties stemmed from the stark changes in their political views, as well as their burgeoning radicalism. Of all the members, only two, Nancy Ling Perry and Joe Remiro, grew up in the Bay Area.

NANCY LING PERRY

Nancy Ling grew up just north of San Francisco in Santa Rosa. At just under five feet tall and weighing approximately 100 pounds, the petite Perry did not exactly fit the stereotype of an urban guerrilla. She left the Bay Area in 1966 to attend Whittier College, Richard Nixon's alma mater. But after her freshman year she returned home to attend the University of California, Berkeley. She graduated from Berkeley in 1970 with a bachelor's degree in English literature. While attending Berkeley, Ling fell in love and married an African American jazz musician by the name of Gilbert Perry. Their marriage was tumultuous. Although Gilbert Perry was himself unfaithful, he often accused Nancy of infidelity, and even painted a scarlet "A" on the door of their cottage after he moved out. The couple separated in 1971, but divorce papers were never filed.[2] After her graduation from Berkeley, Nancy began using and selling drugs. During the summer of 1973, she overcame her drug habit and dedicated her time and energy to the Symbionese Liberation Army.

JOE REMIRO

In many ways, Joe Remiro's life mirrored that of Nancy Ling Perry's. However, instead of pursuing an education, he chose the army and soon found himself in Vietnam as a member of a long-range reconnaissance patrol (LRRP). Toward the end of his tour in Vietnam, Remiro began experimenting with hallucinogenic drugs, and he continued to experiment with drugs after his tour. Upon returning to the Bay Area, Remiro eloped with a friend from high school, Kathy Exley. Much like Nancy Ling Perry's marriage, his also ended quickly.

Despite his time in the military, Remiro did not support the war in Vietnam. In September 1972, he helped found the Oakland chapter of the Vietnam Veterans Against the War—it was called the Winter Soldiers Organization. He had hoped that the Vietnam Veterans would serve as a revolutionary vanguard, advocating for change in government policy and control. In March 1973, when Remiro discovered that the other members of the Winter Soldiers Organization did not share his appetite for revolution, he left the chapter and turned his attention to the injustices surrounding California prisons.[3] In April 1973, Remiro volunteered at Wounded Knee, the scene in South Dakota of an armed confrontation between members of the American Indian Movement and the government that played out on the Sioux reservation. While there, he helped by running ammunition from bunker to bunker during firefights.[4] In addition, Remiro became an active member of Venceremos.

PATRICIA SOLTYSIK

SLA member Patricia "Mizmoon" Soltysik joined Remiro in his efforts to reform California's prison system. From Goleta, California,

Soltysik found freedom at the University of California, Berkeley from an angry and repressive father.[5] Berkeley liberated Soltysik in other ways as well, altering her worldview and exposing her to new and exciting experiences as she began to experiment sexually with both men and women.

It was at her home on Parker Street in Berkeley that Donald DeFreeze hid out after his escape from Soledad Prison in March 1973. Soltysik's home was also where the SLA formulated its initial plans.[6] Meanwhile, while attending Berkeley, Soltysik embraced a radically feminist demeanor, even engaging in a sexual relationship with Camilla Hall.

CAMILLA HALL

In 1968 Camilla Hall came to California from her hometown in Minnesota searching for acceptance. By the time she moved to Berkeley, she was openly gay.[7] While at Berkeley, Hall discovered the legendary Channing Way, a communal neighborhood featuring a "rare collective identity."[8] The collective and tolerant spirit of the neighborhood was exactly the vibrant and welcoming atmosphere Hall had hoped to find in the Bay Area. When Camilla Hall met Patricia Soltysik, the latter had recently ended a relationship with Christopher Thompson, a Black Panther Party participant who seemed to know everyone involved in the SLA but never became personally involved. Hall gave Soltysik her nickname, "Mizmoon," during their intimate relationship—a relationship that ultimately failed because of Soltysik's inability to stay faithful to Hall. While they were dating, Soltysik continued to have sex with men, including Donald DeFreeze after he arrived in Berkeley. There is some speculation that Hall may have joined the SLA not because members of the SLA shared her political views but because of her love for Soltysik.[9]

WILLIE WOLFE

Camilla Hall may not have been very invested in the SLA, but other members, such as Willie Wolfe, played an important role in the development of the SLA's ideology. Wolfe, the son of a successful anesthesiologist, arrived in Berkeley from Connecticut in January 1971. Unlike his father and brothers who attended Yale, Wolfe seemed academically indifferent after he concluded his prep school studies at Mount Hermon.[10] Wolfe traveled around the United States and Europe instead of enrolling at the Ivy League school. He finally settled on Berkeley, convinced that "this is where it's at."[11]

At Berkeley, he began taking classes in anthropology. According to Russell Little, it was in his anthropology class that Wolfe became interested in prison reform.[12] In March 1972, Wolfe attended a Black Cultural Association (BCA) meeting for the first time; it was held at Vacaville Prison. He was, according to his biographer, at the prison working on "a story about a new prison program designed to give black convicts pride in their blackness and hope and help for making it on the outside."[13] Wolfe would later convince Little and other residents of the Peking Man House to become involved in the BCA and prison reform movement.

RUSSELL LITTLE

The only southerner to join the SLA, Russell Little was born and raised in Pensacola, Florida. After graduating from high school, Little attended junior college for a year before receiving a scholarship to the University of Florida in Gainesville. He initially planned to major in electrical engineering; however, as Little tells the story, "my second year [at the University of Florida] would have to be called the turning point in my life—politically and socially. I took a course in philosophy that fall, 1969, which seemed to drive home some of the contradictions which I had and was experiencing. The course was taught by a young Marxist graduate student with background similar to mine."[14] Like Wolfe, Little was influenced by the courses he took in college and the people who taught them. According to Little, it was at this time in his life that he turned his back on the "Great American" myth, prompting his shift in majors and perspective on life.[15]

Little's new worldview led him to join other young college students throughout the United States in protests against the war in Vietnam, the shootings at Kent State and Jackson State, and the arrests of members of the Black Student Union at the University of Florida.[16] In the course of these protests, Little became convinced that America needed to change.

RUSSELL LITTLE AND ROBYN STEINER

The war in Vietnam, the reelection of Richard Nixon, revelations regarding the FBI's domestic spying known as COINTELPRO, and eventually the Watergate scandal served as proof to radicalized students in the 1970s that the U.S. government was broken. In the summer of 1971, Russell Little and his girlfriend, Robyn Steiner, took a trip out west to Berkeley. His first impression was not a positive one. Neither he nor Steiner could find work, and the anticipated riots following the violent prison death of George Jackson never materialized. Jackson was arrested in 1961 as a teenager and spent the rest of his life in prison. He helped establish the Black Guerilla Family prison gang in 1970 and wrote two books, *Blood in My Eye* and *Soledad Brother.* Jackson's death became a catalyst for leftist groups to question the large number of African Americans incarcerated in California and to protest the state's prison conditions. In many ways, Jackson had become a "political prisoner" instead of a convict, and his prison writings contributed to the SLA's founding fundamentals.

Because of their disillusionment with Berkeley, Little and Steiner returned to Florida for the fall semester.[17] Little spent the following year reading and studying national liberation movements and traveling throughout the country with Steiner. In August 1972, Little and Steiner returned to Berkeley, where they moved into the Peking Man House commune. There, individuals practiced and preached Maoist-influenced politics. Through Willie Wolfe, Little and Steiner became involved in the prison reform movement and the BCA at Vacaville Prison.[18]

ANGELA ATWOOD

Another SLA member with a background that did not point toward joining a revolutionary movement was Angela DeAngelis Atwood. Angela DeAngelis grew up in the small town of North Haledon, New Jersey. She was the oldest of three daughters in a tight-knit Italian family. Her father served as business manager for Local 999 of the Teamsters Union.[19] When her mother died in 1965, Angela assumed most of the household duties. Angela's upbringing resembled that of the other SLA members—growing up in a middle-class family in a predominantly white neighborhood. A devout Catholic in her youth, Angela possessed an outgoing, vivacious personality that made her very popular in high school. There, she maintained excellent grades and was captain of the cheerleading squad.[20] When it came time to choose a college, she decided to leave home to attend Indiana University. It was at Indiana that Angela met future fellow members of the SLA Bill and Emily Harris and her future husband, Gary Atwood, an aspiring actor who was heavily influenced politically by the writings of Russian communist revolutionaries Gorky and Trotsky. Angela and Gary married in 1970.

Gary's leftist politics created a wedge between Angela and her family in New Jersey, and she became alienated from them.[21] In the summer of 1972, Gary and Angela Atwood moved to the San

Francisco Bay Area. Gary dropped out of the University of Indiana and accepted an unpaid position with a government-funded theatre as an alternative service arrangement for conscientious objectors. Although Gary was able to avoid military service, the couple was forced to rely on Angela's meager waitressing job for support. Their financial situation strained the relationship, and their marriage soon fell into disrepair. By 1973 Gary had returned to Indiana. Angela, however, would remain in the Bay Area.[22] Though they never legally divorced, the marriage was over.

BILL HARRIS

Before Angela and Gary's separation, Bill Harris had moved with his wife, Emily, from Indiana to the Bay Area. This was not their first trip to California. Emily had spent a summer working at Disneyland, and Bill had enjoyed a seven-and-a-half-week California sojourn in 1965. Bill's parents provided a solidly middle-class upbringing and anticipated that Bill would attend college, which he did. By all accounts, his first two years at Indiana University were exceptional, except for his lack of academic achievement. Upset by his poor academic performance, Bill's father refused to continue paying his tuition until Bill became serious about school.

Harris then spent two years in the Marine Corps and served in Vietnam. However, a torn ligament in his knee—the product of an otherwise uneventful touch football game—effectively disqualified him for a combat role.[23] Nevertheless, Bill's time in the military left him questioning America's role in Vietnam and the future role of government. The racism he observed there also left him indignant. After returning to Indiana University in 1968, Bill joined the Vietnam Veterans Against the War and became a vocal leader in the antiwar movement on campus.[24]

EMILY HARRIS

Emily was raised in the Chicago suburb of Clarendon Hills, Illinois, in the comfortable confines of an upper-middle-class family. An excellent student, she was a member of the Chi Omega sorority at Indiana University. Bill and Emily met on a blind date in 1968. Before meeting her husband-to-be, Emily was described by classmates as a "non-political sorority sister."[25] But as her relationship with Bill grew, so did her interest in politics.

Just like the Atwoods, the Harrises married in 1970. As the war in Vietnam was winding down and radical New Left politics was beginning to decline on college campuses, Bill and Emily decided to move to the San Francisco Bay Area. There they reconnected for a brief time with their friends Gary and Angela Atwood. In fact, after Bill returned from his 1965 trip to California, he "knew he would return."[26] Apparently, Emily felt the same way: "We left Indiana for the Bay Area in 1972 because we wanted to learn more about what was happening in a place that seemed to us as midwesterners to be the nucleus of radical activity."[27]

To the rest of the world, Berkeley did indeed fit that description. However, Tim Findley, an investigative reporter for the *San Francisco Chronicle,* dismantled the narrative of this generation of young people as radicals when interviewed for the documentary film *Guerrilla: The Taking of Patty Hearst*: "I don't think that most of the young people involved, who considered themselves part of the counterculture, saw themselves so much as revolutionaries, or renegades, as people think they did, or as the establishment kept accusing them of being. They actually saw themselves, if they did not admit it as such, as patriots."[28]

It would be absurd to suggest that the SLA's actions were patriotic. However, SLA members strongly believed they were fighting for their country on behalf of those whose voices had been silenced by the corrupt authority and policy of the U.S. government. Berkeley proved to be a great starting place for the SLA, but, despite their good intentions, the founding members of the SLA could not possibly relate to those they were fighting for. To legitimize themselves, the SLA needed a leader, someone with "real life" revolutionary experience.

A key component of Venceremos was the need for "Third World" leadership of the organization. Following in its footsteps, the SLA was looking for an African American or Chicano to lead its revolution. When Donald DeFreeze arrived in Berkeley, his status as a political prisoner and escapee of the California penal system gave the white members of the SLA just the person they were imagining. The SLA needed DeFreeze to lend it credibility. Without him, the SLA would have never existed. Ironically, however, DeFreeze's radical actions and demands would also alienate the SLA from other leftist organizations and most of the American people.

2
CINQUE MTUME

BY 1972 THE SOCIOPOLITICAL CLIMATE IN Berkeley defined all aspects of the SLA and its members except for one—Donald DeFreeze. Some have questioned DeFreeze's role in the SLA and whether he served as a plant, an agent provocateur, or a figurehead.[1] How could an uneducated former prisoner have led a group of well-educated white people into a revolt against their country?

At that point, the future soldiers of the SLA were actively seeking an opportunity to rebel. Many made the choice by simply moving to the Bay Area. However, it was not until DeFreeze came along that the SLA could take shape, uniting the various individuals and their political agendas to form one coalition. In a carryover from Venceremos, DeFreeze had the two requisite qualities of leadership: he was an African American, and he had escaped from prison. It would only take a few months for DeFreeze and a handful of Bay Area radicals to form America's first domestic terrorist organization.

EARLY LIFE AND MARRIAGE

Donald DeFreeze was born and raised in Cleveland, Ohio. Unlike the other members of the SLA, he was the product of a deeply troubled home. The eldest of eight children, young Donald served as his father's personal punching bag on more than one occasion. As a teenager, DeFreeze stole a gun. When police caught him with the firearm, DeFreeze told them he intended to use the gun to kill his father.[2] During this period of his life, he was constantly in trouble and involved in many small crimes. He eventually dropped out of high school, left Cleveland, and bounced around New York and New Jersey.

At the age of eighteen, DeFreeze met and married Gloria Thomas, who was already the mother of three young children. He appeared to settle down in New Jersey. However, like most other members of the SLA, DeFreeze's marriage proved to be an unhappy one, prompting him to start "playing around with guns and fireworks and dogs and cars" as a distraction. In the fourteen-page autobiography he wrote in 1970—intended to sway a judge into giving him a lighter sentence—DeFreeze wrote that he did these things to "get away from life and how unhappy I was." He blamed his wife for his legal troubles, maintaining that because she "wanted nice things . . . the next thing I know I had become a thief."[3] Russell Little later supported this assertion, claiming, "Defreeze couldn't live the American dream that you see on TV just by working, so he also became a thief."[4]

In 1967 DeFreeze and his family moved to California in search of a fresh start, but his fascination with guns and explosives led to conflicts with law enforcement on more than one occasion. In June 1967, he was arrested for possession of a bomb and a handgun. In December, he was arrested again. This time, DeFreeze robbed a prostitute after paying for her services. The prostitute escaped and contacted police. She then brought them back to the motel where he had fallen asleep. The police arrested him and searched his car in the motel parking lot. To their surprise, they discovered twelve stolen handguns—just a small part of a haul of 200 guns stolen from a Los Angeles gun shop. DeFreeze told the police his wife knew the person who sold him the stolen guns and could lead them to where he lived. In return, DeFreeze requested leniency. However, when he arrived at his apartment with the police, Gloria was not there. While they waited for her return, DeFreeze jumped out of the apartment's second-story window and escaped. His freedom was short-lived, however. The police quickly recaptured him at a friend's home after Gloria tipped police to his whereabouts.[5]

When released on bond, DeFreeze fled to New Jersey along with his family. From there, they moved to Cleveland where he found himself in trouble once more. On October 11, 1969, he was arrested trying to flee from an attempted robbery of the Cleveland Trust Bank after police received a call about a man on the roof of the bank. When the police arrested him, DeFreeze gave them a false name, Steven Robinson. His mother bailed him out of jail before law enforcement could verify his identity. Taking to the road again, DeFreeze uprooted his family and returned to southern California.[6]

PRISON AND THE BCA

DeFreeze's freedom in California did not last long. On November 15, 1969, a little over a month after his arrest in Cleveland, he robbed a woman at gunpoint, stealing her purse, which contained a $1,000 cashier's check. Two days later, DeFreeze attempted to cash the check at a Bank of America in Los Angeles, but the check had been reported stolen. During the transaction, DeFreeze became nervous and fled the bank. The bank security guard chased him down. A running gun battle ensued as the Los Angeles Police Department quickly joined in the pursuit. During the exchange of gunfire, DeFreeze was wounded in his left hand and foot.[7]

Meanwhile, prior to his trial DeFreeze had become embroiled in a bizarre case in New Jersey in which he was accused of helping New Jersey Black Panther Party leader Ralph Cobb kidnap the black caretaker of a New Jersey synagogue. When accused of being a member of the Black Panther Party, DeFreeze replied, "I have been questioned about being a member of the Black Panthers or US [an African American organization that emphasized African heritage] or a member of the Muslims, and I have never been a member of anything but a Church!" DeFreeze went on to say that he was "too nervous" to be involved in such aggressive activities.[8] Either way, at his trial for his botched bank transaction, DeFreeze finally had his day of reckoning with the judicial system and was sentenced to five years to life in prison.

During his incarceration from 1970 through early 1973, DeFreeze underwent a dramatic change. He became politically aware of the world around him for the first time and became involved in the Black Cultural Association in Vacaville Prison. As part of his transformation in prison, DeFreeze assumed a new name, Cinque Mtume. After he interviewed DeFreeze in jail, the lawyer for the Black Panther Party observed that he had "difficulty reconciling my image of DeFreeze, a hustler, with Cinque."[9] If DeFreeze had been involved in either the Black Panthers or Ron Karenga's Black Nationalist organization, US, it would have been on the periphery

Figures 3-4: Police mugshot of Donald David DeFreeze aka Cinque Mtume. San Francisco, California, 1974. (Associated Press)

and through the sale of stolen guns or homemade bombs—his specialties prior to incarceration. All in all, Vacaville Prison served as the chrysalis for DeFreeze the petty criminal to morph into Cinque the revolutionary.

DeFreeze aspired to a leadership role in the BCA, but he came to the organization without a reputation as a prison leader. In June 1972, he caused a commotion when he tried to gain the leadership of the organization via election. When he was banned from running for election because he had not attended the requisite number of meetings laid out in the BCA constitution, he challenged the BCA ruling and complained to prison officials.

The inmate leader of the BCA, Robert Jackson, already had a replacement in mind, so when DeFreeze complained to prison officials, the other members of the BCA labeled him a snitch. After the commotion of the BCA election, the outside coordinator of the BCA, Colston Westbrook, brokered a deal that would end the internal sniping. DeFreeze would establish a subunit of the BCA called Unisight. This new group would focus on the assimilation of African American prisoners into their families after their release from prison.

Unisight gave DeFreeze an opportunity to demonstrate his new leadership capabilities. It also helped him establish connections on the outside because Willie Wolfe and Russell Little became involved in this group. Both Wolfe and Little were impressed with DeFreeze. In fact, Little wrote a letter to the California State Parole Board in October 1972 urging that DeFreeze be paroled, despite the fact that he was not then eligible for parole. By that time, the last vestiges of the old Donald DeFreeze had disappeared and Cinque had taken his place.[10] Unisight was significant for him and the SLA. It helped establish the connections DeFreeze used to escape from prison, and it also established a framework for support outside of prison that would later morph into the SLA.

Much like Donald DeFreeze, the BCA itself was undergoing changes in the latter months of 1972. These changes had a clear impact on the development of the SLA. BCA coordinator Colston Westbrook was coming under escalating attacks from other members of the group, and rumors were swirling around Westbrook that he was involved with the U.S. Central Intelligence Agency (CIA).[11]

Finally, in December 1972 the BCA's executive board requested the removal of Westbrook. Prison officials agreed, and Jim Mayfield replaced Westbook.[12] In disbelief, Westbrook stated that "the Maoists" had "taken over" the BCA.[13] Meanwhile, the influence of outsiders such as Wolfe and Little grew as their relationship with prisoners strengthened. Furthermore, their politics were decidedly left of center and heavily influenced by Mao Zedong.

ESCAPE

In December 1972, the State of California transferred DeFreeze from Vacaville Prison to Soledad Prison. Even though Soledad was nearly 200 miles south of Vacaville, the move did not cut DeFreeze off from the network of Bay Area contacts he had established. Indeed, it was his friends from the BCA and Unisight who proved instrumental in his successful escape from Soledad on March 5, 1973, the establishment of a safe house, and the eventual development of a new revolutionary group, the Symbionese Liberation Army.

Upon his transfer to Soledad, DeFreeze was reclassified as a minimum security risk, meaning prison officials did not see him as much of a threat or an escape risk. As a result, DeFreeze was assigned to work outside the main prison complex on a boiler located at the Correctional Officers Training School. His first day on the job would be his last. On March 5, 1973, as soon as prison guard Jim Tucker dropped him off at the site, DeFreeze climbed over the fence surrounding the compound and departed on foot. His escape went unnoticed for approximately twenty minutes.[14] Meanwhile, DeFreeze managed to travel to the small farming town of Gonzales, just a few miles north of Soledad.[15]

DeFreeze quickly found refuge with a Mexican American family in Gonzales, who willingly provided him with food and a place to sleep for the night even though they were not part of the escape plan. The next morning, DeFreeze phoned Mayfield, asking him for a ride into the Bay Area. Mayfield willingly picked him up and gave him a change of clothing.[16] But, although Mayfield came to DeFreeze's aid, they agreed that because of their past relationship and Mayfield's close association with the BCA, it was best that DeFreeze find another place to stay.

Mayfield chauffeured the escapee around the Bay Area, but DeFreeze quickly exhausted his list of safe contacts. None of DeFreeze's friends or allies was willing to harbor a fugitive. It also became evident that many of the people who spoke of revolution with the inmates of Vacaville Prison were not wholeheartedly invested, especially when it meant helping an escaped convict. Desperate, Mayfield and DeFreeze drove to the Peking Man House in Berkeley.

David Gunnell was the owner of the commune. DeFreeze found Gunnell to be "kinda freaky."[17] Gunnell initially seemed reluctant to house DeFreeze for the night, possibly because DeFreeze had announced that he was ready to start the revolution.[18] Much like those who visited the prisoners in Vacaville, most of the counterculture youth surrounding Berkeley were more about talk than action. Discussing revolution and partaking in revolution were two very different things.

Many of the students at Berkeley wanted to make a difference, but they had never been thugs and thieves like many of the radicals who had been imprisoned, including DeFreeze. And yet, despite his reluctance about DeFreeze's mission, Gunnell allowed him to spend the night, and later, within the commune, DeFreeze met the revolutionary-minded individuals he had been searching for. Unfortunately, these soon-to-be members of the SLA, who probably joined DeFreeze with good intentions, would spiral out of control under Cinque Mtume's direction.

THE TRANSFORMATION: DONALD DEFREEZE TO CINQUE MTUME

By the time of his escape, Donald DeFreeze had morphed into Cinque Mtume. He had transformed himself from a small-time thug into a revolutionary leader. According to the legendary African American prison inmate George Jackson, "This camp (prison) brings out the very best in brothers or destroys them entirely. But none are unaffected."[19] To survive incarceration, DeFreeze developed a new persona. Cinque did not play the part of a loner. Instead of shunning associations with groups as DeFreeze had done in his teens, Cinque joined the BCA, sought an active leadership role within it, and developed Unisight from it.

Although they never met, Cinque was heavily influenced by the rhetoric of George Jackson, himself a revolutionary prison leader. Jackson was one of the Soledad Brothers accused of killing a prison guard in response to the death of an African American prisoner. After publication of his *Soledad Brother: The Prison Letters of George Jackson* in 1970, his death in a controversial escape attempt from San Quentin's Adjustment Center in 1971, and the posthumous publication of *Blood in My Eye* in 1972, Jackson's fame and influence grew exponentially.

Cinque bought into Jackson's exhortations about the need for a violent revolution. *Blood in My Eye* centered on the issue of a violent overthrow of the U.S. government. According to Jackson, in the early 1970s it was "time to move, we must show them that resistance is possible, and that there is a hard-left cadre willing to lead it."[20] Jackson's ideas made a deep impression on Cinque as he began the process of changing from small-time criminal to prison revolutionary.

The revolution, from Jackson's perspective, required a vanguard. Jackson admired Cuban leader Fidel Castro and French journalist Regis DeBray, and he believed that revolution in America required a committed revolutionary group to begin the revolt. According to

Jackson, "There have never been any spontaneous revolutions. They were all stages, manufactured by people who went to the head of the masses and directed them."[21] Jackson believed that "revolutionary consciousness can be raised to the highest point by stimuli from the vanguard elements."[22] He sided with the elements of the New Left that advocated direct action against the federal government. Jackson also agreed with DeBray about the Foco theory of revolution—a revolution in which a group of individuals would step forward to lead and inspire the masses, like Castro's revolution in Cuba. For Cinque, a liberation army would be that vanguard.

DeFreeze's transformation into Cinque while in prison and his absorption of Jackson's writings while in his cell demonstrated the impact that Jackson would have on the politics and revolutionary strategies of the SLA, which differed from the groups that had come before it. In fact, Patricia Hearst would recall that icons of the New Left such as Angela Davis, Huey Newton, and Jane Fonda were disliked by the SLA. George Jackson, by contrast, was viewed as a hero.[23] Members of the SLA strongly encouraged Hearst to read the works of Jackson.[24] The SLA's extremist views and violence were a direct result of his influence.

But in following the revolutionary ideals of Jackson, as defined and embodied by Cinque, the SLA fell victim to a major flaw in his writings. For the SLA to succeed as the vanguard of revolution, it required something incredibly vital that it did not possess: a dependence on the Bay Area's leftist movements and their willingness to participate in the violent overthrow of the U.S. government.[25]

3
THE LAUNCH

AFTER CINQUE MTUME'S ARRIVAL AT THE Peking Man House, Russell Little and Willie Wolfe began the process of locating a new safe house for their friend. Because of the documented ties among Cinque, Little, and Wolfe from the BCA and the Unisight programs, it seemed inevitable that law enforcement would arrive on their doorstep looking for the escaped convict. By chance, Little ran into a former Peking Man House resident, Christopher Thompson.[1] During this meeting, Little described the situation to Thompson without mentioning Cinque by name.

Thompson knew someone who could help them, his former girlfriend Patricia "Mizmoon" Soltysik. Despite her involvement with the prison reform movement, Soltysik had not put one foot in a prison. Therefore, it was unlikely she would be suspected of harboring Cinque. She also knew many of the members of the Peking Man House and was considered to be politically in tune with them.

Shortly after moving into Soltysik's Parker Street residence, Soltysik and Cinque began an intimate relationship. By the end of March, Soltysik's brother, Fred, and sister, Sue, were both commenting on how happy Soltysik seemed to be with her new lover. Soltysik's happiness with Cinque came on the heels of a bout of depression from dealing with a succession of failed relationships and gonorrhea.[2]

Within four weeks of his escape from prison, Cinque had found not only a safe house, but also comrades to help him formulate plans for a revolution. According to Fred Soltysik, from March through November 1973 his sister worked with Cinque, Russell Little, Nancy Ling Perry, Joe Remiro, and Willie Wolfe on a "serious document that would be a declaration" and the basis for the newest of the New Left organizations.[3] Their newly founded multiethnic organization—the Symbionese Liberation Army (Symbionese from the word *symbiosis*)—was intended to serve as the vanguard of a

Marxist revolution in the United States. The Symbionese Liberation Army manifesto was entitled "The Symbionese Federation and the Symbionese Liberation Army Declaration of Revolutionary War and the Symbionese Program." By establishing the SLA, they sought to replace Venceremos as the preeminent action-oriented New Left organization in the Berkeley area.

The members of the SLA were determined to change the United States. They drafted a series of documents that included a "Declaration of War against the United States," "Codes of War," the terms of military/political alliance with the United Symbionese War Council, and a treatise detailing the seven principles of the SLA. The SLA took its role in the "impending revolution" seriously. To foment their revolution, the members of the SLA decided to emulate Fidel Castro and implement the Foco theory of revolution, which, according to author Dan Berger, "was first advocated by Che Guevara and based on the military success of the Cuban revolution."[4] In this manifestation of the Foco theory, the SLA would become the leader for others to follow. Thus during the formative stages of the SLA, Cinque attempted to align the SLA with other New Left groups under the Symbionese Federation.

As plans for the SLA continued to develop, and activity increased at Soltysik's Parker Street residence, the decision was made to move Cinque to an apartment in East Oakland. The Soltysik bungalow was a hub for revolutionary activities. Foot traffic in and out of the residence worried Cinque enough that new living arrangements became a necessity.[5] Patricia Soltysik would therefore have to commute back and forth between her Berkeley residence and Cinque's East Oakland apartment.[6]

RECRUITING MEMBERS AND ESTABLISHING LEADERSHIP

Most accounts of the SLA focus on Cinque. However, he was not the group's only revolutionary member. Prior to planning its first staged event, the assassination of Marcus Foster on November 6, 1973, the SLA had some success recruiting beyond the "original ten."[7]

According to Vin McLellan and Paul Avery, two Bay Area journalists who covered the SLA during the 1970s, "Wolfe, Little and Perry were already involved with another prison-based revolutionary terrorist group" at the time of Cinque's escape.[8] It is unlikely that Little and Wolfe could fade away so quickly after finding Cinque a safe house. They had been close friends with Cinque prior to his escape, particularly Little. Instead, the prison work of these individuals served as an extension of the newly formed SLA. Many prisoners such as Clifford "Death Row" Jefferson, who later claimed to be high-ranking members of the SLA, had also been involved in the Partisans Vanguard Party through Wolfe and Little.[9]

Although in the early days of the SLA Wolfe had a primary role in bringing together its original ten members, assumptions that he was a central figure in the SLA actually ignore the role Russell Little played in the group's formative stages.[10] The usual narrative begins to change when the statements of those who knew Wolfe are analyzed. When Marilyn Baker asked Christopher Thompson whether Wolfe was a leader and whether Little followed Wolfe into the SLA, Thompson replied, "Hell, no, Willie was no leader. Nobody would go anywhere with Willie. People wouldn't follow Willie Wolfe to the bathroom. He was a loser. He was just a rich white kid playing at politics. No one respected him, not even in Peking Man House."[11] Amanda de Normanville, another individual on the periphery of the SLA who had been actively involved in the BCA, referred to Wolfe as "a follower of David's [David Gunnell of the Peking Man House]." She continued: "David I would listen to; Jean Wah I would listen to; I felt more on the same wavelength. But Willie seemed so young. I would sort of think, Ah Willie, there's Willie, all talk and no action."[12] Wolfe never demonstrated the capacity for leadership, whether in high school, in college, or in the prison reform movement. By contrast, Little, who is often overlooked, played an active role inside and outside the prisons, building trustworthy relationships and boosting SLA membership.

Little and Cinque developed a close rapport working together in BCA subgroup, Unisight, and it was Little who wrote to the parole board on Cinque's behalf. Little was one of two whites Cinque asked to participate in Unisight. When Cinque had exhausted almost all possibilities for assistance following his escape when he had nowhere else to turn, he knew he could trust Little. Indeed, Little never failed to assist Cinque. He served as Cinque's second in command and his closest adviser.[13] In this capacity, it was Little who recruited Nancy Ling Perry and Joe Remiro into the SLA.

Meanwhile, the newly recruited SLA members worked diligently. In May 1973, Soltysik left the Parker Street residence she had shared with her sister in Berkeley and moved in with Cinque in the East Oakland apartment. Nancy Ling Perry also moved in with them. Perry's initial task was to edit the SLA "Codes of War" and other documents. By the spring of 1973, the SLA consisted of five official members: Cinque, Soltysik, Perry, Little, and Wolfe.[14]

MOVING FROM PLANNING TO ACTION

As they sat writing their "Codes of War," the early members of the SLA convinced themselves that the time for action had come. The rise of the SLA coincided with the public revelations of White House involvement in the Watergate scandal. Public trust in President Nixon and his administration began to erode as the scandal continued to grow because of testimony from prominent Nixon staffers and the disclosure of a White House taping system. The members of the SLA concluded that the government had become so corrupt that it no longer represented the people of the United States. It was time, they believed, to implement the Foco theory of revolution popularized by Che Guevara.

Despite the void within the Bay Area's New Left community because of the dissolution of Venceremos, the SLA gained momentum during this time because of Watergate. Yet even as its membership increased, so did its isolation from the rest of Berkeley society. Consequently, no voices were raised to contradict its growing belief that the time had come for revolutionary action in the United States and that the SLA would serve as the vanguard for others to follow.

On August 2, 1973, the SLA assisted in the escape of an African American convict, Thero Wheeler, who had been a member of Venceremos and who had succeeded Cinque as the leader of Unisight following his transfer to Soledad Prison.[15] As described in chapter 4, while incarcerated for armed robbery, Wheeler had the reputation of being a "jailhouse lawyer" and a "heavy" among his fellow prisoners. However, his reputation among law enforcement was tarnished by his membership in Venceremos. Wheeler was surprised to learn that Cinque had been involved in his escape.[16] Because of Wheeler's previous involvement in Venceremos, law enforcement blamed the escape on that disintegrating organization. Wheeler's escape from Vacaville Prison, however, represented the SLA's first successful revolutionary action.

On August 21, the SLA released its declaration of war against the United States. Lost in the shuffle of the many leftist movements that seemingly rose and fell daily throughout the 1960s and 1970s, the significance of the timing of the declaration was overlooked—the group had chosen the second anniversary of the death of inmate and revolutionary leader George Jackson. The SLA was still a relatively unknown part of the ever-evolving revolutionary politics of the Berkeley area, at least to the world outside of it. Consequently, Cinque wanted to announce to the world the existence of the SLA through a communiqué declaring its role in Wheeler's escape. Yet Wheeler went to great lengths to convince Cinque "that the potential dangers [of the communiqué] were much greater than the advantages."[17] Having just gained his freedom, Wheeler wanted to remain as anonymous as possible. Cinque therefore decided to forego the communiqué on Wheeler's escape, but his thirst for notoriety remained unquenched.

4 THERO WHEELER

THE CONFLICT OVER THE COMMUNIQUÉ WAS merely the beginning of a stormy relationship. Thero Wheeler continually undermined Cinque Mtume. According to one account, Wheeler attempted to reach out to other members of the SLA to wrest the leadership from Cinque. Wheeler did not view Cinque as a powerful leader, and he clashed with Cinque on the aim and structure of this new revolutionary cell. After seeing firsthand Cinque's plan for the SLA, Wheeler considered it "really shit." Wheeler felt nothing but disdain for the SLA's simplistic Marxist theories pertaining to revolution.[1] Furthermore, the roles had reversed.

A DETERIORATING RELATIONSHIP

In prison, Wheeler had the reputation of a leader, whereas Cinque was known as a follower. Wheeler became involved in leftist politics while incarcerated for armed robbery, and he joined Venceremos. Since his escape, Wheeler's situation had changed dramatically, and he did not particularly like the position he was in. Cinque was the unchallenged leader of the SLA, and he viewed Wheeler as subservient.[2] It did not take long, then, for the relationship between the two to deteriorate. From Cinque's point of view, Wheeler had been disloyal and ungrateful for Cinque's help in escaping from prison. Plus, Cinque feared Wheeler wanted to take over his organization. After all of the failures in his life, including an unsuccessful bid to become the elected leader of the BCA, Cinque had finally found a group that accepted him as its leader, and he was determined to hold on to his position.

It is not known whether Cinque anticipated the conflict that would arise between the two once the SLA helped Wheeler to escape from Vacaville Prison. However, the SLA needed Wheeler to help

Figure 5: Thero Wheeler during an interview at the California Medical Facility in Vacaville, California on December 31, 1975. (Jim Palmer/Associated Press)

carry out their agenda. Cinque had difficulties convincing African Americans to join the SLA. Therefore, the SLA hoped that by assisting Wheeler, it could utilize his contacts, reputation, and credibility to gain access to the people Cinque could not reach.[3] Thus the feeling among the collective had been that freeing Wheeler and adding him to the organization would increase its stature and increase recruitment. However, despite Wheeler's involvement in the SLA, he was unwilling to aid in member recruitment: "I couldn't seriously recruit for him [Cinque] because he was off into suicide and bullshit. The people I knew just wouldn't accept the SLA."[4]

Wheeler, like many veterans of Venceremos and other radical organizations, believed that the SLA came across as an overly aggressive, violent, and politically confused group. The "Codes of War" and the act of declaring revolutionary war against the United States appeared overzealous at best and inviting trouble at worst. Such an act proved to be more than what other leftist and revolutionary groups in the Bay Area were prepared to rally behind. Rumors swirled that Cinque was acting as an agent provocateur for law enforcement because of the aggressive nature of the SLA, its actions, and its writings.[5] However, the more likely reason Wheeler was so combative toward Cinque and the SLA was because talking about revolution was easy inside prison walls. On the outside,

Wheeler faced the actual prospect of fighting the U.S. government, and he balked at the SLA's provocation.

THE ISSUES THAT DIVIDED

Although Wheeler was present during the planning stages of the assassination of Oakland superintendent of schools Marcus Foster in November 1973, he severed ties with the SLA before it was carried out, and he was long gone by the time the SLA made the decision to kidnap Patricia Hearst. However, in the brief time that Wheeler spent with the SLA he continually contradicted Cinque. Further aggravating the situation among Wheeler, Cinque, and the other SLA members, Wheeler's girlfriend, Mary Alice Seim, joined him in the Bay Area soon after his escape. Seim, who also had previous ties with Venceremos, was an heiress to a California lumber and real estate fortune. According to some of Seim's associates, she gave Wheeler "a couple of thousand dollars," which he in turn shared with the SLA.[6] If Wheeler had any illusions that the money would provide a seat at the leadership table, they were quickly dispelled. However, finances had been an ongoing problem for this nascent revolutionary organization. Soltysik's paycheck from her work as a janitor at the Berkeley Public Library and the money Perry earned working at Fruity Rudy's fruit drink stand had been the primary sources of funding for the organization until Wheeler arrived.[7] Wheeler believed that robbing banks could provide the money needed for revolution, while delivering a blow against "the centers of capitalist oppression.[8] However, Cinque was not yet ready to start robbing banks because the SLA was still in a formative period. Consequently, he found himself at odds with Wheeler once again.

Money was not the only issue that pitted Cinque and Wheeler against one another. Wheeler's reluctance to seek publicity frustrated Cinque. Wheeler had been a member of Venceremos and had learned from its mistakes. He believed the SLA should act, but it should not call attention to the organization by announcing its involvement. He also believed the SLA should avoid situations such as the October 1972 Ronald Beaty jailbreak. As Wheeler knew from personal experience, that jailbreak, which led to the shooting of two prison guards and the death of one, spelled the end for Venceremos.[9]

Despite his strong will and reputation as a leader, Wheeler was unconvincing. He failed to recognize the personal relationship Cinque had developed with the other members of the SLA. Even though they knew Wheeler, they did not love and respect him as they did Cinque. Little and Wolfe had forged a close bond with Cinque through their involvement with the BCA and Unisight. Soltysik and

Perry had developed a close relationship with Cinque that was both physical and intellectual. They worked closely with him on various documents relating to codes of conduct and the development of a Symbionese Federation. In all of the confrontations between Cinque and Wheeler, members of the SLA sided with Cinque.

At one particular point in their conflict, Wheeler vetoed Cinque's plan to assassinate *San Francisco Examiner* reporter Ed Montgomery. Cinque's hatred of Montgomery stemmed from an article the reporter wrote about Wheeler, mentioning his recent escape from prison.[10] Cinque planned to write a letter to Montgomery, presumably letting him know he was an SLA target. Wheeler told Cinque he would write his own letter to Montgomery denying his involvement in any plan to kill him. This conflict was like previous disagreements over the communiqué Cinque wanted to release announcing the SLA's involvement in Wheeler's escape from jail. In each case, Wheeler convinced Cinque not to act in a way that would gain publicity for the SLA. But Cinque, like the others in the SLA, sought the public's attention.

The distrust between Cinque and Wheeler inevitably led to more heated confrontations, and Cinque reached a point where he could no longer tolerate Wheeler mocking his leadership of the SLA.[11] In September 1973 during this power struggle, Wheeler decided to move out of the SLA safe house in Oakland and into an apartment with his girlfriend and her child. This arrangement did not sit well with Cinque. In early October, Cinque, along with Perry and Soltysik, decided to pay a visit to Wheeler's new apartment.[12] However, the visit quickly went off the rails when Cinque and his companions pulled out their guns and aimed them at Wheeler and Seim. Cinque was angry because of Wheeler's physical separation from the SLA and therefore Cinque's control. He told Wheeler there would be no auxiliary members of the SLA, and he gave Wheeler an ultimatum: return to the safe house or be shot along with Seim and her child. Throughout the confrontation, Wheeler remained calm as he tried to convince Cinque that he was still committed to the cause and an active member of the SLA.[13] Reluctantly, Wheeler and Seim returned to the SLA safe house with her child.

After a few days, Wheeler and Seim were allowed to leave the SLA safe house to pick up their necessities from their former residence. They did not return to the safe house but fled separately, each with the deep conviction that Cinque and his followers had a rendezvous with a destiny they did not want to share. As Wheeler aptly stated, "It [the SLA] didn't have nothing to do with reality, man, all it could do was get you killed."[14] Shortly after Wheeler and Seim fled, the remaining SLA members moved out of the Oakland safe house and into a new one in Clayton, California—a residence

Wheeler knew nothing about.

Wheeler's absence reinstated Cinque as the unquestioned leader of the SLA. It also meant that Cinque and the organization could proceed with their goals without having to address opposing viewpoints. Cinque yearned for notoriety and publicity. Once Wheeler left, no other member of the SLA challenged Cinque's radical plans for seeking publicity.

Unfortunately, with Wheeler gone the SLA would also lose access to funds from Seim. Seim's money, though, had only amounted to a band-aid for the SLA's long-term financial needs. The SLA needed money for safe houses, vehicles, arms, and ammunition if it was going to continue its activism, but its monetary needs were much greater than its means. In the latter months of 1973, to concentrate on the development of the SLA, Perry and Soltysik quit their jobs. Their small paychecks were the SLA's only dependable sources of income. However, because in early October—after Wheeler and Seim fled—the SLA rented an apartment in Oakland just a half-mile from the Oakland school administration building,[15] it is clear that the SLA was receiving funds from undisclosed parties during its formative stage.

Indeed, Wheeler mentioned in interviews that Cinque had received financial support from a Bay Area radical with known ties to Venceremos but with unknown ties to the SLA. In addition to the funds provided by this mysterious source, Cinque and the SLA were resorting to various crimes to acquire money. According to *The Voices of Guns*, "In the early fall, the SLA had burglarized the homes of at least three prominent leftist activists, stealing guns, ammunition, and ammo-loading equipment."[16] They even stole a wallet from Venceremos member Janet Cooper and later used her name and identity to rent a red AMC Hornet that was used in the Hibernia Bank robbery on April 15, 1974.

By the fall of 1973, even though Cinque had dismissed Wheeler's earlier proposition that the SLA target banks because they were the "center of capitalist oppression," it appeared to be steadily moving in that direction.[17] What most likely offended Cinque about Wheeler's proposition was not the idea of robbing a bank itself; rather, it was the person who proposed it. Whether Wheeler meant to, he had in fact challenged Cinque's leadership of this fledgling revolutionary group. As money became increasingly scarce for the SLA, the group concluded that they had to resort to illegal means of getting the money needed to fund the revolution—just as Wheeler had predicted in August.

It is significant that during this time Cinque and his followers began the initial planning to assassinate Marcus Foster. Prior to the assassination of Foster, Wheeler claimed that many of his supporters, mainly those involved in Venceremos, had provided money during the initial stages of the SLA's development.[18] Wheeler also claimed that the Hibernia Bank robbery meant that Cinque had severed relations with his previous principal financial supporters—further proof of their alienation. However, the SLA's financial difficulties began long before that robbery in April.

On September 30, 1973, Soltysik and Perry robbed Seifert's Floral Company in Oakland. They stole between $400 and $600 from the shop but had to abandon their van used in the getaway because onlookers were seen writing down the van's license plate number.[19] Further demonstrating the SLA's financial desperation, on October 12, 1973, Joe Remiro, with gun in hand, approached Donald Sullivan from behind on Berkeley's Telegraph Avenue and demanded the keys to his 1969 Chevy van. The van was later found near the Clayton safe house stripped of almost everything, including the engine.[20] The members of the SLA had become thieves and criminals, following in the footsteps of their leader, Cinque.

With Thero Wheeler no longer a threat, Cinque could continue his version of revolutionary activism unopposed. Not only did Cinque want notoriety for the SLA, demonstrated by the lengths to which he and the other members would go to gain public attention, but he also hoped that their actions would kick-start a national revolution in much the same way Fidel Castro did in Cuba. Wheeler's negative statements about Cinque and the SLA point to their radicalism. He believed that his continued involvement in the SLA would only result in his death. If Wheeler, an ex-con and veteran member of Venceremos, feared and did not support the actions of the SLA, then what made Cinque think that its actions would spark a national revolution?

In hindsight, Wheeler's descriptions of the SLA were accurate. The SLA's actions proved on the world stage that it was overly aggressive, violent, and politically confused. The SLA was the vehicle by which Cinque demonstrated to the rest of the world that he was no longer a frightened petty criminal trapped in a marriage with a domineering, emasculating wife. Donald DeFreeze, the unsuccessful man with no follow-through, no longer existed. Through the SLA, DeFreeze emerged as Cinque, and for a fleeting time, through his followers, the earliest members of the organization he had created, he achieved a taste of the recognition he had so long yearned for.

5 THE ASSASSINATION

THE ACCEPTED VERSION OF THE FORMATION of the SLA consists of Cinque moving around the Bay Area, unsuccessfully attempting to sell his vision of the revolution. This version has merit in terms of assembling additional hard-core cadres. Groups of sympathizers did exist, but their allegiance did not match that of the original ten. Meanwhile, other cells of SLA sympathizers had good reason to withdraw from the group from November 1973 through February 1974. In November 1973, the SLA became the subject of condemnation throughout the Bay Area for its assassination of Oakland superintendent of schools Marcus Foster.

THE VICTIM: MARCUS FOSTER

The SLA first came to the attention of law enforcement and the San Francisco Bay Area radical scene with the assassination of Marcus Foster on November 6, 1973. David Horowitz wrote that "the act itself was so brutal, so morally unjustifiable and so politically incomprehensible that most Bay Area radicals assumed the SLA to be a cover for some right-wing or police group."[1]

Foster, a native of Atlanta, Georgia, who overcame southern poverty, had earned his reputation as a highly respected educator in Philadelphia. There, he was recognized for turning a struggling inner-city high school around in three short years. His fine work at Simon Gratz High School led to his promotion to associate superintendent for community relations of Philadelphia schools. He also became a trustee of the University of Pennsylvania and was named Philadelphia's "Man of the Year" in 1968.[2]

In mid-1970, a move to Oakland gave Foster an opportunity to escape from his community relations position in Philadelphia.[3] A talented educator, Foster wanted the opportunity to lead, and the Oakland job was a chance to do just that. Foster was a unique individual who found himself at home with people from all walks of life. As a close friend described him, "He was a good and dutiful student, but could run with the boys on the corner of ghetto Philly."[4] Furthermore, "he was steeped in the Bible," but he could "shoot pool like Minnesota Fats."[5] In other words, Foster had the ability to appeal to and communicate with a wide variety of people. This ability benefited him greatly when he was given the reins of Oakland schools. The composition of the school board was overwhelmingly Caucasian, whereas the enrollment in Oakland schools in 1973 was 64.2 percent African American, 21.1 percent Caucasian, 7.7 percent Latino, 5.7 percent Asian; and 1.1 percent Filipino and other minorities. Oakland was a city in transition, and Marcus Foster had been hired because of his ability to communicate and bridge the growing gap between African Americans and the Caucasian numerical minority that still wielded more power than its numbers justified.

According to Thero Wheeler, the decision to assassinate Marcus Foster was finalized during a SLA meeting in mid-October 1973. Wheeler reported that after watching a television news story about Foster and security issues in Oakland schools, Cinque proclaimed that "we [the SLA] are gonna off that nigger."[6] However, it is much more likely that Cinque's response was influenced by a report delivered by Willie Wolfe following an October 9, 1973, Oakland school board meeting and not based solely on Cinque's reaction to a news story.[7] Meanwhile, although Cinque acted rashly on occasion, the SLA's standard methodology involved detailed planning—but not always accurate information.

THE MOTIVE

In the time leading up to the Oakland school board meeting on October 9, 1973, an Alameda County grand jury had been investigating drug abuse, vandalism, and efficient use of school funds. As a case study for its report, the grand jury chose to focus on Oakland schools. The grand jury's decision to focus on those schools may have been influenced by the on-campus stabbing of an Oakland Tech student by a nonstudent in May that year.[8] The final report, issued during the summer, recommended that the Oakland police and the school authorities develop guidelines on the proper division of responsibilities when law enforcement arrived on a school campus. The report also recommended a police presence on school campuses throughout Oakland to combat future violence and other illegal activities.[9]

The California Council on Criminal Justice (CCCJ) provided

Oakland schools with a $275,000 grant to add greater security measures in view of the recent stabbing. However, the CCCJ wanted Oakland schools to allocate a significant portion of those funds to ensure that all security staff had police experience and that the funds targeted the city's junior and senior high schools.[10]

Figure 6: Oakland superintendent of schools, Marcus Foster. April 1970, Oakland, California. (Associated Press)

Foster strongly disagreed with the idea of police in Oakland schools. Instead, he hoped to enlist "parents from the neighborhood" to serve as the security coordinators instead of police.[11] Consequently, in the meeting on October 9 Foster decided to retract his vote in favor of the CCCJ proposal because of the clause calling for security aides on school campuses to have a law enforcement background.[12] Before the school board meeting, Elaine Brown, chairwoman of the Black Panthers, told Marcus Foster that the Black Panther Party "would be happy, for a fee, to provide security for the schools."[13] Foster, however, turned down the Black Panthers by insisting that he was not interested in adding new security at any of Oakland's schools.[14]

Meanwhile, Oakland schools were taking another look at the notion of issuing identification cards to keep nonstudents off school campuses. Just two years earlier, Foster and the school board had made a financial decision to cut identification cards from the school budget without any reference to ideology or politics. Cutting the identification card program saved Oakland schools approximately $17,000.[15] However, like Foster's refusal to approve placing security officers on school campuses, when the issue of reinstating student ID cards arose, it led to public criticism of Foster—particularly from a local citizen, Vera Silverman, and a group known as "Save Our Schools."[16] Silverman claimed that reinstating the ID cards in schools would serve the same purpose as the ID cards used by the South African government: to allow law enforcement to track and imprison "all the black and brown" students once the revolution began.[17]

In September 1973, Robert Blackburn, Foster's handpicked deputy superintendent, met with students at an all-city council meeting. The council was comprised of elected high school student leaders. During the meeting, Blackburn asked the students for their thoughts on reinstating the ID card program for students. The students responded positively. They found ID cards useful when checking books out at the library, getting into football games, and accessing Alameda County transit buses. Overall, then, the students favored the return of the ID cards.[18] Save Our Schools and the SLA raised a clamor about the possible political motivations behind the ID cards instead of acknowledging the students' comments on their practical use.

When Silverman from Save Our Schools attended the school board meeting on October 9, she opposed implementation of the student ID cards and criticized Superintendent Foster, though her anti-ID card attack lacked the drama that had been attributed to it.[19] Silverman did move to the front of the audience and cut up a child's ID card in protest, but she did not have a great deal of impact on the majority of the crowd.[20] Willie Wolfe also attended the October 9 meeting and witnessed Silverman's and the Black Panther Party's opposition to the ID cards and police involvement in the Oakland schools. As the eyes and ears of the SLA at the meeting, he reported his findings to his fellow revolutionaries a few days later at an SLA meeting. In Wolfe's report to his fellow revolutionaries, Silverman and the Panthers played a much more confrontational role in opposing Foster than had actually transpired.

Wolfe's report encouraged the SLA to target Foster. On November 3, 1973, in the most confounding move in their brief history, the SLA decided to assassinate Marcus Foster. The SLA believed it was acting on behalf of the opposition and that the Black Panther Party and the group Save Our Schools would legitimatize their actions. They began conducting surveillance of Foster's daily activities.[21] To facilitate their surveillance, Nancy Ling Perry, using the alias Lynn Ledworth, rented an apartment in Oakland at 1621 7th Avenue, which was within a half-mile of Foster's office. In what would become a standard method of operation, the SLA kept a close eye on their target and trained daily for the assassination.

Foster's ability to succeed within the white power structure undoubtedly led to Cinque's animosity toward him and jealousy. Understandably, the surviving members of the SLA have never fully explained the reasoning behind their assassination of Foster. At best, they concluded that the assassination of Foster had been a "serious error," while also stating that "killing Foster put a quick stop to the intended programs" of reinstating ID cards.[22] In retrospect, however, the SLA's arguments against ID cards and the presence of police on school campuses may appear premature or even ridiculous.

Election day, November 6, 1973, was, as one Foster biographer noted, "a typical, eleven-hour day" for Foster in almost every way but one.[23] The SLA used handguns and shotguns to cast its vote with bullets. The assassination of Marcus Foster made little sense when it occurred, and to this day little has been done to elucidate this baffling event. At the time of his death, Foster had become a popular leader of Oakland schools. He had developed the ability to work with the myriad of ethnicities and cultures that populated the city of Oakland. In addition, he had demonstrated the political skills needed to deal with a diverse city and a powerful school board mostly composed of Anglo citizens. However, the SLA's obscurity proved beneficial because it left Foster unaware of his vulnerability to their opposition.

The day Foster died began when Deputy Robert Blackburn picked him up at 8 a.m., but ended in a hail of bullets just after 7 p.m. His official day started with an Oakland City Council "work session" where he proposed that the city reopen high school gyms after school to keep Oakland youth off the streets. Later in the day, he chaired a school board meeting. After the meeting, Foster and Blackburn left the Oakland Board of Education building and headed toward Blackburn's Chevy Vega in the parking lot. As he left the building with his friend and boss, Blackburn noticed two young men loitering against the building in the shadows.[24] Glancing over, he got a good look at both of them.[25] As Foster and Blackburn continued walking toward the car, Blackburn sped up to open the passenger door for Foster. When Blackburn reached the rear of the vehicle and Foster crossed in front of him, the two loiterers caught up with Blackburn and Foster and began shooting at Foster. Then, Cinque emerged from the bushes with a sawed-off shotgun and began firing at Blackburn. Both of Cinque's blasts hit Blackburn; the first spun him around, and the second made contact as Blackburn attempted to escape back toward the Board of Education building.[26] Blackburn recalled hearing the handguns fire and seeing the muzzle flashes from the attack on Foster before being shot in the back by Cinque from about fifteen feet away.[27]

Despite the pain from his own injuries, Blackburn continued to stagger back toward the Board of Education building in search of help. Upon arriving inside the building, he cried out for help. David Tom found Blackburn lying in the hallway, bleeding profusely. He yelled out to a janitor to call the police while he checked on Foster. Tom found Foster face down and unresponsive in the parking lot and discovered that he no longer had a pulse.[28]

In the end, then, the SLA succeeded in murdering Foster, but it failed to kill Blackburn. Although the police found a wealth of information at the crime scene, they could not immediately pinpoint a suspect. Initial witness testimony did not provide police with a consistent description of the murderers. The interviews only confused police with conflicting height, weight, and ethnicity descriptions of the suspected shooters.

The autopsy, by contrast, provided police with a trademark clue to the killers. When Dr. Allen McNie performed Marcus Foster's autopsy the day after the murder, he found a bullet that had passed through Foster's heart, but then it slowed down so much that when it hit the pen and pencil clipped to Foster's shirt pocket it came to a complete stop. After examining the bullet, McNie noticed a strange odor that he quickly confirmed to be cyanide.[29] The SLA had drilled tiny holes in the tips of the bullets, inserted small amounts of potassium cyanide, and then sealed the holes with wax.[30] Upon learning the existence of cyanide in the bullets, the Oakland police officer in charge of the Foster murder investigation, Detective Sergeant John Agler, urged the coroner and toxicologist to keep the information confidential. Agler informed only the police chief of the unique bullets. Consequently, when cyanide-laced bullets were found at the site of Patricia Hearst's abduction, the police were able to quickly zero in on the SLA as the perpetrators.

Foster's murder investigation might have proceeded more slowly regardless of the evidence found at the coroner's office, but Cinque continued to seek publicity. A group calling itself the "Symbionese Liberation Army: Western Regional Unit" sent Berkeley radio station KPFA its first public communiqué. The communiqué presented a "Warrant Order: Execution by Cyanide Bullets" for Marcus Foster and Robert Blackburn.[31] As a result, the Oakland police had the name of the organization responsible for the brutal attack.

Throughout the San Francisco Bay Area, radical organizations had sprouted and died periodically, usually with little fanfare, but this one, the SLA, seemed different, particularly for its willingness to announce its complicity in the murder of a respected educator. The Warrant Order communiqué smacked of arrogance, as well as contempt, for law enforcement. Furthermore, the SLA communiqué demonstrated an increasing need for recognition from both law enforcement and the media.

THE AFTEREFFECTS

Much to the SLA's dismay, the community reaction to the murder of Marcus Foster was not what it had expected. The first communiqué announced that the murder was an order from the "Court of the People," but the people of Oakland were grief-stricken and angry about the murder of their school superintendent. Furthermore, Foster's murder brought together members of the Oakland community who in the past had difficulties working together. Mayor John Reading stood beside Black Panther chairman Bobby Seale at the Beebe Memorial CME temple as they paid their last respects to Foster.[32] The greatest blow to Cinque's vision was the outpouring of grief from the Bay Area's African American community. The Black Panther Party in Oakland described the murder of Foster as "brutal and senseless."[33] In fact, initial reactions to the murder, particularly within New Left circles, maintained that the Foster assassination had been the work of a right-wing, fascist, or government conspiracy.[34]

News of the Foster assassination rapidly reached California prisons. Within one day of the shooting, inmate Al Taylor told his prison psychiatrist that "they" should not have killed Marcus Foster. When the doctor asked who "they" were, Taylor responded, "the Lebanese Liberation Army [Taylor had confused the SLA's title]." Prison inmates were extremely critical of the Foster murder and may have issued an order for Cinque's "execution."[35] Instead of being heralded as active revolutionaries in the wake of their first successful act, the SLA found the period between the Foster assassination and the arrests of SLA members Joe Remiro and Russell Little in January 1974 (described in the next chapter) to be one of introspection and further isolation for the SLA.

The arrests of Remiro and Russell following the assassination led police to the SLA safe house in Clayton, which was full of information about the cell. The core of the SLA quickly headed underground, whereas those who had any affiliation early on with the SLA rapidly and quietly severed any remaining ties. The February 22–28, 1974, edition of the *Berkeley Barb,* an alternative newspaper sympathetic to New Left causes, published a letter from former members of the SLA, who declared that they "resigned collectively" following the assassination of Marcus Foster. Furthermore, they stated, "The revolutionary role of necessary violence is the opposite of what the SLA believes, and practices."[36] These former members felt it necessary to go into hiding to avoid retribution from the SLA and law enforcement.

Perhaps what is most interesting in the open letter from the former SLA members is the recruitment timeline they provided, which lends a great deal of authenticity to their claims. These former members were first approached in June 1973, which matches the timeline of Cinque and Soltysik's move from the Parker Street bungalow to the apartment in Oakland. After the move, the SLA began reaching out to other radical organizations to join the Symbionese Federation. According to the article, these former SLA members, who had joined the SLA in August, felt they had found a place "in a revolutionary organization that was on its way beyond the Left, old and new."[37] The August timeline is important because it coincides with the escape of Thero Wheeler and signals the true beginning of the SLA as an active entity. The only challenge to the letter's credibility was the writers' apparent innocence regarding the use of violence. The Federation had established a War Council, and on August 21, 1973, the SLA had issued a declaration of war. This document clearly reflects the general attitude of the original members of the SLA—that violence was the necessary next step on the path to revolution. The evidence, which demonstrates that the SLA contacted other revolutionary groups and peoples, presents a picture of the SLA that is very different from the one previously constructed.

6

TRIUMPH TO TURMOIL

BEFORE THE ASSASSINATION OF MARCUS FOSTER, the SLA had some success recruiting beyond the "original ten." After the assassination, however, the SLA found itself in a precarious position. As noted in chapter 5, the almost universal condemnation of the SLA by community leaders throughout the San Francisco Bay Area and the New Left eroded those affiliations.

Forced to abandon the Oakland apartment it had used as a base for the assassination, the SLA moved on November 8, 1973, to the suburbs: 1560 Sutherland Court in Concord, California.[1] In hindsight, Russell Little realized that "the SLA should never have had a safe house in Concord because we didn't fit into that middle-class suburban community."[2] And yet Concord seemed like a safer option than either Oakland or Berkeley. The fledgling revolution would have to be placed on hold while the SLA members determined their next course of action.

Although no member of the SLA was prepared for the backlash after the Foster murder, Willie Wolfe seemed the most distraught. As the local community and media outlets vilified the murderers, Wolfe began to question his role in the assassination.[3] The youngest member of the SLA, Wolfe was confused and agitated by the reactions of his friends, many of whom were in California prisons. Despite his private doubts, he continued to speak and proselytize about the coming revolution in America. However, he made the decision to return to his family on the East Coast for a brief respite under the auspices of acquiring much-needed funds for the revolution.

On December 20, 1973, Wolfe arrived at his father's house in Pennsylvania—forty-four days after the assassination of Marcus Foster. He told his family he planned to marry his Swedish girlfriend, Eva Olsson, and told them that this was the purpose of his visit. Wolfe's parents were wealthy, and his cover story may have been a way to ease into a discussion of acquiring financial assistance from his father.[4] Around January 1, Little and Remiro tried to contact Wolfe because Little wanted him to return to the SLA as soon as possible. On January 10, 1974, Bill Harris phoned Wolfe to tell him that Little and Remiro had been arrested and would be charged with Foster's murder and that Wolfe needed to return to the West Coast.

Bill Harris gave Wolfe the information he needed to contact the SLA once back in California. Wolfe then canceled his January 11 meeting with his father and asked his sister, Roxie, to drive him to the bus station, claiming he needed to visit a sick friend in New York. When they arrived at the bus station, Wolfe gave his sister his most prized possession, a duffel bag that once belonged to his father.[5] In his own way, Wolfe was saying his final goodbye to his family and committing himself to the SLA, leaving behind any doubts he may have had about the assassination of Marcus Foster.

THE ARRESTS OF LITTLE AND REMIRO

In many ways, the arrests could have been avoided. Had the SLA acquired a safe house in the city like its former ones instead of in a smaller town, its van might not have looked so conspicuous. It was 1:23 a.m. on January 10, 1974, when Concord police sergeant David Duge spotted a van driving slowly in the general vicinity of the safe house. Duge patrolled the area regularly and was familiar with the routine in this quiet suburb. Midnight traffic was rare, and the slow pace of the vehicle made Duge suspicious. So he decided to pull over the van, and inside he found Little and Remiro.[6] Duge asked Little for his driver's license, which he provided. The license was in the name of Robert James Scalise.[7] False identifications had enabled the members of the SLA to remain anonymous. They were particularly handy when renting a home, apartment, or car without providing their real identity. Ironically, though, Duge became suspicious of the van's passenger, Joe Remiro, who had provided genuine identification. Duge asked the men what they were doing out so late. Little replied they were looking for the DeVoto residence. Duge contacted the police dispatcher to run a check on the names Remiro and Scalise. The check came back clean, and Duge had no reason to detain the men any longer. However, on a hunch he asked the dispatcher if there was a "DeVoto" residence in the area. When the response was negative, Duge decided to take a closer look at Remiro.[8]

Duge had Remiro step out of the vehicle, and he frisked him. He asked Remiro whether he had any knives or guns on his person. Remiro then stepped back and pulled out his gun, a Walther .380 automatic. Duge and Remiro exchanged fire.[9] Remiro continued to

Figure 7: Imprisoned members of the Symbionese Liberation Army, Joseph Remiro, 27, (foreground) and Russel Little, 26, are led from the courthouse in handcuffs on March 13, 1974 in Oakland, California. (Bettmann/Contributer/Getty)

fire as he ran for cover. Duge called for backup, and Little drove off in the van, which by then was rather conspicuous: the rear window had been shot out, and it had a flat tire. Meanwhile, Little had acquired a superficial shoulder wound from one of Duge's stray bullets. He was rounded up and brought into custody. When police searched the van, they found a stash of SLA leaflets. They suspected they were close to capturing Marcus Foster's killers.

Remiro evaded the police for another four hours before surrendering within blocks of the SLA safe house. When the police disarmed Remiro, they found the Walther handgun, which was later found to be one of the weapons used to murder Foster.[10] There is some speculation that while Remiro was evading the police he was able to warn his SLA brethren.[11] Indeed, his peaceful surrender suggests that he did at least warn his fellow SLA members at Sutherland Court. It was against the Codes of War for an SLA soldier to surrender, as the Los Angeles Police Department would discover later in the year: SLA soldiers who "surrender to the enemy" would face the death penalty.

However, instead of condemning Remiro for his meek surrender, the SLA lionized its two captured soldiers. With newfound energy, it began planning an action that, it hoped, would lead to its comrades' release from prison. It would be absurd to suggest that the SLA advised Remiro to surrender. However, with their arrests, Cinque and the SLA finally received the media attention they so desperately wanted.

EFFECTS AND FALLOUT OF THE ARRESTS

The period between the Foster murder and the arrests, while Wolfe was back east, served as a period of consolidation for the SLA. Although it did not expand beyond its original ten members, it solidified its organization, enhanced its armaments, and most important, survived the public backlash from the Foster murder. Law enforcement found little help within the New Left communities in its search for the killers. Consequently, as 1974 began, the SLA had reason to be optimistic about its fledgling revolution. It remained at large and untouched by the Oakland Police Department's ongoing murder investigation.

Little and Remiro's arrests had a crippling yet stimulating effect on the remaining members of the SLA. They still advocated for a revolution; however, the arrests of two of their comrades forced them to alter their tactics and set temporary goals.[12] Furthermore, the revolution still needed money. Until the arrests of Remiro and Little, the SLA could count on the income from Bill and Emily Harris and Camilla Hall as they continued to work. Cinque, Soltysik, and Perry remained underground, essentially becoming professional revolutionaries. And yet despite financial difficulties, the SLA continued to seek new allies. An undated schedule found at the Concord safe house lists meetings with medical personnel, "Seara," "Arco," "Chicano Brother," and "Bro Hi." "Arco" gave Cinque a method for converting a carbine into an automatic weapon with "a high cyclic rate of fire."[13]

The fallout from Little and Remiro's arrest was substantial for many reasons. For one thing, Oakland police found one of the murder weapons and two likely suspects in the Foster murder case. In addition, law enforcement given the task of gathering information on the SLA now had a starting point for uncovering the affiliations of SLA members, and the police began to piece together Little and Remiro's activities. The van also provided clues about the SLA's past and planned activities in addition to the cache of SLA leaflets. They discovered the van was registered to Nancy Gail Ling (Perry), and they traced the motor to a van stolen at gunpoint in Berkeley on October 12, 1973.

The police now had two SLA members in custody and the identity of another,[14] but they never followed up on searching for a DeVoto residence—the residence Little mentioned when questioned by Duge. Around 6:00 p.m. on the evening of Little and Remiro's arrest, the safe house at 1560 Sutherland Court caught fire. The remaining members of the SLA, except Wolfe, set the fire and proceeded to flee in the vehicle Willie Wolfe's father had purchased for him. The attempted arson was unsuccessful, however. The SLA members had sealed up the house before they left, unwittingly suffocating the fire before it was able to engulf the structure. The only thing the fire succeeded in doing was producing a black billowing trail of smoke, which led law enforcement directly to the hideout. But then it was the police's turn to blunder because they failed to cordon off the residence. By the time reporter Marilyn Baker arrived on the scene, the residence had become a circus: "As kids and neighbors paraded by clutching their Symbionese trophies, I kept pulling more papers from under the pile on the bed."[15] The police not only missed the opportunity to capture most of the SLA members, but also allowed the public to enter the safe house and remove possible evidence.

Within the safe house, police did find fingerprints belonging to Cinque, Perry, and Soltysik. Law enforcement's list of SLA member names was rapidly expanding. The police were able to link the Chevrolet that Nancy Perry used in the escape from the Concord safe house to Willie Wolfe and then link Wolfe to the SLA. In addition, the police "removed more than a dozen cartons of letters and files along with an address book and other miscellaneous documents."[16] This rich haul of information, which included Patricia Hearst's name on a list of potential SLA targets, did not seem to be significant at first, though one document listed Marcus Foster as executed. Next to the name Charles W. Comer, president of the T.A. White Candy Company, was this note: "kidnap or execute: warrant prepared." Beside Hearst's name was the citation "arrest warrant issued." References to Patricia Hearst were also found in a spiral notebook belonging to Nancy Ling Perry.[17]

THE PERRY LETTER

The SLA had been tracking Patricia Hearst and planning some action against her and others as early as January 1974. Unfortunately, police did not consider the notes, lists, or other materials significant enough to warn those whose names appeared on them. Even after the Foster murder, the police did not consider the SLA to be a major threat. In this way, law enforcement grossly underestimated the SLA and the lengths to which its members would go to free their comrades Little and Remiro.

The remaining members of the SLA still strongly believed that a revolution was eminent, and the "arrest warrant" issued for Patricia Hearst signaled a shift in the SLA's actions. Stung by the harsh criticism arising from its murder of Marcus Foster, the SLA moved from political murders to politically motivated kidnappings. During one of their group meetings, members of the SLA had seen the movie *State of Seige,* which exalted the Uruguayan terrorists known as the Tupamaros. The Tupamaros engaged primarily in political kidnappings and armed propaganda, and they would serve as a role model for the SLA in the next phase of its development following the arrests of Little and Remiro.[18]

Because her name had already become publicly associated with the SLA, Nancy Ling Perry lent her name to a letter the SLA sent to various media outlets sometime between January 11 and January 31.[19] The letter provided some insight into the SLA's version of U.S. history and its view of the assassination of President John F. Kennedy. In an Oliver Stone-like storyline, Perry referred to a military coup that had occurred in 1963-64, allowing the "militarily armed corporate state" to take over "the existing government" as it "blatantly destroyed the constitution that some of us still believed in."[20] In the letter, the SLA attempted to present itself as patriotic Americans whose movement supported and defended the U.S. Constitution.[21]

In her letter, Perry also included an autobiography, a justification of the murder of Foster, and an assertion that the fire at the Concord residence was meant only "to melt away any fingerprints that may have been overlooked."[22] The *Berkeley Barb* had a challenging time translating Perry's rambling letter. In fact, its article ridiculed the letter and even compared it to speeches written for "Nixon, LBJ, or Reagan." The article claimed Perry was "in too far" and went on to lampoon Perry's justification for the fire at Concord safe house by pointing out that "fingerprints don't melt." In fact, written just days before the abduction of Patricia Hearst, the *Berkeley Barb* article still wondered whether Foster's murder was an act of a "CIA dirty tricks team . . . or is the SLA a bunch of sincere people long on revolutionary theory but short on tactics and common sense."[23]

While the *Berkeley Barb* was mocking Perry and her letter, the SLA was reorganizing and training for its next action. With amazing speed, the SLA rebounded from the arrests of Russell Little and Joe Remiro and the abandonment of its only shelter. Little's arrest did complicate its ability to organize because he was the only member of the SLA who knew the identities and whereabouts of *all* of the group's members and sympathizers. Without Little, people such as "Arco," the person who had modified the group's .30 caliber M-1 carbines, were now lost to the organization because no one else knew who they were or how to find them.[24]

Cinque, Perry, and Soltysik left the Concord safe house in the late afternoon of January 10. Less than two days later, they had located a new base of operations. The remaining members of the SLA, except for Camilla Hall, joined them underground. Bill and Emily Harris quit their jobs, abandoned their personal vehicle, and vacated their apartment, leaving behind most of their personal belongings. Angela Atwood followed the Harrises underground, where they were reunited with Willie Wolfe upon his return from the East Coast. On January 12, Emily Harris and Patricia Soltysik posed as Joanne James and Judith Lawrence and rented a home at 514 Winchester Drive in Daly City, just outside of San Francisco.[25] The owner of the property kept a key, and for a while he continued to stop by the residence to make repairs to the newly rented house.[26] Although a typical renter may have appreciated this level of attention, it did not bode well for the SLA's plan to sequester a kidnapping victim in their rented house. It soon became obvious that the Winchester Drive property was not suitable, and the SLA began to search for an alternative.

On January 15, 1974, the owner of a house at 37 Northridge Drive in Daly City placed an ad in the *Industrial City Newspaper*. The homeowner later testified that he was "contacted on January 20, 1974 by two white females, Toni Wilson and Candi Jackson." He claimed he was unable at that time to identify either of the women as SLA members.[27] The owner's wife and one of his two sons, however, would later identify Patricia Soltysik as Toni Wilson.[28]

By January 23, the SLA had abandoned the Winchester Drive house and relocated to the Northridge Drive property. Soon after moving into their new safe house, the SLA changed the locks on the front door and installed a heavy-duty bolt lock to ensure that the owner of the Northridge property could not barge in unannounced. They proceeded to cover the windows "with a heavy material which was nailed to the wall." They even nailed the drapes to the window frames so that no one outside could peer inside.[29]

Perhaps the most interesting renovation to the Northridge property was the modification of the closet doors in the master bedroom. The closet, which measured four feet by six feet, was fitted with new doorknobs that prevented the door from being opened from the inside.[30] With the renovations to the closet complete, the SLA was finally ready for its next act. The closet would serve as the "People's Prison," and wealthy California heiress Patricia Campbell Hearst would be its first inmate in an attempt by the SLA to coerce the release of its jailed comrades, Russell Little and Joe Remiro.

7 THE KIDNAPPING

WITH THE KIDNAPPING OF PATRICIA HEARST, Cinque Mtume gained the media attention he craved and a sense of power that he had never experienced before. And yet the SLA was not able to translate this power into a positive outcome. For one thing, it had never determined an actual value for its captive. Indeed, seduced by the sudden media attention, it was unable to determine a single course of action after the abduction. Therefore, despite the efficiency of the kidnapping itself, the SLA's actions from that time through the May 1974, shootout in Los Angeles demonstrated a central weakness of the organization—its inability to achieve a specific agreed-on goal.

As noted, the SLA had been watching Patricia Hearst for a long time, predating the arrests of Little and Remiro.[1] Three weeks before the kidnapping, Hearst and her fiancé, Steven Weed, hosted a party at their Berkeley apartment. At the party, both Hearst and Weed spotted three "rough types, not college students—sinister." Because they each figured the three were friends of invited guests, they never confronted them or asked them to leave. Following the kidnapping, Weed identified Patricia Soltysik as one of the party crashers.[2]

The SLA kidnapped Patricia Hearst—and not her parents—because she was more accessible. She lived in Berkeley near her kidnappers, whereas her parents lived in an upscale neighborhood where members of the SLA would stand out. Patricia was an heiress to the Hearst fortune, so there would be money there for her release, and the family business included newspapers and other media-related assets, so the SLA would stand to gain its much sought-after national attention. Patricia Hearst seemed the perfect candidate for a political kidnapping.

February 4, 1974, the day of the kidnapping, the SLA had everything in place except for enough getaway vehicles. According to the *Oakland Tribune*, no one in the cell knew how to hot-wire a

Figure 8: Patricia Hearst. San Francisco, California, 1974. (Tony Korody/Polaris)

car, so they were forced to steal one directly from an owner. The would-be revolutionaries "stood on the dark side of Berkeley's Shattuck Avenue Co-op parking lot" looking for a car to "borrow." When the SLA members first spotted the 1964 Chevy convertible they would end up using, they laughed derisively at the vehicle and referred to it as a "junker." However, after several unsuccessful attempts to appropriate a different vehicle, the carjackers came back to the Chevy, which was parked nearby on Josephine Street.[3] As Peter Berenson, the owner of the Chevy, began removing groceries from the car, two females from the SLA approached him. One said, "Give me the keys. We want your car, not you." The two women and another assailant then knocked him down, tied him up, and blindfolded and gagged him. He was thrown in the back seat of the car and covered with a blanket.[4] At the same time as the carjacking, the driver of a blue Volkswagen parked directly across the street from Hearst and Weed's apartment at 2603 Benvenue Street, a few blocks from the Berkeley campus.

The SLA wanted to ensure that its target remained at her Benvenue apartment until all aspects of its plan were in place. The Volkswagen remained across the street from Hearst's apartment with the motor running from at least 7:00 p.m. until the kidnapping, leaving with the other SLA vehicles associated with the abduction. Its license plate was covered in mud and not visible. A blonde woman who bore a striking resemblance to Camilla Hall, based on descriptions from eyewitnesses, was identified as one of the two people waiting in the car.[5]

A QUICK, EFFICIENT EVENT AND ITS INTERMEDIATE AFTERMATH

The kidnapping of Patricia Hearst was the first political kidnapping in U.S. history. It was quick and efficient: within a four-minute period, from 9:17 p.m. to 9:21 p.m., Cinque Mtume, Bill Harris, and Angela Atwood charged into the apartment. They beat and tied up Hearst's fiancé, as well as their neighbor, Steven Suenego, who just happened to be leaving his nearby apartment at that moment.

They also snatched Hearst's wallet and tied her up.[6] Just before the SLA members left the apartment with Hearst, Weed somehow leapt to his feet and ran around the apartment, exiting out the back door screaming for help. Bill Harris picked up Hearst, threw her over his shoulder, and left the apartment complex.[7]

Figure 9: Fiancé Steven Weed, 26, reaffirms his promise to withhold testimony against Patricia Hearst's abductors at a news conference on February 9, 1974. Weed is badly beaten and joined by Patricia's mother, Catherine Campbell, on the steps of the Hearst mansion in Hillsborough, California. (Bettmann/Contributer/Getty)

When Harris arrived at the stolen getaway car, he found the trunk locked. While he was removing the keys from the ignition to unlock the trunk, Hearst was trying to hop away.[8] Reflecting on the kidnapping in later years, Harris mentioned Weed and Hearst's different reactions to it. Unlike her fiancé, who screamed and whimpered until Cinque knocked him down and supposedly out, Hearst reacted in a cool and defiant manner.[9]

Initial reports of the abduction, based on Weed and Suenaga's accounts, described the kidnappers as two black men and a white woman.[10] Consequently, the FBI focused on Cinque and Thero Wheeler as the primary suspects, despite the fact that Wheeler had left the SLA before the Foster assassination.[11] Ultimately, the FBI had no hard evidence linking the kidnapping to the SLA until officers found a box of .38 caliber bullets underneath a bookcase in Hearst's apartment.[12] The tips of the bullets had been drilled, filled with potassium cyanide, and capped with wax. At the time of the kidnapping, only law enforcement was aware of the significance of the cyanide-tipped bullets and their relationship to the Foster assassination. The box of bullets solidified the FBI's suspicions that the SLA was involved in the kidnapping.

Two days after the kidnapping, the SLA announced its involvement in an "arrest warrant" sent to Berkeley radio station KPFA and station manager Paul Fisher. The document announced that Hearst had been "arrested" because of a "warrant issued by: The Court of the People." It went on to state that Hearst had been "removed to a protective area of safety" and that any attempts to rescue her would lead to her execution.[13] The SLA attached Patricia Hearst's Mobil Oil credit card—in her father's name—to the communiqué, further substantiating the claim that the SLA was responsible for the kidnapping and had Hearst in its possession.

KIDNAPPERS' DEMANDS

To the Hearst family's bewilderment, instead of a ransom the SLA demanded that "all communications from this court MUST be published in full in all newspapers and all other forms of media. Failure to do so will endanger the life of the prisoner." The SLA wanted media attention, not money. Although Randolph Hearst and Steven Weed had hoped for a demand from the captors that they could easily fulfill, the next communiqué outlined the "good faith gesture" that had to be met before negotiations for Hearst's release could begin. The public nature of the negotiations between the SLA and Randolph Hearst made them unique. Randolph Hearst did not have the opportunity or the ability to contact Cinque directly. Instead, Cinque and the SLA preferred to use his media empire as their middleman. In doing so, Cinque maintained control of the process, while keeping Hearst and law enforcement in a defensive and reactive state.

After nearly a week of waiting, on February 12, 1974, the SLA sent an audio communiqué to radio station KPFA. In this message, both Cinque and Patricia Hearst spoke. Hearst's role was to reassure her family that she was alive and unharmed. Cinque spoke first on the communiqué. He identified himself as a "black man who holds the rank of General Field Marshall in the United Federated Forces in the SLA." Cinque stated that Hearst had been kidnapped because of her parents' sins. The Hearst family needed to provide a good-faith gesture before negotiations could begin.

Cinque told the Hearst family to host a food giveaway—that is, give at least $70 in high-quality foods to each person who presented a welfare card, parole or probation papers, or jail or bail release slips. Hearst was instructed to begin the food giveaway by February 19, and to hold the food distribution on Tuesdays, Thursdays, and Saturdays. Distribution centers were to be placed in the poor communities of San Francisco, Oakland, East Los Angeles, Compton, and Watts. Furthermore, the SLA demanded that there be no police interference whatsoever.[14] The request for a food program opened a new phase in the relationship among the SLA, the Hearst family, and the media. Using the food distribution program, the SLA hoped to reconnect with the Bay Area's African American community,

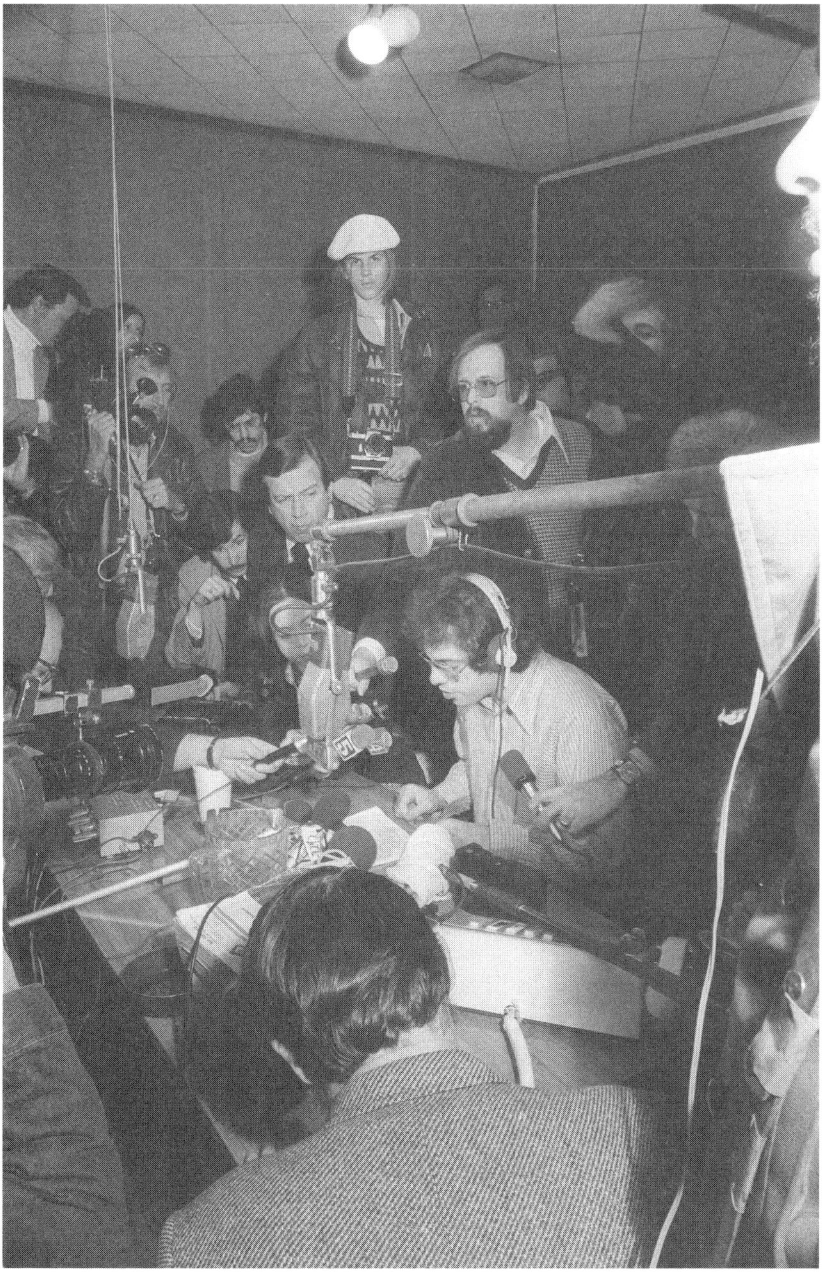

Figure 10: KPFA Radio's Paul Fischer reads a letter from the SLA to the media on February 12, 1974 in Oakland/Berkeley, California. (Clem Albers/San Francisco Chronicle/Polaris)

a relationship that never materialized because of the Foster assassination.

Patricia Hearst's role in the communiqué was not only to provide evidence that she was alive and being treated humanely, but also to validate the kidnapping, the character of the SLA members, and the demand made by the SLA of the good-faith food gesture. She stated that she was a prisoner in the same manner that Remiro and Little were prisoners—suggesting that the SLA hoped to exchange her for its imprisoned comrades. The tone of Hearst's voice led the FBI to believe that she may have been drugged.[15] Her portion of the tape seemed scripted, and it came across as though she were sympathetic to her captors and their cause, thereby foreshadowing her future role with the SLA.

This communiqué was problematic for William Randolph Hearst in two ways. First, Cinque's food distribution scheme was estimated to cost over $400 million.[16] Second, any exchange of his daughter for Remiro and Little was beyond his control. Meanwhile, the SLA had greatly overestimated Hearst's wealth. According to Steven Weed, Patricia Hearst had at one time estimated her father's wealth at approximately $15 million. However, after Weed reviewed the Hearst family accounts in 1974, he estimated the family to be worth $1.4 million. During the period between the release of the first communiqué and the taping of the second, Cinque and Perry interrogated the captive on the amount of her father's wealth. Unaware of the facts, Hearst was in no position to repudiate the assumptions of wealth attributed to her family by the SLA.[17]

The SLA wanted the Hearst family or Gov. Ronald Reagan or any other government entity to offer to swap the SLA's captured soldiers for Patricia Hearst. Of course, Hearst did not have the power to release Remiro and Little from prison, and Governor Reagan, who did have that power, refused to do so because it would set a precedent. When the negotiations for the release of their comrades failed to transpire, the SLA faced a difficult decision: How valuable was their captive?[18] In the end, Patricia Hearst was valued at $2 million worth of food donations from her father. The Hearst Foundation would place another $4 million into an escrow account to continue the food program known as People-in-Need (PIN) once the SLA released Hearst. In the meantime, however, the SLA lost interest in the PIN program, which seemed to have more to do with making a positive impression on the poor of northern California than any real desire to negotiate the release of Patricia Hearst. Although the program provided the initial gratification of being able to manipulate Hearst, by the end of March the SLA was making new plans for his daughter.

The SLA's first public arrest warrant suggested to the Hearst family that Patricia Hearst's kidnapping would be unlike any other kidnapping in recent memory, and the communiqué of February 12 erased any remaining doubts. The SLA wanted to embarrass Hearst by refusing to negotiate the release of his daughter before he undertook a good-faith gesture. Cinque and his comrades knew that if they maintained possession of Hearst, they could manipulate her family. The question was, just how far would Randolph Hearst go to secure the safe return of his daughter?

Even though the SLA's demands were unrealistic and beyond his financial means, Hearst cooperated with the SLA's demands to the best of his ability—even stating he would suggest another option within the next twenty-four to forty-eight hours.[19] Neither the SLA nor Patricia Hearst believed her father. The thought of something being beyond her father's financial means was inconceivable to her.

Randolph Hearst continued to plan for the People-in-Need program to meet the basic parameters of the SLA's request. However, on February 16 the SLA sent a third communiqué, this time to Rev. Cecil Williams of Glide Memorial Church, and it featured both Patricia Hearst and Cinque Mtume. In it, Hearst told her father that the SLA was not making an unreasonable request or trying to feed the whole state.[20] She also mentioned that the SLA was angry about Governor Reagan's comments on the upcoming food program.[21] She would, she said, remain "okay as long as the SLA demands are met and as long as the two prisoners in San Quentin are okay. And as long as the FBI doesn't come in here."[22] And once more, the SLA hinted at the release of their two friends in custody. Why the SLA did not blatantly request a prisoner exchange is unknown. Neither Hearst nor any government agency attempted to insert Remiro and Little into the negotiations for Hearst's release.

Not wanting to project any signs of weakness in its negotiating position, the SLA desperately searched for alternative demands to continue negotiations with Hearst. The February 16 communiqué called on Reverend Williams and representatives of the American Indian Movement, Black Teachers Caucus of Nairobi College of East Palo Alto, United Prisoners Union, and National Welfare Rights Organization to serve as observers of the food program and intermediaries between the SLA and the Hearst family. Other organizations, such as the Black Panther Party, the *Kalayaan* (newspaper), and the radical newspaper *Getting Together*, refused to participate. The groups that chose to participate issued a joint declaration stating that they did not condone terrorist activities.[23] By involving these outside organizations, the SLA attempted to legitimatize its actions. And through the involvement of these organizations it hoped to clear itself of any wrongdoing in the assassination of Marcus Foster, while demonstrating that the kidnapping of Patricia Hearst was necessary for humanitarian reasons. The kidnapping would benefit those without a voice in U.S. politics.

Reactions among members of the New Left were tepid at best. They proved willing to involve themselves in an activity that they hoped would lead to the release of Patricia Hearst, but they remained wary of the SLA, particularly because of its violence.[24] Many of these New Left organizations that did not advocate for the violent overthrow of the government had difficulty understanding how the kidnapping would lead to positive political changes for the United States.

In response to the SLA, Hearst announced on February 19 the establishment of a tax-exempt charitable organization under the leadership of Secretary of State Ludlow Kramer in Washington State.[25] In Washington, Kramer had established a food program known as Neighbors-in-Need (NIN), which served as the model for People-in-Need. Hearst donated $500,000 to the PIN program, while another $1.5 million was donated by the William Randolph Hearst Foundation. Thus Hearst responded in a proactive and compliant manner, but he was in a no-win situation. There was nothing he could do to appease the SLA because its demands were unreasonable and beyond his financial means.

The SLA's third communiqué on February 16 represented a tactical shift and a final push to squeeze as much money as possible from Hearst. It also reflected the realization that a trade for Little and Remiro would not occur.

Meanwhile, Cinque's tyrannical power ballooned as he himself began to receive media attention. When the media named Donald DeFreeze, a.k.a. Cinque, as one of the SLA suspects, he launched into a tirade:

> You do indeed know me. You have always known me. I'm that nigger you have hunted and feared night and day. I'm that nigger you have killed hundreds of my people in the vain hope of finding. I'm the nigger that is no longer just hunted, robbed, and murdered. I'm that nigger that hunts you. Yes, you know me. You know me, I'm the wetback. You know me, I'm the gook, the broad, the servant, the spic. Yes, indeed you know us all, and we know you—the oppressor, murderer, and robber. And you have hunted and robbed and exploited us all. Now we are the hunters that will give you no rest. And we will not compromise the freedom of our children.[26]

This was Cinque's personal declaration of war against the oppressors of the world. His diatribe signaled the apogee of his manipulation of Randolph Hearst. Cinque realized that Hearst had limits, and that there was little more he could offer aside from his media platform. The SLA released only three more communiqués before leaving the Bay Area for Los Angeles.

ROCKY IMPLEMENTATION OF THE PIN PROGRAM

The SLA's fourth communiqué on February 21 made it very clear to Hearst that he was in a precarious situation. When Cinque rejected and criticized Hearst's $2 million food program, he claimed it was "not at all a good-faith gesture but rather is an act of throwing a few crumbs to the people, forcing them to fight over it amongst themselves."[27] Cinque demanded that another $4 million be added to the program. The SLA had the Hearst family by the throat and did not want to relax its grip. It not only asked for more money, but also wanted the food to be distributed in seven largely ethnic neighborhoods in San Francisco, Oakland, and East Palo Alto with no identification requirements. They designated the Western Addition Project Area Committee (WAPAC) as chair of the People-in-Need coalition—that is, it would have veto power over any and all decisions on the PIN program.[28] WAPAC had a reputation throughout the Bay Area as a "hard-line black radical group," despite its status as a federally funded urban development project.[29] If Hearst did not meet these new demands, the SLA threatened to block further negotiations for the release of Patricia Hearst.

Instead of shutting down the food program after the SLA's criticisms, Hearst continued it. The first food distribution occurred on February 22, 1974. Trucks arrived late at the distribution sites in San Francisco, Richmond, East Palo Alto, and East Oakland. The Nation of Islam owned the initial food distribution centers used by PIN. Crowds gathered at the distribution centers early in the morning in anticipation of receiving the free food, and thousands of people were already in line by 9 a.m. Unfortunately, the trucks did not leave the warehouse until just after noon.[30] Ludlow Kramer predicted that 20,000 people would receive food during the first day of distribution, but his estimate proved to be off the mark. In fact, only 9,000 people received food in the initial giveaway, according to Kramer's final tally.[31]

With thousands of people standing in line for hours and not enough food to go around, the potential for disaster was enormous. It was an extremely unorganized affair at all four locations, but only one location—East Oakland—had trouble. By the time the PIN trucks arrived at the Oakland distribution site, the anticipation had grown to such a level that the waiting mass of people rushed the trucks. Volunteers were pushed aside as individuals leapt onto

Figure 11: A waiting crowd mobs a delivery truck loaded with groceries to be distributed by PIN program started by Randolph Hearst. February 25, 1974, Hunter's Point section of San Francisco, California. (Tony Korody/Polaris)

trucks and began tossing food to the rabble. Indeed, they swarmed the trucks—pushing, shoving, and fighting. What was supposed to be a good-faith gesture to Cinque's unreachable demographic resulted in twenty-one people reporting injuries.[32] In the aftermath of the first distribution, the Nation of Islam sent PIN a bill for $154,000 for 150,000 pounds of fish and 820 cases of eggs that were handed out from their own warehouse because of the inadequacy of the PIN distribution. PIN then settled with the Nation of Islam and sent it a check for $99,026.[33] No further PIN distributions occurred at Nation of Islam warehouses.

PIN was, then, off to a rocky start due in large part to the SLA's demands. Quickly assembled, the food giveaway program was staffed only by volunteers. Consequently, the program was plagued by organizational problems. Though later food distributions were not beset with mayhem like the first, the initial impressions of the program were difficult to shrug off.

The same day that PIN kicked off its food giveaway program, Hearst responded to the SLA's demand for another $4 million. Accompanied by his friend and colleague Charles Gould, publisher of the *San Francisco Examiner*, Hearst declared at his meeting with the press that the latest SLA demand was beyond his "financial capability."[34] Following Hearst's statement, Gould stepped forward and stated that on behalf of the Hearst Corporation he was "prepared to contribute to People-in-Need a total of four million dollars for a food distribution program for the poor and needy, provided Patricia Hearst was released unharmed."[35] Hearst needed a commitment from the SLA for the release of his daughter, and this was the offer. PIN would receive $2 million upon freeing Patricia Hearst and another $2 million in January 1975.

The SLA responded to this last offer with silence, possibly because it did not know how to respond to the pushback. The purpose of the food program from the SLA's perspective had already been met. The SLA had received the requisite attention from the media. It had humbled Hearst, and, in the opinion of the SLA, the food giveaway demonstrated the support it had earned from the poor and the needy.

Despite Cinque's silence, Hearst continued with the PIN food distribution. Volunteers continued to arrive at the PIN warehouse to assist with the preparations for future food distributions.[36] With the flurry of activity surrounding the food giveaway, supplies disappeared from the warehouse by the truckload. The situation became so bad that even the security guards were filling their vehicles with food.[37]

Despite the chaos surrounding PIN, a second food distribution was scheduled for February 28, 1974. By most accounts, this second food giveaway was less dramatic than the first as an estimated 30,000 people received "top quality" food. Arnold Townsend of WAPAC disagreed with Kramer's numbers. According to WAPAC estimates, only 15,000 received a bag of food, and each bag had an estimated value of $8.[38] The third food distribution occurred on March 5, and it included twelve distribution sites. Despite the loss of nine trucks, 35,000 people received food, according to Kramer, although Townsend and WAPAC estimated that only 25,000 received food. Despite the discrepancies in numbers, the consensus was that a sizable number of people received free food.

Commenting on the PIN program at a private luncheon for the Bull Elephants on March 6, Gov. Reagan said, "It's just too bad we can't have an epidemic of botulism."[39] Reagan's outrage at the extortion funding PIN food distribution reflected the feelings of many. He probably did not wish illness upon thousands of Californians; it is more likely that he disagreed with Hearst's eagerness to meet the demands of the SLA. A food program was necessary, but this one was forced, not genuine. Despite Reagan's negative remarks, the PIN program continued with another food distribution at fourteen sites on March 8. Thirty-five thousand people received food packages valued at approximately $20 per package.[40] The fifth and final food distribution was held on March 25.

In all, PIN distributed food to over 100,000 people throughout the Bay Area. All of this had been accomplished with the $2 million provided by Hearst and the Hearst Corporation. Despite the ad hoc nature of the PIN organization and the nearly impossible deadlines imposed by the SLA, the food giveaway was an enormous success. If the food program had truly meant anything to the SLA, then Patricia Hearst would have been released, and PIN would have received another $4 million from the Hearst Corporation, thereby ensuring continuation of the program. However, the food program was merely a ruse—an opportunity for the SLA to gain media attention, recruit new followers, and emasculate Hearst. Instead of seizing the opportunity to continue PIN, it criticized the failures of the initial distribution in East Oakland. Clearly, further media attention took precedent over aiding the poor.

On March 9, more than two weeks after its previous public statement, the SLA released another communiqué. The recording was taped to the toilet in the women's restroom at Foster's Restaurant in San Francisco. Phil Buchanan, an on-air personality from radio station KSAN received a phone call from a woman who gave him directions to the location of the audiotape. The package contained a California State Automobile Association card bearing the name of Patricia Hearst.[41]

This communication introduced Angela Atwood as General Gelina.[42] Atwood began her monologue with a scathing rebuke of the leftist elements that had condemned the SLA's actions: "It has been claimed that we are destroying the left." Those who condemned the SLA "were cowards afraid of revolutionary violence."[43] What Atwood and her fellow revolutionaries failed to realize, possibly in part because of their isolation, was that the individuals associated with the New Left were under constant surveillance by law enforcement. The FBI and other law enforcement agencies used the abduction of Patricia Hearst as a pretext to follow, interview, and keep watch over those who were associated with leftist causes and organizations. Radical elements within the New Left felt just as threatened by the SLA as by law enforcement because of its unpredictable nature and use of violence.[44]

Atwood went on to blast the food giveaway, stating that "PIN showed contempt for the people through disorganization and distribution of surplus commodities instead of quality fresh meats, vegetables and produce." She complained about the "measly two million dollars" allotted to the PIN program, and then blamed Hearst for not following the guidelines established by the SLA. The $4 million to be added to the PIN program was "a sham," she claimed. In closing, Atwood stated that no further communication would occur until Remiro and Little were interviewed on national television.

Patricia Hearst followed Atwood on the audiotape. In an

emotional, angry response to her family, Hearst stated that the FBI was the enemy, and she feared it was trying to kill her. She said she did not believe her father did not have the money the SLA requested for the food program. Because of Governor Reagan's comments about PIN recipients contracting botulism, Hearst said she was no longer being treated as a person, but instead as a political pawn. Like Atwood, Hearst condemned the food program. She asked her cousin and sisters to speak out in her behalf, particularly her cousin William (Willie) Hearst. She also said the SLA had provided her with George Jackson's book *Blood in my Eye,* and that through her readings she had gained a greater understanding of "fascism in America." To protect her from the FBI, the SLA had issued her a shotgun and would provide her with ammunition if the FBI attacked the safe house.

By this point, Patricia had developed a relationship with Willie Wolfe, and she had begun to read books by George Jackson, Regis DeBray, and others.[45] As the SLA attempted to bring Patricia Hearst into the fold of its organization, other leftist groups continued to condemn it. Russell Means, an Indian activist and radical leader of the American Indian Movement (AIM), became fed up with the SLA after the release of the fourth communiqué. "My fears have been realized," said Means, "and it looks like they're going to continue to make demand after demand. The SLA is a punk organization."[46] Means's response to the SLA's fourth communiqué reflected the feelings of many within various "radical" organizations of the mid-1970s.

In the end, the food program did little for the SLA. The $2 million good-faith gesture did not lead to the release of Patricia Hearst, nor did it lead to negotiations for the release of Russell Little and Joe Remiro. The SLA did not receive any praise for or recognition from feeding the poor. "No one," wrote Patricia Hearst, "had come out with any kind of praise for the SLA bringing about the distribution of food to the poor."[47] The SLA had not improved its reputation since its dubious beginning with the Foster assassination. The SLA wanted support from the New Left, and realized it needed some sort of positive publicity, but PIN did not bring the support or positive reinforcement it expected. Therefore, the SLA abandoned the program. By the end of March, Cinque and his followers were preparing to make an announcement that would ensure their longevity in the limelight.

8 THE MEDIA

AS SOON AS POLICE OFFICERS REALIZED the kidnapping victim from the 2603 Benvenue apartment was a member of the Hearst family, handling the media became a primary concern for everyone involved in the case. Initially, a voluntary news blackout occurred at the request of Randolph Hearst—he was hoping a ransom could be paid, or the culprits found, before word of the kidnapping spread. However, Hearst's hope for a news blackout quickly came to an end when William F. Knowland, former U.S. senator and publisher of the *Oakland Tribune*, notified Berkeley police on the morning of February 5 that his paper would run the Hearst kidnapping story in its afternoon edition. When Berkeley police notified the other media outlets of Knowland's decision, the media circus began. KGO radio in San Francisco made the first official radio announcement of the kidnapping.[1]

A slew of headlines followed. The Hearst case monopolized the front pages of the nation's newspapers until August 1974. Because she was the granddaughter of a media giant, it seemed only natural that the kidnapping of Patricia Hearst would play out on the front pages of newspapers throughout the country and be the lead story on television news programs. As the president and editor of the *San Francisco Examiner*, Hearst knew his daughter's abduction was big news, particularly in California, where the Hearst family had served as uncrowned royalty since the nineteenth century. The sensationalistic journalism popularized by William Randolph Hearst found its perfect story in his granddaughter's kidnapping.

MEDIA ACCESS

When news of Patricia Hearst's kidnapping was released to the public, a virtual city sprouted up outside the Hearst home in

Hillsborough, California. The Hearst's front yard became a campground for news outlets as they waited like vultures for the most recent developments on Patricia Hearst and the SLA. The SLA's tapes and communiqués fueled this dramatic environment as the media reported on every utterance. Never before had a terrorist group had this type of access to and control of the media—which the SLA continually exploited and provoked.[2]

On February 12, John Lester, the reporter covering the kidnapping for the San Francisco Bay Area's ABC affiliate Channel 7, was called into the main house to meet with Hearst. The media kingpin asked Lester to round up the news crews so he and Catherine Hearst could respond to the recent SLA demands for a food program. By the following morning, Lester was being called the Hearst family spokesman in the *San Francisco Chronicle,* and he went on to serve as their spokesman throughout the kidnapping.[3] Lester's involvement is indicative of how closely the media were associated with access to the Hearst family, the FBI, and other law enforcement officials.

In the first communiqué following the kidnapping, the SLA demanded that "all communications from this court [the Court of the People] MUST be published in full, in all newspapers, and all other forms of media. Failure to do so will endanger the safety of the prisoner."[4] Randolph Hearst took the threat very seriously, and so the *San Francisco Examiner* published every communiqué as well as the transcript of every audiotape. This was a small price to pay to ensure the safety of his daughter. Many other media outlets followed suit. No one wanted to be responsible for any harm to Patricia Hearst.

In media history, 1974 could be described as *the* year of investigative journalism. While Bob Woodward and Carl Bernstein were becoming famous for their investigation of the Watergate break-in and the Nixon administration, many journalists such as Paul Avery, Vin McLellan, Tim Findley, Les Payne, Jerry Belcher, Don West, Shana Alexander, and Marilyn Baker were reporting on the Hearst kidnapping. Their insights and investigations led to several articles and books, with varying degrees of accuracy, on the kidnapping. The reading public's insatiable appetite no doubt encouraged publishers to produce as many accounts of the case as possible.

With its every communiqué published and its every audio recording played for public consumption, the SLA surpassed all other movements within the New Left in media access. The closest comparison, albeit for a much shorter time span, may have been the protests outside the Democratic National Convention in Chicago in 1968. Even then, with students shouting, "The whole world is watching," the whole world was not. A strike in Chicago prevented the media from transmitting the images live. The footage was aired about a half-hour after the events occurred.

The media placed the SLA on center stage for all to see and hear. Whether the media were reporting news or being manipulated by a group of Berkeley leftists playing revolution remains in question. However, the public maintained a keen interest in the case, and so the media catered to its demands. At the same time, the press was enabling the SLA's addiction to attention. Cinque and his followers knew that any public action or statement generated instant publicity. After the Hibernia Bank robbery, for example, which would occur just a month after the last kidnapping communiqué, SLA members would turn on their radios and television sets to catch the latest news of their "appropriation." In fact, everyone "was swept up in the awe and public surprise as radio and television programs were interrupted with the sensational news of the daring daylight holdup of the Hibernia Bank by the SLA."[5]

DID THE SLA'S MESSAGE WORK?

Although the SLA's audiotapes were played on the radio and their communiqués were printed in newspapers, its message calling for an armed revolution against the fascist U.S. government did not generate enthusiasm from the American people. The SLA's message of communism and revolutionary violence went against the American norm. George Jackson may have struck a nerve with the members of the SLA, but not with middle-class America. In the end, the SLA's odd mixture of Marxism, Maoism, and prison politics could not convince Americans to take to the streets and overthrow the government. Instead, the SLA's message created a curiosity based not on interest but on an odd sort of voyeurism. The outlandish statements and actions of the SLA caused many Americans to forgo serious debate about poverty in America in favor of a more unique and entertaining form of "guerilla street theatre."

Indeed, a deeper look into the issues and concerns of the New Left led not to the embrace of these ideas by the middle class, but instead to their almost total alienation from it and the SLA and its goals. What remained of the New Left in 1974 did not look favorably on this new revolutionary group as well; moreover, sympathizers to the New Left blamed the SLA for its dissolution. In his scathing editorial in the May 1974 edition of *Ramparts* about the SLA and its violent proclivities, David Horowitz viewed the emergence of the SLA as "directly attributable to the collapse of the organized Left at the end of the sixties and its continuing failure to regroup itself and revive.[6] Bruce Franklin, the former leader of Venceremos and a Stanford University English professor, referred to the kidnapping of

Patricia Hearst in an interview as "counter-revolutionary." He then went even further, stating, "I can't imagine what political movement the SLA is part of." In an interview at Glide Memorial Church in San Francisco, Angela Davis responded to the actions of the SLA by saying, "If you want to build a mass movement against racism, poverty and imperialism, you don't do things that alienate people. You do things that will help draw people into your struggle."[7] As a member of the New Left, the SLA opened up all New Left organizations to public ridicule. It was singlehandedly destroying the reputation of New Left organizations, some of which were making positive changes n the community.

The various media outlets played a vital role in the Hearst kidnapping case by providing an outlet for the communiqués and other announcements from the SLA. In addition, journalists, news anchors, and broadcasters acted as spokesmen for negotiations between the Hearst family and the kidnappers. In the end, however, neither side benefited from these public negotiations. Moreover, the constant media attention left both the Hearst family and the SLA vulnerable to public scrutiny. A once influential and wealthy family now appeared powerless in their negotiations with the SLA.

9
THE FBI

DESPITE THE HITS TAKEN BY THE FBI's reputation from the revelations surrounding COINTELPRO, the actions of the SLA, the high social standing of its kidnapping victim, and the constant attention of the media forced the agency to experiment with innovative technologies and strategies in abduction and hostage situations while maintaining its poise. The kidnapping of Patricia Hearst was an opportunity for the FBI to regain the trust and loyalty of the American people.

Within hours of the abduction of Patricia Hearst on the evening of February 4, 1974, the FBI entered the case it called HEARNAP.[1] Upon receiving the news of his daughter's abduction, Hearst called FBI director Clarence Kelly. Kelly confirmed that the kidnapping did indeed occur, but he did not have any details at that time that he could pass along.[2] By 1 a.m. the same night, the FBI had begun its unofficial involvement in the case as agents sat in on a briefing with the Berkeley and Oakland Police Departments.[3] Twenty-four hours after the kidnapping (that is, when enough time had passed for the kidnappers to have theoretically crossed state lines, making the case a federal crime), the FBI began its official involvement in the case and led the investigation.

COINTELPRO

The kidnapping of Patricia Hearst occurred at a tumultuous time in the agency's history. On March 8, 1971, a group calling themselves the Citizens Commission to Investigate the FBI broke into a resident agency of the FBI in Media, Pennsylvania, and pilfered documents from file cabinets housed on-site. Not long afterward, copies of the stolen documents arrived in the mailboxes of selected members of Congress and the media.[4] The *Washington*

Figure 12: Charles Bates, FBI special agent in charge answers questions from the media in front of the Hearst home on May 18, 1974 in San Francisco, California. (Anonymous/Associated Press)

Post responded by publishing a story about the break-in and the documents that were stolen; the documents were related to FBI informants in leftist groups and on college campuses.[5] NBC reporter Carl Stern's decision to submit a Freedom of Information Act (FOIA) request led to public revelations about the FBI's counterintelligence programs, or COINTELPRO. Even though his initial FOIA requests for COINTELPRO documents was denied, Stern pursued the case in federal court, finally winning release of the materials on September 25, 1973. By February 1974, the FBI had undergone many changes arising from the revelations pertaining to COINTELPRO, the death of director J. Edgar Hoover, and the FBI's role in the Watergate investigation.

The COINTELPRO documents were proof of the FBI's involvement in illegal domestic surveillance. Initially created to counter threats from communists, the program evolved until by the 1960s it had become involved in monitoring and disrupting the people and organizations involved in antiwar protests. After the break-in in the Media office, Hoover suspended the work of COINTELPRO; however, the damage had already been done to both the FBI's reputation and its ability to effectively monitor domestic left-wing organizations. As for the SLA, COINTELPRO likely had a minor impact on the organization because the SLA had isolated itself from society long before COINTELPRO would have tried to infiltrate the organization. On the other hand, revelations about the domestic counterintelligence program did lead to allegations that Cinque Mtume had served as an agent provocateur for law enforcement's crackdown on the New Left in California.[6] Even though corroborating evidence had not been uncovered, the subsequent surveillance and interrogations of members of New Left organizations and New Left sympathizers had allowed this allegation to remain a part of the SLA's history.

Clarence Kelly, a former Kansas City police chief, was appointed director of the FBI during this difficult period for the agency. Under Kelly's leadership, agents could incorporate new technologies into their investigations, and African Americans and females could join the agency. The San Francisco special agent in charge who led the HEARNAP investigation, Charles Bates, had previously served as assistant director for the General Investigative Division in Washington, D.C. Bates was also in charge of the FBI's investigation of the Watergate break-in, beginning in June 1972. According to W. Mark Felt, deputy associate director of the FBI, Bates had been transferred out of the Washington, D.C., office along with four other high-ranking members of the agency for either leaking information to the media or for pursuing the Watergate investigation too forcefully as interim FBI director L. Patrick Gray saw it.[7] (Felt's comments about the leaking of information are ironic given that *Washington Post* reporter Bob Woodward revealed in his book *The Secret Man* that Felt was the informant Woodward and fellow reporter Carl Bernstein dubbed "Deep Throat" in their reporting on the Watergate scandal.[8]) Gray had served in numerous positions within the Nixon administration and was considered nothing more than a political appointment by career FBI personnel. He later became ensnared in the Watergate investigation for his role in destroying documents and "turning data on the (Watergate) investigation over to White House Counsel John Dean."[9]

AN FBI IN SEARCH OF REDEMPTION

The kidnapping of Patricia Hearst was the case the FBI needed to redeem itself. It quickly identified the SLA as the perpetrators of the crime. Within hours of the abduction, the box of cyanide-laced bullets was found underneath the bookshelf in the apartment of Steven Weed and Patricia Hearst. The day following the abduction, the FBI began questioning Weed. During the interrogation, he was asked if he owned a firearm, to which he replied with an emphatic "No." He claimed the bullets, which matched the ones used in the assassination of Marcus Foster, must have been dropped in the apartment by the kidnappers.[10] The Mobil Oil credit card in the name of Randolph Hearst that accompanied the SLA's February 7 arrest warrant for Patricia Hearst eliminated any doubt that may have remained.[11]

Within two days of the kidnapping, the FBI had pulled together a list of likely members of the SLA—among them, Angela Atwood, Bill and Emily Harris, Nancy Ling Perry, Willie Wolfe, and Donald DeFreeze.[12] Patricia "Mizmoon" Soltysik would soon be added to the list. Camilla Hall, because of her past relationship with Soltysik, also became a suspected sympathizer. The FBI's list of potential SLA members also included about twenty other names.[13] By February 28, the list of suspected SLA members had grown to about thirty-five and included Gary Atwood (Angela's estranged Trotskyite husband), Nancy Lou Boehm, William James Carter, Charles Robert Conley, Elizabeth Ruth Ehrlich, Cynthia Anne Garvey, David William Gunnell, James "Doc" Holliday, Roy Nelson Hofstedder, Willie Waco Jackson, Clifford "Death Row Jeff" Jefferson, Anita Landenburg, Katherine Francis Moynihan, Raymond Sparks, and Robyn Sue Steiner. At least fourteen other names were included on the list but redacted for personal privacy by the FBI.[14]

Despite the FBI's diligence, the agency was criticized for its inability to locate the SLA after the kidnapping. In the FBI's defense, SLA members had proven to be very successful in developing alternate identities and obtaining false identification cards. In addition, Angela Atwood and the Harrises had made good use of their background in the theater by altering members' appearance so they would not be noticed carrying out everyday tasks in public.

Camilla Hall, however, did remain aboveground—at least at first. During the period when she was blindfolded at the Daly City safe house, Patricia Hearst recalled hearing of "Gabi, who lived aboveground and brought supplies to the combat team."[15] Even though she participated in the kidnapping, Camilla "Gabi" Hall helped the SLA with its activities outside the safe house. Once the FBI identified Soltysik as a member of the SLA, Hall, who was Soltysik's former lover, became a suspected SLA associate.

The FBI discovered that Hall kept a savings account at a Berkeley branch of the Central Bank. In late February, the FBI asked the bank's manager to immediately notify its Berkeley office (which was just across the street from the bank) if Hall came into the bank. Bank personnel were not to inform Hall that the FBI wanted to talk to her. Unfortunately, the bank manager either forgot or did not think the request important enough to inform the bank tellers, because on March 1 Camilla Hall entered the bank and withdrew the $1,565 she had in her savings account, and no one from the bank contacted the FBI.[16] The agency endured a great deal of criticism for its incompetent investigation of the SLA, but in this instance, even though it had taken the proper steps, its efforts were hamstrung by the forgetfulness of a branch manager.

On March 4, Hall sold her blue 1967 Volkswagen bug, the car suspected of being the lookout car for the Hearst kidnapping.[17] When she arrived underground with cash in hand, her SLA comrades no doubt greeted her warmly. After all, the revolution needed money. Meanwhile, the FBI lost the only aboveground link to the kidnappers. Ironically, a clerk in the stenography pool in the FBI's San Francisco office unwittingly purchased Hall's blue Volkswagen. For weeks, then, the car was parked just outside the FBI offices before it was finally discovered.[18]

Although the FBI had no knowledge of the whereabouts of the SLA, it maintained contact with the friends and family members of the SLA soldiers, hoping that some clue to their location would surface. Earlier, on February 14, Bill Harris had sent a letter to his mother asking for money. Along with the letter, Bill enclosed a stamped, preaddressed envelope in the name of Janet Cooper. Bill's letter and preaddressed envelope were placed in a larger envelope, which Emily Harris sent to two friends from college. Emily asked her friends to hand-deliver the enclosed envelope to Bill's mother for reasons she and Bill would explain later.[19]

Friends and colleagues of the Harrises had been contacted months earlier in conjunction with the Marcus Foster murder investigation. Therefore, when Emily's friends received the letter, they decided to open it to determine whether they should forward it to Bill's mother. After reading the letter, they decided to contact the Oakland police. The Oakland Police Department and the FBI decided to forward the letter to Bill's mother and stake out the post office address on the enclosed envelope. Bill's mother sent her son a check for $250, but it was never picked up. In fact, it never arrived at the Santa Clara post office because Bill Harris wrote the wrong postal code on the stamped preaddressed envelope, and it ended up in a general delivery mailbox in Santa Barbara, California. So the FBI struck out again. In these two instances, the FBI had planned correctly by contacting Camilla Hall's bank and staking out the post office. Unfortunately, both opportunities were thwarted by simple, yet significant details.

TAKING A NEW APPROACH

Unlike their approach in the latter part of the Hoover era, the FBI did seek alternate methods and technologies to help it locate Patricia Hearst's captors. However, after almost two months of frustration in their attempts to locate the SLA and its captive, Patricia Hearst, the FBI began to consider more drastic measures. Physical surveillance of known SLA associates had not been productive. On March 25, FBI agent W. R. Wannall sent a memorandum to fellow agent E. S. Miller broaching the topic of electronic surveillance of individuals who might know the SLA's whereabouts. Wannall knew the FBI needed to obtain approval of electronic surveillance, but without providing the court with probable cause as it was "traditionally understood."[20] In fact, the traditional uses of electronic surveillance had undergone tremendous change because of the Watergate break-in and allegations of the illegal use of electronic surveillance by Presidents Nixon, Kennedy, and Lyndon B. Johnson, along with Attorney General Robert F. Kennedy and FBI director Hoover.

The key question then became whether the FBI could pursue a domestic intelligence operation using electronic surveillance methods without new legislation from Congress because of the so-called Keith decision. In 1972 U.S. District Judge Damon S. Keith had ruled against the legality of domestic electronic surveillance. The Supreme Court then upheld the decision, acknowledging that warrantless electronic surveillance was not necessary to "protect the nation from subversion by domestic organizations."[21] Wannall hoped that a sympathetic U.S. District Court judge might approve the use of electronic surveillance because of Congress's inability to produce new legislation on this issue and the FBI's immediate need. The legal counsel for the FBI commended the efforts of Wannall and Miller, but emphatically stated, "The Hearst kidnapping case should not be used as a test vehicle to establish the authority of the FBI to undertake electronic surveillance in domestic cases for intelligence purposes."[22]

Because the Hearst kidnapping was the first political kidnapping in U.S. history, the FBI chose to consider the implementation of any weapon in its arsenal to locate the SLA. The changes that took place within the FBI during the HEARNAP investigation are further demonstrated in the circumstances involving Murray Miron, a professor of psychology at Syracuse University.

On March 12, a member of the Federal Aviation Administration's (FAA) Air Transportation Security Team contacted Richard J. Gallagher, assistant director of the FBI's Criminal Investigative Division, to tell him that Miron had expressed an interest in assisting the FBI on the HEARNAP case and that he had worked with the

FAA and the CIA in the past.[23] Miron, who was head of Syracuse University's Psycholinguistics Center, wanted to produce an analysis of the SLA's audio communiqués for the FBI. Earlier FBI leadership would have likely rebuffed Miron's involvement in the investigation. However, the new FBI director, Clarence Kelly "wanted the FBI to explore new ways of doing things."[24]

Miron specialized in communications involving individuals suffering from mental health issues and aberrant behavior. As a consultant, he had provided psychological profiles of foreign personalities for the CIA and hijackers for the FAA.[25] Miron's analysis focused on keywords used by the speakers. The FBI referred to his methodology as "a blend of intuitive and empiricism" based on the Semantic Differential Technique pioneered by the University of Illinois.[26] Miron cautioned that the analysis generated by his computer program could not replace the experience of the investigator in the field. However, the more input he had for his computer program, "the more definite" he could be in his conclusions.[27]

In retrospect, Miron's analysis proved to be extremely accurate. In a meeting with the FBI on April 3, he provided accurate insight into the SLA. He observed that Patricia Hearst was "using SLA as therapy" and "telling the SLA her problems."[28] Former SLA member Bill Harris echoed this sentiment when he recounted that Hearst told members of the SLA about her difficult relationship with her mother and her problems with her fiancé.[29] Miron went on to mention that Hearst had "adopted the ideas of the SLA because she was suggestible and that she would require psychiatric treatment once she had been freed.[30] He did not conclude that either the members of the SLA or Cinque, despite the Foster assassination, had developed into cold-blooded killers. Therefore, he did not believe they would kill their captive-turned-revolutionary. Instead, the SLA was determined to "commit suicide by establishing the condition in which their destruction at the hands of someone else is inevitable."[31] The analysis Miron presented at the April 3 meeting chillingly foreshadowed the events that would take place in Los Angeles on May 17, 1974. Although his analysis did not lead to the quick capture of the SLA, it did give the FBI a greater understanding of the group's dynamics. Also, the FBI's receptiveness to Miron's work demonstrated its willingness to incorporate new methodologies in fighting crime.

EMBRACING ADAPTABILITY

Contemporary accounts of the Hearst kidnapping case have largely not been kind to the FBI. In these accounts, the FBI investigation of the kidnapping has become more of a "Keystone Cops" affair.[32] However, portrayals of the FBI's tactics in searching for Hearst and the SLA have been somewhat accurate. The FBI, much like the Oakland police investigating the Foster murder, needed a break to solve the case. The SLA had effectively isolated itself and was impossible to locate by conventional means.

By the time the SLA successfully robbed the Hibernia Bank in San Francisco on April 15, the FBI realized it needed greater mobility so it could react much faster to future moves by the SLA. The FBI therefore rented two helicopters and pilots, who remained on standby from 7 a.m. to 7 p.m. and were in the air three to four hours each day. Two FBI agents joined the pilots to act as observers. This rapid response unit first took to the air on April 29, and it remained active until the SLA's shootout with police in Los Angeles on May 17. The helicopters and pilots cost the FBI about $6,000 each for a six-day week.[33] Although they did not lead to an SLA sighting, use of the helicopters demonstrated the new thinking and adaptability of the FBI agents investigating the HEARNAP case.[34]

In early May, when the FBI's use of helicopters to patrol the skies above San Francisco became more common, Cinque became paranoid that every helicopter was manned by the police searching for the SLA.[35] SLA members left their Golden Gate apartment at the end of April and eventually wound up in a dilapidated home in the Hunter's Point section of San Francisco. Hunter's Point, one of the poorest areas of San Francisco, was beset by crime. The large police presence in the area convinced Cinque that the SLA was surrounded by law enforcement and that police had put up roadblocks around the city of San Francisco, particularly at the bridges, in order to locate them. According to Patricia Hearst, "On more than one night, Cin went out into the backyard and shook his clenched fist at a helicopter roaring overhead," assuming it was on the lookout for the SLA.[36]

During its investigation, the FBI also used trained dogs to recognize Hearst's scent and to verify whether she had visited specific places (it was called "Operation Sniff"). Once the SLA had been sighted in Los Angeles in May 1974, the FBI flew "Operation Sniff" dogs to that city. After the shootout with the Los Angeles Police Department on May 17, law enforcement officials used the dogs to determine whether Patricia Hearst had been in the house and if she had been one of the victims. The FBI's dogs would later be employed to confirm that Hearst spent a portion of the summer and early fall of 1974 at a farmhouse in Jeffersonville, New York, with several SLA members.[37]

In the wake of the FBI's involvement in COINTELPRO, intelligence on radical organizations in northern California was scarce. Whispers about the bureau's misdeeds under Hoover's leadership, as well as allegations that the agency gave the White House preferential treatment during the Watergate investigation, placed the FBI in an extremely difficult position at the outset of the HEARNAP investigation. In such a high-profile case, the FBI used all of its resources to locate the kidnappers. One hundred and nineteen special agents were permanently assigned to the case—sixty-eight operating out of the San Francisco office and fifty-one out of Berkeley—in addition to the thirty-seven agents on special assignment working with the HEARNAP investigation. Most of the agents were busy investigating alleged Hearst and SLA sightings reported from around the country—over four hundred between April 29 and May 8, 1974.[38] Having little else to work with, the FBI and other law enforcement agencies waited for the SLA to make a mistake. It took over three months, but they finally made that one error that allowed the police to locate the cell. On May 16, law enforcement finally got its big break, and by May 17 the SLA—as a movement—had perished in flames in its only direct clash with the police.

10

THE SLA: FROM CAPTORS TO COMRADES

THE DALY CITY SAFE HOUSE ON Northridge served as Hearst's prison. It brought her into daily contact with the members of the SLA and introduced her to the SLA's lifestyle as "urban guerillas." A walk-in closet served as Hearst's prison cell from her arrival on February 4, 1974, until the group's move to Golden Gate Avenue in San Francisco on either March 20 or March 21.[1] Although factors such as the length of time Hearst spent isolated and blindfolded, her sexual relationships with SLA members, and the way in which the audio communiqués were taped have been vigorously debated, her confinement in the Daly City closet has never been disputed.

Hearst's "cell" measured four feet by six feet and was about six and a half feet in height.[2] To soundproof the closet, her captors nailed shag carpeting to the walls. A three-inch-thick foam pad on the floor served as her bed. Initially, Hearst was locked in the closet with her hands tied so she could not escape.[3] In her trial testimony describing the closet, Hearst claimed it had a "musty odor of body sweat and filth." She likened it to an "underground coffin" and expressed her first reaction to her confinement as "utter terror."[4] She thought of the news story of the girl who had been kidnapped in Georgia and buried in a box with an air tube.[5] Hearst told the story of her fear of the closet with a great deal of assistance from defense lawyer F. Lee Bailey.[6]

Patricia Hearst maintained that her only thought after her abduction was to stay alive. Every action from the abduction until her arrest was a calculated decision toward that end. Hearst described her abduction as a series of events beginning with her isolation and sensory deprivation, followed by a series of audio communiqués taped in the closet. She also said she was raped by

Willie Wolfe and Cinque. According to Hearst, she was kept in closets at both the Daly City safe house and the Golden Gate Avenue apartment where the SLA moved to in March 1974 (a move that is described shortly) for a total of eight weeks.[7]

The SLA never considered the Daly City safe house a permanent residence. When Camilla Hall went underground with the cell in early March, the group decided to find a new safe house. One factor in the decision to move was the fact that the SLA no longer needed a "jail cell" for Patricia. She had begun taking meals with the group and was slowly assimilating. According to Hearst's trial testimony, she participated in group mealtime discussions.[8] Allowing Patricia Hearst to become a member of the SLA did not occur dramatically or suddenly, but over lunches. However, even after she became a member, she claimed she still felt endangered and knew her only real hope was rescue.[9] That said, when asked why she took up arms for her former tormentors rather than escape from them on May 16, the only explanation she could provide for her actions was that she acted "instinctively."[10]

FROM CAPTIVE TO SYMPATHIZER

Eventually, Patricia Hearst began to sympathize with the SLA's cause and become an active participant. She would not just play a big part, but would become known as the "Queen of the Revolution." Her shift in political and social allegiance began when her father told Cinque that his demand for another $4 million to be added to the PIN food distribution was beyond the Hearst family's financial means.

His daughter did not believe him. Despite her ignorance of the family's finances and the intricacies of her grandfather's will, it was unfathomable to her that her father could not come up with another $4 million. Her father's response enraged her, and she began confiding in her captors about her poor relationships with her family and her fiancé.[11] She described her mother, Catherine Hearst, as an alcoholic, who was also addicted to prescription drugs.[12] Hearst thought her mother cared little for her safety or return; she felt as if her family had betrayed her. Her sudden acceptance of the SLA, then, was not based solely on feelings of abandonment; she was also being independent and strong-willed, while displaying a bit of a rebellious streak.

Later, during the pretrial period of her incarceration, many psychologists interviewed her. One of the doctors hired by the defense, Margaret Singer, also interviewed a close friend of Hearst's, Mimi Swanton. Swanton described how Hearst had avoided an exam at Santa Catalina High School by claiming that her mother had cancer. In an interview with a prosecution psychologist, Hearst displayed "feelings ranging from dislike to hatred of her parents but certainly no feelings of closeness or identification with their values."[13] Her lifestyle choices—attending the University of California, Berkeley, living with Steven Weed before their wedding, and using marijuana—demonstrated that she was far from the innocent white girl the media and her parents made her out to be.

Prior to her kidnapping, Hearst had been having doubts about her relationship with her fiancé, Steven Weed. Her uncertainties about the impending marriage stemmed from her dissatisfaction with her subservient role in their relationship. She also found her fiancé "somewhat boring at times."[14] While in prison awaiting trial, Hearst told psychologists that in the month before her abduction she began having thoughts of suicide because she felt forced to go through with the marriage to Weed even though she really did not want to.[15] These feelings of remorse and hatred, which Hearst discussed freely with her doctors, did not dissipate following the kidnapping, and she shared these feelings freely with her captors as she began to form a bond with them.[16] The kidnapping provided her with an opportunity to free herself from her situation. As negotiations for her release dragged on, a change in her temperament was evident in the audio communiqués released by the SLA; she had severed her ties to her parents and her fiancé.

Hearst's role in the first three communiqués was largely symbolic, aimed at giving her friends and family evidence that she was still alive. However, on the March 9 tape she no longer sounded like she had been drugged. Instead, she came across as assertive and angry with her family. She expressed disdain toward her father for not agreeing to the SLA's demands for a $6 million food program as a good-faith gesture. She also voiced her sense of betrayal. She thought her father had succumbed to what she believed was the FBI's philosophy—that she and the SLA had to be extinguished. Indeed, Patricia Hearst echoed Atwood in the communiqué by proclaiming that the FBI was her greatest danger. In a moment of desperation, she even reached out to her fiancé, Steven Weed, for help. However, what truly demonstrated that Patricia Hearst was speaking of her own volition was her appeal to her cousin Willie Hearst. Her appeal to Willie seemed to confirm that she had given up on her parents: "Willie, I know you really care about what happens to me. Make Mom and Dad let you talk. You can't be silent."[17] Although she spoke of her own free will, the SLA fed her information in the hope of influencing and manipulating her.

Cinque, along with other members of the SLA, had regaled Hearst with stories of how law enforcement had inflicted violence and abuse on the Left and African American prisoners. George

Jackson's *Blood in My Eye* aroused her interest in the poor conditions prisoners were facing in jails throughout the country. She was very receptive to the teachings of the SLA and had begun to see the FBI as her greatest danger. These factors led her to announce in the March 9 communiqué, "Because of these dangers, I have been transferred to a special security unit of the SLA combat forces, where I am being held in protective custody. I have been issued a twelve-gauge riot shotgun, and I have been receiving instructions on how to use it."[18] Because she had not been physically transferred to another location, observers speculated that by early March she had either completely bought into the SLA program, or a portion of her statement had been written for her. She concluded her portion of the communiqué by stating that she still wanted to be released and that those who wanted to help her should focus on preventing the FBI from attacking her.

In her autobiography, Hearst recalled that the entire communiqué had been crafted under Atwood's direction and that "the clever personal touches Gelina [Atwood] added to the script" led many to believe Patricia Hearst had converted to the SLA.[19] However, that was not the case. The thought of Hearst taking up arms with the SLA remained highly improbable and unrealistic. Thus newspaper articles reacting to the communiqué did not mention the possibility that she had switched her allegiance.

PERSONAL RELATIONSHIPS

When Patricia Hearst began opening up to Angela Atwood and Willie Wolfe about her personal and family life, she found the love and acceptance she had not found at home from her family. Although the SLA may have cleverly manipulated her, Hearst played an active role in her own transformation from kidnap victim to revolutionary. The March 9 communiqué does not mark the date on which she willingly joined the SLA, but it does serve as a significant point in her evolution to becoming the most famous revolutionary figure in the United States at the time.

Hearst's words to her family were harsh in the March 9 tape, but she did say she hoped to be released soon. She was angry because she believed her father had not done all he could have done to ensure her release and safe return. The relationship between Patricia Hearst and her father had been extremely close prior to her abduction. The rigidity of her mother, Catherine Hearst, was counterbalanced by the flexibility and tolerance exhibited by Randolph Hearst. If anything, Hearst had been a "daddy's girl." Thus the line in the sand that her father drew in response to Cinque's demands shook Patricia to her core. She felt abandoned by the one person in her family who had always given her help when she needed it.[20]

Although Hearst's friends and family described her as independent and strong-willed, she also demonstrated the capacity, particularly in her relationship with Steven Weed, to be submissive. In fact, her relationship with Weed is a prime example of the duality of her character. She pursued Weed while he was teaching math at her high school when she was only a junior. However, despite her being the aggressor in initiating the relationship, Weed became the dominant figure. Hearst chose to attend the University of California, Berkeley because Weed was attending the university and completing his graduate work. As a couple, Weed's social circle became Hearst's.[21] Overall, despite her strong will, Hearst had allowed Weed to consume her.

At the time of her kidnapping, her internal struggle pertaining to her relationship with Weed had reached a boiling point. Later, psychiatrist Joel Fort, during his testimony at the Hibernia Bank trial, mentioned the perception of Patricia Hearst as desperate to end her relationship with Steven Weed, and she validates Fort's observations by mentioning in her autobiography her doubts about her impending marriage to Weed.[22] However, during her portion of the March 9 communiqué, her fiancé was spared her shrill comments. Instead, she chose to direct her anger and frustration at her parents.

The single-minded pursuit of revolution must have seemed exhilarating given Hearst's less than thrilling portrayal of her pre-kidnapping life with Steven Weed.[23] Her relationship with her parents had not been idyllic as well. She clashed with her mother, Catherine, who, like her daughter, was described as strong-willed and stubborn. The fact that they did not get along during Hearst's teen years was no secret. Patricia chafed under the control of the nuns at Santa Catalina High School, which her mother had insisted she attend. As Patricia became more independent, she seemed to go out of her way to make her mother uncomfortable. In fact, her relationship with Weed can best be described as exhibit A of her rebellion against her mother. Not only did she live with Weed out of wedlock, but she also attended the University of California, Berkeley instead of Stanford.

After the March communiqué, the SLA remained silent for almost an entire month. On March 20 or 21, the SLA moved out of its house in Daly City and into an apartment in San Francisco on Golden Gate Avenue. Their unfamiliarity with Daly City, as well as Cinque's growing sense of restlessness and paranoia, contributed to the SLA's decision to move.[24] The move occurred in the evening to keep prying eyes away—and just a few days before the next month's rent was due.

The new apartment did not have a yard and was not nearly as spacious as the Daly City safe house, but it brought the kidnappers closer to the heart of San Francisco. If the SLA had any hopes of adding new recruits, they knew they had better chances in an urban setting. Indeed, the move back to the city from the suburbs represented a new beginning for the revolutionary group. The SLA redirected its focus to planning its next move and educating its newest member—Tania, Queen of the Revolution.

11 TANIA, QUEEN OF THE REVOLUTION

ON APRIL 3, 1974, PATRICIA HEARST announced her decision to join the SLA. She would remain estranged from her family until her arrest on September 18, 1975. Her deliberate isolation from her family demonstrated her commitment to the revolution. Indeed, at no point, from April 3 until her arrest, did she try to contact her friends or family.

Hearst's decision to join the SLA emerged after a series of developments following her kidnapping and imprisonment. Those developments included her immersion into the radical politics of her captors and the failure of her father to negotiate her release.

The silence between the SLA and the Hearst family from March 9 to April 2 served as a period of profound change for Hearst and the organization. She began sharing meals with her captors, reading books they recommended, and participating in their daily routines, including the self-critique sessions during which members of the organization discussed their weaknesses and how they could improve themselves. Hearst also became romantically involved with Willie Wolfe, and by late March she had begun taking her turn on guard duty at night:

During a lengthy cross-examination by attorney F. Lee Bailey at the Hibernia Bank robbery trial, Dr. Joel Fort explained Patricia's motivation for joining the SLA:

> She was—something was missing in her life. She was a strong, willful, independent person, bored, dissatisfied, in poor contact with her family, disliking them to some extent, dissatisfied with Steven Weed, with whom she had been with for about three years at the time of kidnapping—and

Figure 13: The iconic image of Patricia Hearst, "Tania", in front of the SLA banner holding a machine gun. April 1974, San Francisco, California. (Tony Korody/Polaris)

> the interaction of that, that kind of vacuum, of something missing, a missing excitement, a missing sense of meaning or purpose in life with what seemed on the surface to be offered by the SLAers as she got to know them and as she became impressed, as she described in the Tania Interview, with their commitment, and as she described to me being impressed by their willingness to die for their beliefs—I think action was very important to her.[1]

In fact, Hearst referred to the SLA members' willingness to die in the pursuit of their goals in her initial audiotape following the kidnapping, which was released on February 6, 1974. As she put it, the SLA members "have been honest with me, but they are perfectly willing to die for what they are doing."[2] Throughout her autobiography, Hearst mentions the SLA's commitment to their revolution. By the time the group moved south to Los Angeles, she characterized life in their new safe house as more focused on death than ever before. "Death stalked the foul air in that safe house," Hearst wrote. "More than ever before, all of them talked of death. Hardly a day or night went by but that someone mentioned death and others quickly took up the subject."[3] Instead of being repulsed by the group's fascination with death, however, or the "foul air," she became enthralled by the revolution and admired the SLA's dedication to a cause.

Her decision to join the SLA, according to Hearst's own account, was made in late March, after the move from Daly City to the Golden Gate apartment in San Francisco. Hearst had been transported to the new safe house unceremoniously in a brand-new thirty-gallon trash can. A few days later, Cinque approached Hearst with two choices—either join the SLA or be released. Cinque viewed the possibility of "Tania" joining the revolution as a "great propaganda coup if the prisoner wants to stay."[4] He and the SLA based this crucial ultimatum on their unending quest for greater notoriety.

THE DECISION

Hearst's decision to join her revolutionary captors has always been shrouded in controversy and mystery. Did she willingly join the SLA? Hearst herself has steadfastly maintained that she only joined the SLA as a desperate survival measure, claiming she "knew too much" and the SLA could not release her.[5] However, subsequent events, such as her full, verifiable participation in the Hibernia Bank robbery and her later role as a shooter at Mel's Sporting Goods, along with her decision to contact neither family nor friends after the demise of the SLA in Los Angeles (when she had ample opportunity to reach out to them), contradict her version of events.

Less than a year after their arrests, Bill and Emily Harris would attempt to explain the process Hearst went through before deciding to join the SLA.[6] The Harrises downplayed the conditions of Hearst's confinement immediately following the kidnapping. Instead, they mentioned that very early during her captivity they gave her a copy of George Jackson's *Blood in My Eye*. The reeducation of Patricia Hearst began in the earliest days of the kidnapping, although the SLA did not contemplate her conversion until March. The housing situation ensured she would remain near with her captors. By getting to know the cell members and their reasons for joining the SLA, Hearst became sympathetic and immersed in their belief system. The Harrises also emphasized Hearst's relationship with Willie Wolfe, his patience in reading to her and explaining his experiences, and how he developed a true relationship with her.[7]

Despite later protestations that she did not like anyone from the SLA, both the *New Times* interview of Bill and Emily Harris and her own autobiography paint a portrait of Hearst and Wolfe as two close friends. Because of their similarities in age and upbringing, Willie Wolfe and Patricia Hearst would have naturally gravitated toward each other. Perhaps the Olmec monkey that Willie gave Patricia is the strongest evidence of their close relationship. She would mention the artifact in the last audio communiqué following the shootout in Los Angeles. Even later, the prosecuting attorney would use the artifact to damage Hearst's testimony on the stand during the Hibernia Bank robbery trial because the artifact had been in her possession at the time of her arrest. If Wolfe had raped her and if she had hated him so much, as she claimed, then it could be argued that it was unlikely she would treasure a keepsake from him.[8]

In addition to their comments on the relationship between Willie Wolfe and Patricia Hearst, the Harrises, in thinking about Hearst's decision to join the cell, revealed that she had begun to fear law enforcement.[9] Soon after her abduction, the Oakland police thought they had located the SLA safe house, and so they quickly attacked the residence with a SWAT unit taking the lead. In this instance, law enforcement's actions reinforced what Cinque had told Hearst and the group might happen. He often warned them that the FBI always comes in "with guns blazing at revolutionaries."[10] Attorney General William Saxbe had said during a press conference that the FBI would attempt to liberate Hearst as soon as it discovered her whereabouts,[11] and law enforcement's aggressive actions scared her. Furthermore, the thought of the FBI possibly killing those with whom she was closest, such as Wolfe and Angela Atwood, may have increased her sense of fear and resentment of the FBI.

THE APRIL FOOL'S COMMUNIQUÉ

It became evident by the end of March that Hearst had no intention of returning home. However, the hype revolving around her release had to be maintained to hold the attention of the media. The lengthy period of silence was broken on April 2, when John Bryan, the editor of an "underground newspaper," the San Francisco *Phoenix*, received a birthday card, roses, and a portion of Patricia Hearst's California driver's license. In the bundle, which was supposed to be delivered the previous day, was the seventh communiqué from the SLA, entitled "Negotiating the Release of Prisoner." The text stated that "further communications regarding subject prisoner will follow in seventy-two hours. Communications will state the state, city, and time of the release of prisoner." The communiqué was dated April 1, 1974.[12]

In the days leading up to the release of the "April Fools" communiqué, two appeals were made for the release of Patricia Hearst. The first appeal came from an unexpected source—the imprisoned SLA soldiers, Joe Remiro and Russell Little. They released a letter to the media on March 28 dealing with many issues, including their theory that the FBI wanted to kill Patricia to discredit the SLA. They also said she should not be held responsible for the actions of the Hearst Corporation, and she might look back on her captivity as a "worthwhile experience."[13]

On the very same day, Randolph Hearst volleyed back, announcing a new plan that would provide the additional $4 million for the PIN food program, which had concluded its distributions on March 25. He had been searching for some way to reopen discussions with the SLA and provide it with the additional funds it had requested. Thus he had secured from the Hearst Corporation an agreement to place $4 million in an escrow account to be distributed to the food program in two separate $2 million payments upon the release of his daughter. He did not oversee the escrow account. Three trustees not affiliated with the family or the Hearst Corporation were given responsibility for disbursing the funds as soon as one condition had been met—the release of Patricia Hearst to her family.

The request did not lead to the reengagement of negotiations with the SLA. The revolutionaries had seen many developments during the silence, including a new safe house and the addition of a new member to the cell. They had moved beyond the food program and had no desire to resurrect discussions based on what they viewed as a failed effort.

On March 29, Randolph Hearst, along with the FBI's Charles Bates and others, met with reputed SLA member Clifford "Death Row Jeff" Jefferson. Jefferson had spent most of his life in various

California prisons. He had befriended Willie Wolfe, Russell Little, and Cinque, and considered himself a high-ranking member of the revolutionary organization. Randolph Hearst met with him at the prison in the hope of securing his assistance in the release of his daughter. After the meeting, Randolph Hearst sat at a prison typewriter, crafting a public appeal from Jefferson and fellow inmates, as well as Black Cultural Association members Al Taylor and Raymond Scott.[14] However, personal appeals from close associates, just like the promise of more money for the food program, had no effect. Unbeknownst to Randolph Hearst, what the SLA truly craved had always been the attention of the nation's media outlets.

Because of all the recent activity by Randolph Hearst and the public appeals for his daughter's release, Cinque decided to play an April Fool's Day prank on everyone by hinting that her release was imminent.[15] The *Phoenix*'s publisher received the "announcement" in appreciation of a fabricated SLA interview he ran in his newspaper in March.[16] The Hearst family did not realize that the communiqué was the SLA's version of an April Fool's joke. They were excited at the thought of the homecoming[17] and prepared a room at their Hillsborough residence for Hearst's return.

THE REALITY: NO RELEASE

On April 3, word of their daughter, for which the Hearst family had been anxiously awaiting, arrived at radio station KSAN in San Francisco. However, this communiqué completely altered their own and the public's perception of the Hearst kidnapping case. At the beginning of the audiotape Patricia announced that she had not been "brainwashed, drugged, tortured, hypnotized or in any way confused," as it had seemed in her earlier statements. She then said, "As George Jackson wrote, 'It's me, the way I want it, the way I see it.'"[18] Hearst therefore came out swinging, prefacing her remarks with the assurance that these were her own words, a statement she later refuted during her trial for the Hibernia Bank robbery.[19]

Enclosed with the communiqué was a Polaroid photograph of Patricia Hearst in a crouch, wearing a beret and armed with a sawed-off M-1 carbine, a rifle scope tied to its barrel. Her pose was intended to give the impression that she had fired the weapon. Behind her was a large red SLA flag bearing the group's symbol, the seven-headed cobra.[20] In the days that followed, this photograph of Patricia Hearst as urban guerilla became more representative of the SLA than its flag's symbol. Almost overnight, Oakland and Berkeley were flooded with copies of the photograph with a caption at the bottom that read "We Love You, Tania."

After taking the photograph, the members of the cell, adopting a practice similar to that of the U.S. military, proceeded to "unceremoniously cut off" Hearst's hair, leaving "no more than a half-inch growth" around her head.[21] Any hope that Patricia Hearst would be arriving home vanished. Hearst, still seething with anger toward her parents, publicly declared that they had no concern for her safety and that the "People In Need program was a sham." Her parents, she asserted, had attempted to deceive the SLA and the people with their phony statements of concern for her safety.[22] She even called her father a corporate liar and compared him to Adolf Hitler.[23]

The main source of her anger was her parents' inability to quickly obtain her freedom because of financial constraints, and the most frustrating aspect of the kidnapping for Randolph Hearst was his inability to negotiate a prompt and satisfactory offer for the release of his daughter. As a prisoner, Hearst had not been able to sift through the news accounts of the negotiations on her behalf. Instead, she received bits and pieces of news offered to her by her captors and so she never understood the impossible tasks faced by her father. Furthermore, during the negotiations Governor Reagan announced that Catherine Hearst had accepted a second term on the University of California's Board of Regents. Hearst believed her parents had moved on without her. Thus the anger in the communiqué was her reaction to what she perceived as her parents cutting all ties to her. Her world had been torn apart, and with her new comrades she found comfort, meaning, and excitement, all of which had been missing in her former life. Feeling as though she had nowhere to go and excited at the prospect of a fresh start, Hearst chose to stay and join the revolution.

On the communiqué, after Hearst renounced her family and stated her decision to join the revolution, Cinque stepped to the microphone and announced that the SLA had issued death warrants for Christopher Brother Thompson, Colston Westbrook, and Robyn Steiner, former associates of SLA members. According to Hearst in later accounts, the death warrants had caused a great deal of angst among members of the cell. Angela Atwood and Nancy Ling Perry had tried to convince Cinque to rescind the death warrants. When a member of the group mentioned that Little "would be very upset when he learned of the death warrant" for Steiner, Cinque responded, "Both Osi (Little) and Bo (Remiro) deserved to have death warrants issued against them. They had violated the Codes of War by allowing themselves to be captured."[24]

As expected, the April 3 communiqué did not sit well with Little or Remiro. Little said that the SLA's issuance of death warrants demonstrated "an unbelievable amount of arrogance," and that "it was a culmination of a lot of negative trends that had developed."[25]

In 1976 Little would observe, "It's obvious now and should have been obvious then that there's no way in hell Hearst was ready to become a guerilla." In Little's opinion, what the SLA "should have done was send her home and let her tell her story to the press."[26] Remiro called the decision to allow Hearst to join the SLA "another example of the media effect taking precedence over more important considerations."[27]

By this time, Cinque had become addicted to the media attention and made it a central part of his decision making. The death warrants also demonstrated Cinque's growing paranoia. They had the unintended consequence of pitting Little and Remiro against the SLA. Steiner, who had dated Little for years and had joined him in the move to Berkeley, had decided to leave the SLA prior to the Foster assassination. She returned to Florida to continue her education and remained silent about her former affiliation with Little and the SLA. The decision to issue the warrant on Steiner "freaked out" both Little and Remiro. In Little's words, "Here's this woman that I had lived with over two years and loved with all my heart and my best friends put out a death warrant on her. It was like a nightmare."[28]

The death warrants were in fact meaningless. The SLA had no way of enforcing them, and the individuals named, particularly Steiner, had not given law enforcement any information. Furthermore, Thompson, Westbrook, and Steiner did not have any current knowledge about the whereabouts of the SLA and no way of contacting them. If anything, the death warrants only served to further isolate and frighten the SLA's potential allies in the New Left. If Cinque and the SLA had any hopes that Hearst's decision to become a member would produce New Left sympathizers, it was mistaken.

Hearst's announcement did prolong the media attention Cinque so desperately craved. As a newly minted revolutionary, Patricia Hearst announced her new name—Tania. Like the other members of the SLA, she renounced her given name in favor of a symbolic revolutionary name. Tamara Bunke, the original revolutionary "Tania," had fought and killed alongside Che Guevara in the jungles of Bolivia. Along with her name, Cinque bestowed upon Hearst the book *Tania: The Unforgettable Guerilla* so that she could learn more about her namesake. However, naming Hearst "Tania" did not sit well with other members of the cell. The name had previously belonged to Robyn Steiner, and, Bill and Emily Harris thought Hearst had not yet earned the name of such a famous revolutionary. However, neither argument had much of an impact on Cinque.[29]

THE REACTION TO THE NEW REVOLUTIONARY

The news that Hearst had joined her captors did indeed create a stir—not only among her friends and family, but also in the media throughout the country. The kidnapping case and its details, which seemed to have been ripped from the pages of a novel, suddenly had another level of intrigue. Taken within the context of the youth revolt of the 1960s and the early 1970s, the Hearst story became yet another example of rebellious youth trading in their PF Flyers and innocence for a new worldview that was destined to clash with their parents' values.

The SLA gave Hearst herself a chance to branch out beyond her family lineage and experiment with a different lifestyle. When Patricia Hearst hit the airwaves as "Tania," a new soldier of the SLA, she became the role model for rebellious youth in the 1970s. Meanwhile, the Hearst family battles played themselves out in newspapers and magazines and on television throughout the nation, for all to see and comment on.

Hearst's conversion to Tania, SLA soldier, came as a shock. However, Larry Lee, the news director for KSAN, the radio station that received the SLA communiqué proclaiming Hearst's new allegiance, concluded that "the actions of her mother alone could have driven her to this decision."[30] Lee's comments referred to Catherine Hearst's decision to accept a reappointment to the University of California's Board of Regents and her habit of dressing in all black as if she were in mourning over the death of her daughter. Although it is apparent that Hearst considered each of these actions detrimental to her survival while a captive, it is highly unlikely that she based her decision to join the SLA on her mother's actions. In fact, her relationship with her mother had never been close. It is more plausible that her greatest disappointment occurred when her father announced he could not meet Cinque's demands for additional funds.

Randolph Hearst had always rescued his daughter from tricky situations, including from the discipline and regimentation of the Dominican nuns of Santa Catalina High School in Monterey, California. When Patricia became upset about the discipline being handed out by the nuns, she complained to her father, not her mother. As a result, Randolph Hearst helped his daughter transfer to Crystal Springs High School, a private school for girls within a mile of the Hearst family home in Hillsborough.[31]

Now that Hearst had announced her decision to stay and join the SLA—a decision that broke her father's heart—Cinque wanted to demonstrate her allegiance to the revolution in a tangible manner. The decision came down to an act of necessity. The money from Camilla Hall's savings had dwindled and was almost gone. The need for an influx of cash was now acute. The SLA ultimately decided to rob the Sunset branch of Hibernia Bank on Twenty-Second Street in San Francisco.

HIBERNIA BANK ROBBERY

In an interview with *New Times* magazine, Emily Harris recalled that the Hibernia Bank robbery served two purposes. The first was to provide operational funding—"at that time no one in the SLA was able to work." The second was "to verify that Tania had indeed stayed of her free will."[32] According to Emily Harris, Tania was supposed to play the leading role in the robbery by firing a round into the ceiling and announcing to the crowd, "This is Tania!"[33] Bill Harris, in the same interview, recalled that the SLA wanted the cameras to capture that moment for everyone to see.

The robbery took place on April 15—income tax day in the United States. While training for the robbery, the SLA referred to the bank as "the bakery" because that was where the bread was. Also, they did not refer to the caper as a robbery because revolutionaries do not steal, they expropriate from the wealthy.[34] In her autobiography, Hearst pointed out that her best friend's father happened to be the president of that bank.

Given the SLA's theatrical nature and the desire of its newest recruit to gain credibility from her comrades, Hearst probably played a role in choosing which bank to rob. As for the date of the robbery, it was symbolic. What better day than April 15 to expropriate money from a bank to foment revolution against authority?

Detailed planning for the Hibernia Bank robbery began after the announcement that Patricia Hearst had joined the revolution. The cell members split into two teams: an inside team and an outside team. Using drawings based on reconnaissance of the bank, the inside team practiced for the upcoming "expropriation." Between April 11 and April 13, Camilla Hall and Emily Harris presented an identification card in the name of Janet Cooper to rent four vehicles for use in the robbery.[35] On the morning of the bank robbery, each team gathered in their assigned vehicles. In a green Ford LTD station wagon, the inside team comprised driver Camilla Hall and Patricia Soltysik in the front seat and Cinque, Perry, and Hearst in the back seat.

Following the inside team in a red AMC Hornet, the outside team of Atwood, Wolfe, and the Harrises was assigned the role of providing protection from the police or any other potential interlopers before the inside team left the bank. The red Hornet was parked across the street from the bank in an abandoned gas station, while

Figures 14-15: Cinque, Hearst, (above) and Perry, (left) during the Hibernia Bank robbery on April 15, 1974 in San Francisco, California. (Tony Korody/Polaris)

the LTD circled the bank twice before parking illegally in a bus zone on Twenty-Second Street around the corner from the bank. The inside team exited the vehicle, rounded the corner, headed toward the bank, and on Cinque's signal they entered it. Hall opened the door for Hearst and the two "strolled together through the length of the bank to the rear writing desk."[36] Soltysik quickly followed Hall and Hearst, and then came Perry, who dropped her ammunition upon entering the bank and had to stoop to pick it up. Cinque became impatient waiting for Perry and leapt over her to loudly announce the bank robbery, yelling, "This is a holdup! The first motherfucker who don't lay down on the floor gets shot in the head!"[37]

While Hearst, Perry, Hall, and Cinque rounded up the patrons of the bank, Soltysik demanded keys from the tellers to their cash drawers. Cinque relieved the bank's security guard, Ed Shea, of his .38 caliber Smith & Wesson revolver.[38] All the while, Cinque and Hearst kept track of the time so they could leave the bank before the police arrived.

Hearst had entered the bank with a loaded weapon. The plan called for her to fire a single round in the air to prove to everyone that she knew how to use the weapon and that she was free to use it. In doing so, she would be helping the SLA to show off its new recruit and provide proof that she had joined of her own free will. Also, with proof that she had carried a loaded weapon into the bank, the SLA knew that any claims of coercion could be easily refuted. However, just before entering the bank, she chambered a round in her semiautomatic carbine and it jammed, so she could not eject the bullet or fire a round into the air. Hearst later explained that while in the bank she "happened to notice at this point that the bolt of my carbine was off to one side rather than closed flat. It struck me that the carbine was inoperable."[39] The world would have to wait until May 16 to see her prowess with the carbine.

Meanwhile, in all of the excitement and free flow of adrenaline, Hearst may have forgotten her speech entirely. According to her account, all she could muster was a pathetic "This is Tania . . . Patricia Hearst."[40] At least she still managed to announce her new identity and her involvement in the bank robbery.

While the SLA controlled the bank floor, the assistant vice president of the bank, Jim Smith, watched the robbery unfold from an upstairs break room. He immediately hit the silent alarm button that activated two high-speed, 35-mm surveillance cameras located above the only entrance to the bank. According to an FBI report of the robbery, approximately 400 frames of film were exposed "during the actual robbery," and at four times per second this indicated that the SLA spent approximately two minutes inside the Hibernia Bank.[41]

For the most part, the robbery was executed with skill and precision, until Nancy Ling Perry panicked when two bank customers tried to enter the bank in the midst of the heist. Perry fired at customers Pete Markoff and Gene Brennan, and they hastily left the building. Markoff received a .30 caliber slug in his right buttock that exited through the front of his right leg. Brennan was also wounded while trying to flee—Perry had shot him in the hand. Both men received quick medical attention and recovered fully from their wounds. After about two minutes, the SLA left Hibernia Bank with $10,692.21, along with security guard Ed Shea's .38 caliber revolver.[42]

Speed was key to the success of the robbery. The SLA left the bank before the San Francisco police arrived, and so were able to reach their switch cars unseen and escape. The police found the abandoned red AMC Hornet parked in a no-stopping zone in the middle of the block of 2400 Lawton Street.[43] The green Ford LTD station wagon was discovered at the intersection of 30th and Lawton Streets. Both cars were located because of the San Francisco Police Department's intensive search of the areas surrounding 22nd and Noriega Streets. Based on the SLA's quick disappearance, law enforcement speculated that its safe house was in a nearby area.

But once again, the SLA outsmarted the FBI. The SLA members did not disappear into their safe house, but into the switch vehicles: a green 1973 four-door Ford LTD hardtop and a green 1974 four-door Ford Maverick. The SLA drove to an area near its safe house on Golden Gate Avenue, where everyone except drivers Emily Harris and Soltysik left the vehicles to walk back to the safe house. Harris and Soltysik proceeded to ditch the switch cars at the Japan Center parking garage at 1600 Geary Street in San Francisco, where the cars were discovered by the police discovered during their search of all the parking garages in the city. The police tried to pinpoint the SLA's location in a particular portion of San Francisco, they were thwarted in their efforts when the SLA chose the Hibernia Bank and the Japan Center as the disparate locations of the robbery and the drop-off of the switch vehicles.

The Hibernia Bank robbery served as a chilling reminder of the violent nature of the SLA. Brennan and Markoff did not try to interfere in the robbery, and yet both had been shot and wounded by Nancy Ling Perry. The SLA had been heavily armed, and once again it demonstrated its willingness to use its weapons on innocent bystanders. The action served to further distance the group from any potential allies within the community while continuing to place members of what remained of the New Left on the defensive. Because of their growing isolation, the SLA, either communally or at the behest of their leader, Cinque, continued to make increasingly poor decisions.

During her trial, the actions of Hearst at Hibernia Bank were portrayed by her lawyer F. Lee Bailey as coerced and an attempt on her part to remain alive. They may also be viewed as evidence that Hearst did join the SLA and did willingly participate in the Hibernia Bank robbery. And then there is the fact that the bank president was the father of Hearst's best friend, Trish Tobin. Was this just a coincidence? If the FBI's interview with a later friend of the SLA, Jack Scott, is to be believed, then the bank robbery becomes more than just the "appropriation of money," but the willful act of a newly minted revolutionary.

12 ROAD TO PURGATORY

THE HIBERNIA BANK ROBBERY PROVIDED THE SLA with an infusion of much-needed cash. It also brought the SLA a great deal of attention, making the simplest daily activities nearly impossible. As a result, the collective began to feel trapped within the San Francisco city limits and pressed to find a new safe house. The question remained: Where could they evade discovery by law enforcement?

The bank robbery confirmed, at least in the mind of U.S. Attorney General William B. Saxbe, Patricia Hearst's conversion to the SLA. News of the bank robbery reached Randolph and Catherine Hearst during a brief getaway in Mexico. They quickly returned to the Bay Area. There was no doubt that she had participated in the bank robbery, but was she coerced? Did Cinque threaten her prior to the robbery? Did she carry a loaded weapon? Did the tapes show Cinque aiming his rifle at her?

In the immediate aftermath of the robbery, eyewitnesses claimed that Cinque pushed a female member of the SLA upon entering the bank.[1] Initially, the assumption was that the member had been Hearst, suggesting that she was forced to participate in the robbery. However, the contact occurred between Cinque and Nancy Ling Perry after Perry dropped ammo as she entered the bank. When she attempted to bend over and retrieve the fallen bullets, Cinque swept past her and entered the bank. As more was learned, it seemed that Hearst had indeed carried a loaded weapon into the bank, and no conclusive evidence could be found that she was under duress from any member of the SLA during the bank robbery. According to the prosecuting attorney in the subsequent trial, Hearst appeared to be acting willfully. Her movements, as demonstrated by the bank surveillance tapes, depicted her as "acting with great purpose and verve, immediately swinging her weapon around to train it on a hapless customer who had entered the bank while the robbery was in progress."[2]

In his weekly news conference on April 17, 1974, Attorney General Saxbe announced that Patricia Hearst "was not a reluctant participant" in the Hibernia Bank robbery. Saxbe went even further and expressed his personal view that she was a "common criminal."[3] These comments reached the public via the media and propelled a backlash against Hearst. However, the U.S. attorney for the Northern District of California, James Browning, only announced charges against Cinque, Perry, Soltysik, and Hall for their participation in the Hibernia Bank robbery. Although Hearst was shown to be actively involved in the robbery, the arrest warrant issued for the members of the SLA mentioned her only as a material witness and not as a suspect.[4] The warrants demonstrate the fine line to which Browning had to adhere. As he stated at the time of the bank robbery, "I think this is the first time in the annals of legal history that a kidnap victim has shown up in the middle of a bank robbery."[5] The unique nature of the situation surrounding the bank robbery and Patricia Hearst called for Browning to amass a preponderance of evidence prior to any action on his part.

Despite the delicacy with which Browning handled the case surrounding Hearst's involvement in the bank robbery, Cinque made sure to point out to "Tania" that she was now a revolutionary, just like every other member of the cell. "If the feds get her alive, they gonna put her away in jail for a long, long time. Make no mistake about it."[6] Although Hearst never served the long jail sentence that Cinque predicted, his underlying point was correct. Hearst's participation in the bank robbery made her a bona fide member of the SLA in the eyes of the law. Hearst's role in the bank robbery also changed her status in the court of public opinion. Her active involvement in criminal activities appeared to confirm her statement in the April 3 communiqué that she had indeed changed sides.[7]

LAW ENFORCEMENT CLOSING IN?

Patricia Hearst's change in status caused an influx of attention from both law enforcement and the media. On a superficial level, the SLA still welcomed its exposure. After all, it had transformed its kidnap victim into an urban guerilla and successfully conducted a bank robbery. The SLA enjoyed and even reveled in the media attention, but worried when the faces of those who participated in the robbery appeared in newspapers and newscasts.

The increased attention from law enforcement made Cinque uneasy, and he began to fear that the police were closing in on his band of revolutionaries. In fact, he convinced himself and other members of the cell that both the FBI and the San Francisco police were searching every home in San Francisco looking for them. He also feared that law enforcement had placed roadblocks on all roads and bridges leaving the city with specific instructions to look for the SLA.[8] In reality, however, neither the FBI nor the San Francisco police had blocked the roads or bridges, nor were they conducting house-to-house searches.

EFFECTS OF THE ZEBRA KILLINGS

The police had been on high alert since April 16—not because of the SLA's bank robbery, but because of the death of Nelson "Nick" T. Shields IV. Shields had been shot and killed while making room in his station wagon for a rug he had picked up. The .32 caliber shell casings at the scene, along with witness descriptions of a young black shooter, led police to conclude that this shooting had been the latest in a string of murders known as the Zebra Killings.

The killings created a deep sense of fear and foreboding throughout the city of San Francisco beginning in October 1973, but it reached its zenith on April 16. The Zebra Killers were a group of young African Americans with ties to the Nation of Islam. These so-called Death Angels targeted and attacked whites throughout San Francisco because they believed whites were not human beings but "grafted snakes," "blue-eyed devils," and "white motherfuckers."[9] The Zebra Killings case, then, fed the rising racial tensions in the city. The San Francisco police even set up a special task force, Operation Zebra, to investigate the case.

The reaction of the San Francisco police to the Zebra Killings must have triggered Cinque's growing wariness at remaining in the city, especially after police officers began questioning African Americans who resembled police sketches of the Zebra Killers. The racial profiling quickly came under widespread criticism and was deemed unconstitutional by U.S. District Judge Alonzo J. Zirpoli. Subsequently, the "Zebra Check" of African American males throughout San Francisco was suspended.[10] But because Cinque resembled one of the police sketches, he concluded that "Operation Zebra was a police plot designed to capture him and put an end to the SLA."[11] Cinque's thoughts, pronouncements, and actions became increasingly erratic, dangerous, and out of touch with reality.

With the San Francisco police on high alert because of the Zebra Killings case and law enforcement's assumption that the SLA had a safe house within the San Francisco city limits, SLA members began to feel the adverse effects of constant media exposure and no longer felt safe leaving their apartment. The organization had never developed long-term strategic plans; they never expected the high level of backlash from their actions; and they certainly underestimated the resourcefulness and steadfastness of law enforcement. The robbery had provided them with some money, but they became so concerned about being seen and caught that they did not leave the safe house except when they decided they needed to search for new recruits.

A NEW RECRUITMENT EFFORT AND LEADERSHIP CHANGES

The SLA needed help, and Cinque's response was nothing short of astounding. Just days after the Hibernia Bank robbery, he instituted a new plan "to enlist new recruits into the SLA to help us get food . . . and get on with the revolution."[12] With the unanimous support of the rest of the collective, Cinque wanted to recruit new members by going around the neighborhood and ringing doorbells. Bill Harris did suggest, however, that Cinque be accompanied by a backup team when going door to door. This new plan carried a great deal of risk, but Cinque thought the need for food and supplies outweighed the risk of exposure. In addition, the SLA believed that by now people in the neighborhood "would welcome him with open arms" because of his actions for the people.[13]

According to Hearst, Cinque set out on this mission with Bill Harris and Angela Atwood serving as his backup team in case anything went wrong. A much different version of the mission was that Patricia Soltysik and Nancy Ling Perry dressed up as nurses and went door to door to recruit new members.[14] Regardless of the method and who actually undertook the recruitment, the SLA did contact a group of individuals who sympathized just enough to assist the cell with small purchases. In return, the new recruits received financial compensation.[15]

The new allies of the SLA—Black Muslims Retimah X, Jamella Muntaz, Ronald Tate, and Joel Garrett Webster—were welcomed into the SLA safe house. Angela Atwood escorted them. Following their first meeting, which included an introduction to "Tania," Cinque handed his newfound friends money and a grocery list.[16] By inviting these new revolutionary auxiliaries into the safe house, Cinque knew he had compromised the security of the cell. As a result, he became increasingly worried about the SLA's safety if it remained in San Francisco.

On April 24, the SLA delivered its final communiqué.[17] Cinque began by discussing the bank robbery but quickly moved on to a topic that had been haunting him of late, the Zebra Killings. In his typically xenophobic view of events, Cinque claimed the Zebra operation was an attempt by the San Francisco police to disarm the African American community. It was also an attempt to attack the

SLA because "I am of the children of the oppressed and the children of the oppressor together. He [the white power structure] understands that I am bringing the truth to the children and opening their eyes to the real enemy."[18] More and more, Cinque viewed himself as the embodiment of the revolution and the focus of all attention by the authorities.

The latest communiqué also foreshadowed a change in the hierarchy of the SLA. Not long after the SLA released the communiqué, Cinque named Bill Harris, who was also known as "Teko" within the cell, as his second-in-command, replacing Nancy Ling Perry. Not everyone welcomed this change, and in fact Hearst later said that Cinque unilaterally made the decision to replace Perry with Harris.

The other change involved Patricia Hearst. She announced once again her loyalty to the revolution in a strident manner.[19] According to FBI files, she referred to her parents as the "pig Hearsts" and called her fiancé, Steven Weed, a clown.[20] Although her parents continued to believe she had been coerced into joining the SLA, public opinion continued to move in the direction of the assessment of Attorney General Saxbe, concluding that she had been a willing participant in criminal activities. Future events would provide ample evidence that Heart's break with her family had not been contrived.

MOVE TO A NEW SAFE HOUSE AND A NEW CITY

After the release of the communiqué, the SLA once again sought help from their four auxiliary members. They had been purchasing food for the cell, but Cinque had a new mission for them: he asked them to purchase vehicles, and he asked Muntaz to search for a new safe house. In their support role, the Black Muslims purchased three vehicles, secured a new hideout, rented motel rooms, and helped the SLA move out of the Golden Gate apartment.[21]

In late April, when the initial move occurred, the new safe house was not yet available.[22] Despite their collective fear of being trapped on the peninsula of San Francisco, the SLA remained inside the city limits, first renting a motel room in the Hunter's Point section of the city for two days. Their new house at 1808 Oakdale Street was also in Hunter's Point, their old stomping grounds. Both the house and the neighborhood were worse than before, but it is likely Cinque agreed to move there because he knew the Oakdale residence would serve only as a temporary stopping place.

It is not certain exactly when the SLA moved out of the San Francisco apartment. It is well known, however, that they left behind a mess. Members of the SLA spread trash all around the apartment, wrote slogans on the walls, and left the bathtub full of papers, water, urine, household cleaners, and cyanide. Bill Harris even left a message for the authorities: "Warning to the FBI, CIA, NSA, and CBS—there are a few clues in the bathroom. However, you will have to wait until they dry. An additional word of caution: ½ lb. of cyanide crystals have been added to this 'home brew'—so, pig drink at your own risk. There are also many additional juicy SLA clues throughout this safe house. However, remember that you are not bullet-proof either. Happy Hunting Charles."[23]

On May 2, the building manager and the exterminator hired to deal with a cockroach outbreak in the building were greeted with the filth the SLA left behind. Upon entering the former SLA hideout, the building manager noticed two notes left on the floor of the apartment: one dated April 26 instructing all tenants to make their rent checks payable to D & G Investment Company and another note dated April 29 stating that the apartment building would be fumigated on May 2.[24] Because of these notices and their placement just inside the apartment door, it is likely that the SLA left the Golden Gate apartment on or before April 26, just two days after the release of their final communiqué. Nothing left behind at the apartment provided law enforcement with any new clues about the whereabouts of the SLA. In fact, until the shooting at Mel's Sporting Goods in Los Angeles on May 16, the FBI had no idea that the SLA had left the Bay Area.

For reasons unknown, Cinque was drawn to Los Angeles, despite his past difficulties with the police in southern California. Hearst mentioned that by the time they discussed moving to Los Angeles the SLA had developed "a new sense of fatalism," which she sensed creeping "into all of their thinking."[25] The decision to move to Los Angeles, she reported, emanated solely from Cinque and "caused considerable consternation among the others."[26]

Even though most of the SLA members worried about their lack of familiarity with Los Angeles, Cinque dismissed their concerns, and in preparation for the move had everyone "learning the terrain by studying street maps."[27] One motivation for the move south was Cinque's growing worry that "the whole Bay Area is getting too hot for us" and that the police were closing in on them.[28] Another reason was the decision to break the cell up into three-person teams for safety and to begin functioning independently to recruit new members.[29] Hearst found herself teamed up with Bill and Emily Harris.

Between April 26 and May 8, the four auxiliary members of the SLA bought three used vans—two Volkswagens and one Chevrolet. In return, Cinque gave the Black Muslims the station wagon they had been using to run errands for the cell.[30] These three vans gave the

SLA transport they needed to move their revolution to Los Angeles. Without even so much as a scouting expedition to establish a new safe house, the SLA left San Francisco for Los Angeles at 11 o'clock on the night of May 8, 1974.[31]

Apparently, the SLA's departure from the Bay Area coincided with a renewed effort by Randolph Hearst to secure the return of his daughter. At midnight on May 3, Hearst and the Hearst Corporation's offer of $4 million for the People-in-Need program had expired. On May 8, Hearst decided to turn the heat up even higher on the SLA by offering "$50,000 to anyone who furnished information leading to the safe return of Patricia to her family."[32] Now more than ever, the isolation of the members of the SLA was imminent.

In an act of blind faith, or one of complete obedience, the members of the SLA followed Cinque to Los Angeles. On the morning of May 9, SLA members traveling in three separate vans convened at a small neighborhood park in Los Angeles.[33] They quickly settled into the area once Soltysik and Perry found an "old, dilapidated, unpainted wooden shack" with running water, but no gas or electricity. With this new safe house, located at 833 West 84th Street in the ghetto of Compton, the SLA hit rock bottom in terms of its accommodations.[34] Furthermore, the white members of the cell needed to stay indoors to avoid calling attention to themselves in the predominantly African American neighborhood.

In retrospect, Emily Harris conceded that one of the problems with the move to Los Angeles was the fact that the SLA "didn't understand the nature of the various communities in LA, being used to the Bay Area where the neighborhoods are much more racially mixed. In South Central Los Angeles white people are really visible and draw a certain amount of attention."[35] In fact, the property manager who rented the cottage to the SLA, Kyle "Prophet" Jones, informed Cinque that in this neighborhood "whites were not tolerated and even police came into the area at their own peril."[36] Apparently, the SLA had forgotten about the Watts riots of 1965 and the lingering tensions between the African American community of South Central Los Angeles and the Los Angeles Police Department. For that reason, the multiethnic SLA members experienced racial tension as they attempted to blend into their Los Angeles neighborhood, and member recruitment became far more difficult. By the time their presence in southern California was discovered, the SLA had not developed a single meaningful contact. The New Left and antiwar protests did not resonate throughout the area as they had in the San Francisco Bay Area.

Previously, SLA members had avoided interacting with friends from their past so they would not compromise their security. However, because members had just completed a move to Los Angeles and had an opportunity to start over, they began announcing their arrival by contacting old acquaintances. From Hearst's accounts, upon their arrival in southern California the team of the Harrises and Hearst attempted to contact a former friend from Indiana, Jane Bumb. However, the reunion went poorly. The Harrises also tried to contact the mother of Lumumba (also known as Barron Broadnax), an African American prisoner with whom Emily Harris had developed a deep attachment. But Lumumba's mother, Utommu, was not home. Bill and Emily appear to have sought help in desperation, much as Cinque had done in contacting the Black Muslims. In each case, the SLA willingly compromised security in return for links to the outside world. Their isolated lives underground had begun to take a toll.[37] On May 15, Bill and Emily Harris made one final attempt to contact Utommu, demonstrating their desperation for outside contact.

After everyone arrived at the new safe house in Los Angeles, the group continued to drill in anticipation of future actions against the government. Hearst described an intensified training regimen and a growing focus on death. Unfortunately, all their training had to take place inside the two-bedroom shack. Cinque stressed from the very beginning that all SLA members were to remain indoors during daylight hours unless involved in an approved activity.[38]

The iconic group photographs taken of the SLA at their Oakdale residence with a homemade SLA flag in the background were later discovered in Los Angeles. These photographs were to be used in their upcoming recruiting drive in southern California. Furthermore, Cinque began planning a new phase of operations for the SLA that included a series of "search and destroy" missions focusing on the ambush of police officers and home invasions.[39] Cinque viewed the home invasion component as a recruitment tool: "The people would come to understand our mission and would welcome SLA combat units into their homes."[40]

Once settled, Cinque gathered his small army together for what he considered a major announcement. While drinking his ever-present plum wine, he told his troops that he had just discovered what he was: "I am here on earth to lead the people."[41] This revelation led to his next announcement, recorded later, that he intended to write a book that "would impart to the people all of the wisdom and knowledge and experience that he had garnered during his lifetime." In Cinque's mind, his new book would replace George Jackson's *Blood in My Eye* because "George had lost touch with the people in the street."[42] Ironically, in many ways Cinque was describing himself. The isolation and constant state of readiness for combat had begun to take its toll. Cinque was tired and had begun to drift into his own world.

The SLA's move south went unnoticed by the FBI and LAPD. And from May 9 until the afternoon of May 16, the day-to-day activities of the SLA are largely unknown except for what Hearst provides in her autobiography and mentioned in her interviews with the FBI in 1976. Meanwhile, the end of the SLA was fast approaching.

MEL'S SPORTING GOODS SHOOTOUT

On May 16, 1974, at approximately 4:10 p.m. Bill and Emily Harris entered Mel's Sporting Goods at 11425 South Crenshaw Boulevard in Inglewood, a suburb of Los Angeles.[43] They left Patricia Hearst in the red and white Volkswagen van, which they had parked directly across the street from Mel's. The sporting goods store was their fourth stop on their shopping excursion. They had previously purchased four bags of groceries from the Thriftmart totaling $33.06, and from Boston Stores of Southern California they had purchased six pairs of Levi's jeans for a total of $81.41. In addition, they bought nine 5 × 3 notebooks from Sloan Stationers and spent $12.55 on cigarettes, leather gloves, Sterno, batteries, chewing gum, and aspirin. At Mel's Sporting Goods, Bill and Emily purchased "one blue large sweat shirt, a 25-loop shotgun shell belt, five pair of gray heavy knit wool socks [not including the pair that Bill Harris had placed inside his jacket], two 'bike' knee pads, one black knit watch type cap, two pair of white wool socks and two pair of white tube socks."[44]

As Bill and Emily Harris paid for their items at the cash register, Anthony Shepard, a store employee, informed the other employees that he had seen Harris slip a pair of socks wrapped in cellophane inside his hunting jacket.[45] While Bill and Emily completed their transaction, Shepard picked up his pistol and handcuffs and told his boss, Bill Huett, what had transpired. As Bill and Emily left the store, Shepard and Huett followed them outside.[46] There, Shepard asked Bill Harris to return to the store and pay for the item he had shoplifted. Harris responded angrily that he had not stolen anything and continued walking across South Crenshaw Boulevard toward the van. Shepard then grabbed Harris's arm and shouted, "You are under arrest!" Shepard and Harris then wrestled each other to the ground, and Emily jumped on Shepard's back.

Shepard, a "young man, with a coppery afro, a Fu Manchu mustache, muscular and with a tough guy attitude," was not going to shy away from a confrontation with Bill Harris.[47] Larger and stronger than Bill Harris, he was able to place one of the cuffs on Bill's left wrist, despite having Emily on his back. Bill Harris, during all the wrestling, attempted to pull a small revolver from his waistband,

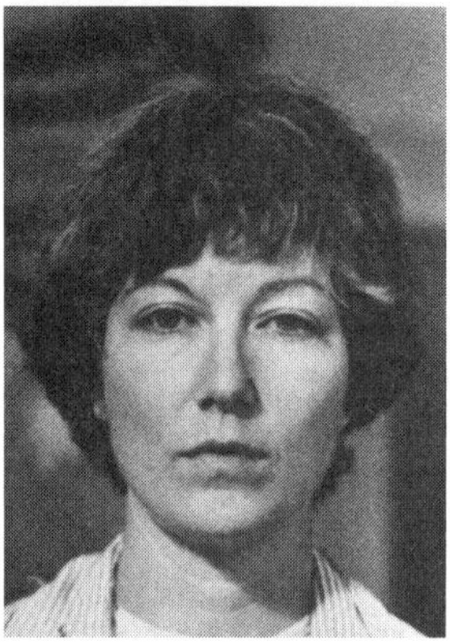

Figures 16-17: Bill and Emily Harris. San Francisco, California, 1974. (Tony Korody/Polaris)

but Huett quickly pried it away from him while other store employees came outside to assist with the arrest. While attempting to place a cuff on Bill's right wrist, Shepard heard gunshots coming from across the street.

Patricia Hearst fired thirty shots toward Mel's Sporting Goods.[48] Twenty-seven shots were from Bill Harris's submachine gun and three shots were from her semiautomatic carbine. She referred to her decision to fire at the sporting goods store in her trial testimony as a reflex.[49] In her autobiography, Hearst stated, "The only answer I could find that satisfied me . . . was that I acted instinctively, because I had been trained and drilled to do just that, to react to a situation without thinking, just as soldiers are trained and drilled to obey an order under fire instinctively, without questioning it."[50] Her attempt to free Bill and Emily Harris from arrest is the best evidence that Patricia Hearst had indeed become a full-fledged member of the SLA.

While Hearst kept their pursuers at bay with her suppressing fire, Bill and Emily Harris scampered across South Crenshaw Boulevard and leapt over a three-foot-high retaining wall on their way back to the red and white Volkswagen van. Shepard pulled out a revolver and fired two rounds at the van as it sped away. During the struggle, Bill lost the handgun that Emily had purchased in her own name before going underground. This handgun would be enough evidence for the police to realize that the SLA was no longer in the Bay Area but had moved to Los Angeles.

After fleeing the store, Bill and Emily Harris looked for new transportation because the clerks at Mel's had seen them drive off in their van.[51] Shepard continued his pursuit of the shoplifter in his car, following the Volkswagen van north on Crenshaw Boulevard, then east onto Imperial Highway to Wilton Place, then along 115th Street, and finally catching up to the van on Ruthelen Street. Shepard then saw Bill Harris commandeer a black and yellow Pontiac. When Harris noticed Shepard a few car lengths behind, he began walking toward Shepard while pointing a weapon in his direction. Seeing this, Shepard quickly slammed his vehicle in reverse and left the area as quickly as possible.[52]

The Harrises and Hearst transferred their weapons to the Pontiac that Bill had taken at gunpoint from Ken Pierre and Marva Davis. In doing so, he announced, "We're the SLA. We need your car. I may have to kill someone today and I don't want to kill you."[53] Three blocks later, the Pontiac stalled in the intersection of 115th Street and Cimarron Avenue. After several failed attempts to restart the car, Bill Harris approached a car belonging to Tom Patin Sr. and Tom Patin Jr. and told them, "We're from the SLA and we need your car, we need it right now." The Patins gave Harris the keys to their light blue 1963 Chevy Nova station wagon,[54] and the three SLA members transferred their belongings to yet another getaway car.

By 4:30 p.m., Bill and Emily Harris, along with Patricia Hearst, had effectively escaped from their pursuers. They had demonstrated the capacity to think quickly and strategically to elude the police following the incident at Mel's. Were it not for a parking citation forgotten in their abandoned van with the address 835 West 84th Street printed right on it, they might have gotten away with it; instead, they had effectively provided the police with the location of the house next door to the SLA safe house (at 833). In addition, a witness at Mel's had positively identified Bill and Emily Harris.[55]

At 7 p.m. that evening, Emily Harris knocked on the door of the Matthews residence in Lynwood, a suburb of Los Angeles. Bill and Emily had spotted a "for sale" sign on the blue 1969 Ford van that sat in the driveway. On the run from police, they needed a vehicle that had not been identified by the police or bystanders. The owner, eighteen-year-old Thomas Dean Matthews, hoping for a quick sale, agreed to allow Emily Harris to test drive the van. After driving two blocks to the corner of Pine Street and Pendleton Avenue, Emily pulled the van over and asked if her two friends could come along on the test drive. Bill Harris then approached Matthews with a drawn automatic rifle, saying, "We're from the SLA. Get in back and do what you're told and you won't get hurt."[56] They placed Matthews in the back of the van and covered him with a blanket. Bill informed their latest victim that they only wanted to use the van for a brief time. If he cooperated, no harm would come to him.[57]

After acquiring their new means of transportation, the first order of business for Bill Harris was to find a hacksaw so he could remove the handcuff Shepard had placed on his wrist. While they looked for a hardware store, Matthews had a chance to talk his captors about the SLA. To begin with, Harris introduced Matthews to the most famous hostage in America, Patricia Hearst.

Bill explained to him that the SLA's goal was to overthrow the government, which, in their view, had been taken over by corporate America after President Kennedy's assassination. Harris then tried to recruit Matthews into the SLA, but Matthews was more interested in his baseball game the next day than the impending revolution.

In his conversation with Hearst, however, Matthews learned a lot. She told him that they had to rob the Hibernia Bank in ninety seconds to get away before police arrived. She also mentioned the SLA's use of cyanide bullets. Hearst was in excellent spirits as she told Matthews about the events at Mel's Sporting Goods earlier in the day. As she recounted, "It was a good feeling to see her two comrades come across the street unharmed." Her demeanor and attitude were those of someone acting of their own accord, not a victim who was acting the part to ensure her survival. She then proceeded to tell their new captive that her kidnapping had been real.[58]

At approximately 8:30 p.m., the van made its way to the Century drive-in movie theatre. The SLA has designated the theatre as a meeting place in case members became separated. Despite all the difficulties they encountered, the team managed to escape police and find their way to the drive-in. As soon as they parked, they used the hacksaw they bought to remove the handcuff from Bill's wrist, followed by a visit to the snack shack. Matthews kept the handcuff as a souvenir.[59] After the trio returned with their food and drinks, they placed a cup upside-down on the pole that held the audio units to let the other SLA members know their location. They remained at the drive-in theatre until 1 in the morning of May 17.

For reasons unknown, Cinque and the others did not follow the procedures that had been established upon their arrival in Los Angeles. Instead, they chose to stay in the general vicinity of their first safe house and did not attempt to leave the city. After leaving the drive-in, the Harrises, with Hearst and Matthews in tow, headed out to the Hollywood Hills to sleep, but Emily persuaded Bill to drive by the house on West 84th Street. When they drove by, they saw that their comrades had abandoned the safe house. The SLA had been dismembered.

By 10 p.m. on May 16, the FBI had notified the Los Angeles Police Department of the SLA's presence in the greater Los Angeles area, confirming that the shootout in Inglewood had included members of the SLA. The FBI also began to stake out the 800 block of West 84th Street. At 2:30 a.m. on May 17, the FBI, LAPD, Los Angeles County Sheriff's Office, and the Inglewood Police Department met and coordinated their efforts to locate and capture the SLA. In recognition of the violent tendencies of the SLA, supervisors from LAPD's SWAT team were involved in these meetings as well. By

4 a.m. that morning, the efforts to locate the SLA were focusing on the residence at 833 West 84th Street.[60] At 5:30 a.m., FBI and LAPD personnel stopped a resident of 835 West 84th Street, who told officers that the individuals who owned the vans parked by his house were male and female Caucasians living at the 833 West 84th Street residence. LAPD and FBI SWAT teams proceeded to surround the suspected SLA residence.[61]

At 8:50 a.m., an LAPD sergeant announced via bullhorn that the 833 West 84th Street residence was surrounded and that all inside should exit through the front door with their hands up. At 8:55 a.m., the FBI's officer in charge (OIC) ordered the use of tear gas, and LAPD SWAT officers fired seven rounds into the residence. The FBI's SWAT team then entered the suspected SLA hideout from the rear, only to discover that the SLA members had left in a hurry much earlier.[62] In fact, they would learn that the six members who had remained at the residence had vacated the area sometime during the evening of May 16. Following the shootout at the sporting goods store, the news that the SLA might be in Los Angeles had been released by television and radio stations. Undoubtedly, Cinque and the others had heard the news and prepared to leave.

Around 4 a.m. on May 17, Cinque, along with Willie Wolfe, Angela Atwood, Nancy Ling Perry, Patricia Soltysik, and Camilla Hall, found a house with its lights on. Cinque decided to knock on the door and seek refuge at the small stucco house at 1466 East 54th Street. The occupants of the house had been drinking wine and playing dominoes when Cinque knocked on the door. Christine Johnson and Minnie Lewis answered the door, and Cinque introduced himself.[63]

He offered the women $100 if he and his friends could stay for a while. The women agreed, and the SLA began unloading their weapons, bombs, and other items from the vans into the house. Freddie Freeman, a friend of Johnson and Lewis's who had been with them when the SLA arrived on their doorstep, told Cinque that he knew of a spot at 1451 East 53rd Street where they could ditch the vans. Freeman helped Cinque drive the vans to the drop-off location, hoping his assistance might encourage Cinque to be just as generous with him as he had been with his friends. However, unbeknownst to Cinque, the spot Freeman had mentioned was a known drop-off point for stolen vehicles, and it was heavily monitored by the LAPD.

Cinque gave Freeman the money needed to purchase new vehicles, and the members of the SLA began scouting out local apartments in the area to serve as a hideout until the police lost track of them. Cinque also used other friends of Johnson and Lewis's to run errands for the SLA, and he encouraged their cooperation by paying them handsomely for their assistance. Brenda Daniels, a friend of

Lewis and Johnson's who just happened to be at the house when the SLA arrived, was given $20 to purchase groceries and cigarettes from the corner market. Meanwhile, Cinque seems to have grown tired of running and hiding from police. He made no concerted effort to conceal his identity, nor did he attempt to move to a new location as the day wore on.

As Cinque and his band were making themselves at home in South Central Los Angeles, the Harrises and Patricia Hearst were continuing their frantic escape. At approximately 6 a.m. on May 17, they acquired a new vehicle. Frank Sutter, in his 1973 Lincoln Continental, pulled over to pick up two young female hitchhikers, but instead he found himself staring down the barrels of two handguns—one held by Emily Harris, the other by Patricia Hearst. Now that they had a new car, Bill Harris told Matthews he was free to go, and even offered to give him gas money for his drive home, but Matthews refused.[64] The three SLA members then drove Sutter's vehicle to where they could purchase another vehicle—one not associated with a crime or any other known SLA activity. They had located a used car from ads in the newspaper and purchased it around 1 p.m. Sutter was then released, but he was out the $250 that Bill Harris had taken from his wallet. In their newly acquired vehicle, the team headed for Anaheim so they could lose themselves among the Disneyland tourists. By 5:30 p.m., they had rented a hotel room and had turned on the television only to find that the FBI and LAPD had surrounded their comrades.[65]

THE FINAL SHOOTOUT

The search Cinque had foreseen had finally happened. LAPD located the SLA's vans that Cinque and Freeman had dropped off on East 53rd Street, and from them it surmised that the SLA was nearby. Based on intelligence from the surrounding neighborhoods, the police believed that Cinque and his followers were hiding at 1462 East 54th Street. However, at around 5 p.m., Mary Carr and her grandson told police that Cinque, Hall, and possibly Hearst were holed up at her daughter's home at 1466 East 54th Street. By 5:30 p.m., the SLA's presence at the 1466 East 54th Street residence had been confirmed, and police began evacuating nearby residents. However, not everyone in the area cooperated, and the residents of 1449 and 1462 East 54th Street remained in their homes throughout the shootout.[66]

The FBI had been the leading investigators on the Hearst kidnapping case and the ensuing search for the SLA in the Bay Area. After the shootout at Mel's Sporting Goods and the assault on the SLA hideout on West 84th Street, sightings began coming in from all over the city. At this point, LAPD and Chief of Operations Daryl Gates had taken the lead on the search for the SLA. At 2 p.m. on May 17, the issue of authority over the case between the FBI and the LAPD came to a head.

William Sullivan, the FBI's lead agent in Los Angeles, insisted that the FBI's SWAT team lead the assault once the SLA had been located. Daryl Gates replied simply, "The answer is no. If there's going to be any shooting in Los Angeles, it's going to be done by LAPD."[67] According to Gates, the FBI did not have a choice. They needed support from Los Angeles police to cordon off the area, provide logistical support, and evacuate people, as well as support from the fire department, ambulances, and other services.[68] Furthermore, LAPD had already had success in dealing with heavily armed and aggressive left-wing groups such as the Black Panthers. The FBI and LAPD resolved their disagreements and determined that in the upcoming shootout, the FBI's SWAT team would serve as a reserve unit only, with the LAPD's SWAT units taking the lead.

At 5:44 p.m., LAPD made an announcement by bullhorn to Cinque and his followers. "Occupants of 1466 East 54th Street, this is the Los Angeles Police Department speaking, come out with your hands up. Comply immediately and you will not be harmed." According to the police report of the shootout, the announcement was repeated immediately and the SWAT teams throughout the area heard each announcement.[69] With no reaction from the SLA forthcoming, another attempt was made to secure their peaceful surrender. This time, an eight-year-old African American boy came out the front door, confirming that the announcements were heard inside the house. He was Minnie Lewis's son, Tony, and he left after the first announcement by the bullhorn.

After two more announcements by bullhorn, Clarence Ross, a drunk neighbor who had been watching cartoons with Tony Lewis, left the premises.[70] According to the eight-year-old, the occupants of the house "had guns and were wearing ammunition belts across their chests."[71] It thus became apparent that the SLA had no intention of surrendering without a fight, and the time had come for LAPD to take direct action against Cinque and his revolutionaries. The decision to act forcefully was not without its risks. LAPD officials had no idea whether Patricia Hearst was inside the small stucco home.

Regardless, the Los Angeles police did not want a standoff that would last into the evening. Even though it had been a decade since the Watts riots, the relationship between LAPD and the African American population of South Central Los Angeles remained contentious and violent at times. The longer the standoff remained

Figure 18: The Los Angeles Police Department launches an assault on the Symbionese Liberation Army hideout. May 17, 1974, Los Angeles, California. (Tony Korody/Polaris)

unresolved, the greater the possibility that the police perimeter could succumb to the growing crowds. Also, Los Angeles police had a history of quick resolutions to standoffs with heavily armed leftist groups. In a shootout with six Black Panthers holed up in a fortified house in South Central Los Angeles on December 8, 1969, LAPD had moved as quickly as possible, serving warrants on two individuals in the house at 5:30 a.m. When the shootout had become a stalemate by 10 a.m., LAPD had received permission to use a grenade launcher provided by the Marines at Camp Pendleton to dislodge the Black Panthers from their "fort."

In that instance, prior to using the weapon, LAPD had made a final attempt to convince the Black Panthers to surrender, "otherwise we're going to take drastic measures."[72] But thus far on May 17, the SLA had shown no intention of surrendering, and LAPD was obliged to take a more forceful approach. Those sympathetic to the goals of the New Left have since characterized the shootout between the Los Angeles police and the SLA as a confrontation instigated willingly by police. According to New Left sympathizers, the SLA were trapped and given no opportunity to surrender.[73] However, the fact that the eight-year-old boy and Clarence Ross had been able to leave the house before the shooting began suggests that the members of the SLA had indeed had that same opportunity. At no point during the initial standoff did any member of the SLA attempt

Figure 19: The burned remains of the SLA hideout where six members of the SLA died. Cinque died of a self-inflicted gunshot wound to the head. May 17, 1974, Los Angeles, California. (Art Rogers/Los Angeles Times/Polaris)

to contact the police.

At 5:44 p.m., when a LAPD officer announced over the bullhorn that the house at 1466 East 54th Street was surrounded and asked the occupants to come out with their hands up, the SLA had two choices, fight or surrender. In the next eight minutes, the police would make seventeen surrender announcements. As the standoff continued into its eighth minute, a SWAT officer complied with the order to fire "two 509 CS Flight-Rite tear gas projectiles through the top of the West window of the SLA residence."[74] Only after the dispersal of gas from the second projectile did the SLA respond with gunfire.

The shootout began at 5:53 p.m. Los Angeles police responded with more tear gas and semiautomatic weapons. The FBI's SWAT team also fired tear gas into the SLA hideout. As the shootout continued, the house caught fire. At 6:41 p.m., smoke was seen billowing out of the house followed by flames. Another announcement was made asking the SLA to surrender.[75] The SLA did not respond. Christine Johnson, who had just awoken from an alcohol- and drug-induced sleep, stumbled out of the burning house. At 6:47 p.m., Los Angeles police made another announcement over the bullhorn, "Come out, you will not be harmed. The house is on fire. It's all over."[76] By 6:50 p.m., the house had become completely engulfed in flames. But the SLA continued to fire at law enforcement from air ducts under the house. With gunfire continuing, the Los Angeles Fire Department did not make any attempt to extinguish the fire.

Nancy Ling Perry emerged from the southwest portion of the house through the crawl space. She advanced cautiously ten feet followed by Camilla Hall, who also emerged from underneath the house. Weapons fire from the house continued, and when Hall came out of the burning residence she began firing at SWAT team members with her pistol. The SWAT team immediately returned fire, killing both Hall and Perry.

By 6:59 p.m. all remaining hostile fire from the SLA had ceased, and the Fire Department was given the green light to fight the fire.[77]

The fire, which led to the deaths of four of the six SLA members, most likely occurred as a result of the mixture of the tear gas, gunpowder, and gasoline in the house. However, according to the official Los Angeles Police Department report, "The cause of the fire was undetermined."[78] The report further states, "The heavy black smoke that was present and the rapid spread of the fire is indicative of a flammable liquid." Within the charred remains of the house police found a two-gallon metal gas can with perforations on the side, along with two pipe bombs, two blasting caps, and other homemade explosives.[79]

WHAT HAPPENED?

Cinque Mtume had led his followers to their deaths. He had mistaken notoriety for popularity, and he had made no effort to maintain the SLA's anonymity while in Los Angeles. In addition, Cinque had made only a half-hearted attempt to find a new safe house in the nearby area. Freddie Freeman, who had helped Cinque hide the SLA vans, viewed the arrival of the SLA as an economic opportunity. Instead of going to work that day, Freeman told his colleagues that he had "an opportunity to earn money from the SLA."[80] At 9:30 a.m. on the morning of the shootout, Freeman received $500 from Cinque to purchase a new vehicle for the SLA. But he never purchased a vehicle, and he did not return to the residence. Cinque had also trusted and given money to Brenda Daniels to purchase bread, luncheon meat, beer, and wine.[81] By noon, rumors had spread throughout the neighborhood that the SLA was on their street. Throughout the day, residents of the neighborhood came by the house to meet the revolutionaries. By 3 p.m., Los Angeles police had blocked off access to the block surrounding the SLA safe house.

The SLA appeared unconcerned. The fatalism Hearst described at the previous safe house had become a self-fulfilling prophecy. Without his second-in-command, Cinque appeared unable to act

Figure 20: Six bodies were found dead at what remained of the SLA hideout in Los Angeles on May 17, 1974. The dead identified by the coroner's office are, top from left: Camilla Hall, 29; William Wolfe, 23; and Donald DeFreeze, 30. Bottom from left: Angela Atwood, 25; Nancy Ling Perry, 26; and Patricia Soltysik, 29. May 19, 1974, New York. (Associated Press)

decisively. In the early afternoon of May 17, Cinque announced with one last ounce of bravado, while drinking a bottle of Boone's Farm wine, "I know I am going to die and all my people know that they will also, but we are going to take a lot of motherfucking pigs with us."[82] In his last known words, Cinque also mentioned that he had returned to Los Angeles to search for his wife and six children,[83] though he would never have this opportunity.

On April 4, 1974, professor of psychology Murray Miron had filed a report with the FBI stating that he believed the SLA was determined "to commit suicide by establishing the condition in which their destruction at the hands of someone else is inevitable." He went even further, saying, "The group as a whole is not capable of their own suicides unless engineered as a dramatic culmination of their indecisive lives as the consequence of the acts of others which they can rationalize as outside their responsibility." [84] Miron's prediction was correct. In the aftermath of the shootout, the police determined that Nancy Ling Perry, Camilla Hall, and Patricia Soltysik all died of gunshot wounds sustained during the shootout.[85] Atwood and Wolfe died from smoke inhalation and burns. Los Angeles County Coroner Thomas Noguchi declared that Donald David "Cinque Mtume" DeFreeze died of a self-inflicted gunshot wound to the head."[86] Cinque had in fact organized his own dramatic death.

13
HEADING EAST

TUCKED AWAY SAFELY IN A MOTEL room near Disneyland, the Harrises and Hearst watched in horror as their friends and comrades were killed in the Los Angeles ghetto. Then, at 11 p.m. on May 17, 1974, just hours after the shootout, Bill Harris turned off the television and announced that he was the new field marshal of the Symbionese Liberation Army and that he expected obedience and loyalty from the surviving members of the SLA, just as they had given both to Cinque. It was up to them to carry the revolution forward on behalf of the people, and it was time to find new members. When he was through speaking, Emily Harris asked Hearst if she would like to join them in bed. Knowing what that meant, Patricia looked at them and said no.[1]

The three SLA members spent the weekend in the motel and gathered as much news on the shootout as possible. They also made plans to leave Los Angeles. Hearst recalled that she was not part of the planning: "I cried so much that I ached with pain."[2] On Monday, May 20, they drove south to Costa Mesa where they found a $40-a-week motel apartment. The plan was to stay put until Memorial Day, May 27, and then head north on I-5 back to San Francisco. The Bay Area was familiar. They knew the streets and the shops, and they had contacts and friends who could help them. Heavy Memorial Day traffic would give them a better chance to travel undetected.

The Harrises and Hearst headed toward San Francisco in an old broken-down car that Emily had purchased for $300. It was a harrowing nine-hour drive with the Harrises in the front seat and Hearst under a blanket in the back. They made it into San Francisco near the Panhandle area of Golden Gate Park before the engine finally died. They pushed it to a garage for repair.[3]

Once the car was in the garage, the three fugitives returned to the Panhandle. Their situation was dire. They may have had as little as $50 between them, and they needed food and a place to

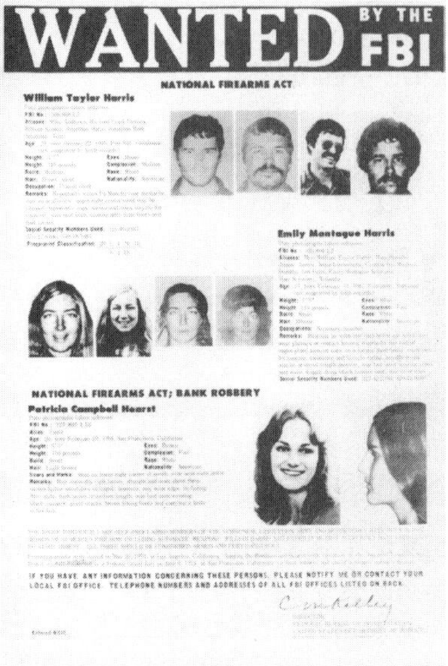

Figure 21: In an effort to expand its manhunt for Patricia Hearst and the two surviving members of the SLA, the FBI distributed wanted posters. Pictured is Bill and Emily Harris, and Patricia Hearst. September 24, 1974. (Polaris)

Figure 22: Kathleen Soliah speaks at the Angel Atwood Memorial held in Ho Chi Minh Park on June 2, 1974 in Berkeley, California. (Associated Press)

spend the night. Looking through her address book, Emily found an acquaintance a few blocks away. She asked for help, but she was rebuffed. Emily had better luck with Mark, a Bloomington, Indiana, friend who lived across the Panhandle. Mark invited them in for the night only and gave them $50.[4]

It was not long before Emily rented a first-floor apartment on Walnut Street, a few blocks from Mills College in Oakland. Emily Harris and Hearst led the way by bus, carrying their red duffel bag filled with weapons and ammunition. Bill Harris followed an hour later. There were no incidents. Walnut Street was home to a racially mixed, working-class society. The Harrises and Hearst easily blended in without attracting too much attention from neighbors.

As soon as these remaining SLA members had settled into their new apartment, they focused on recruiting new members. Much of the work fell on Emily Harris who was more skilled at disguising herself and could move about on the streets undetected. According to Hearst, Emily had become the "intelligence officer," and she proved to be more adept than the others in planning.[5]

Meanwhile, Bill Harris and Hearst remained in the apartment. They spent much of their time making the so-called Eulogy Tape intended to honor their slain comrades. Bill Harris, as the field marshal, controlled content; he gave the SLA's take on the Los Angeles debacle and sought to rally "radicals and oppressed people everywhere" to their cause. Meanwhile, Hearst expressed her love for each of the fallen SLA soldiers. She singled out Cinque for having "taught me how to show my love for the people."[6]

Emily Harris's search for support from the Berkeley-Oakland radical community continued, and the frustration over the lack of response was disheartening. One radical friend from Venceremos refused to talk with her. Another contact was a pediatrician at the Children's Hospital who did meet with her, but he refused to do anything that put him at risk.[7] It very quickly became clear that while the East Bay was "home" to the SLA, it could not count on active support. The Foster murder in November 1973 had created a permanent, formidable wedge between the SLA and any New Left sympathizers.

KATHLEEN SOLIAH

Nevertheless, on June 2, 1974, a rally to honor the SLA dead was held in Ho Chi Minh Park (Willard Park) in Berkeley, just three blocks from the Benvenue address where Patricia Hearst had been kidnapped in early February. Several Bay Area radicals attended. The flamboyant but shady Wilbur ("Popeye") Jackson was one of the 400 who showed up. He was a leader in the prison reform movement and had been active in Randolph Hearst's PIN food giveaway program. Sarah Jane Moore, an accountant in the PIN program and an FBI informant, stood on the stage behind the speakers. She spoke to those in attendance about Jackson's activities, as well as the PIN program. Aspiring actress and revolutionary, Kathleen (Kathy) Soliah, age twenty-seven, helped organize the event. When she took over the microphone and claimed she was a member of the SLA, she caught the attention of Bill and Emily Harris, who were seeking to find just such a soldier, ready to work.

Like Nancy Ling Perry, Soliah and her siblings, Josephine (Jo) and Steven, had come from a solid, close-knit, conservative Republican family. She was very popular and active in high school activities. She later enrolled at the University of California, Santa Barbara, and there she met Jim Kilgore, a talented athlete and sportswriter. Kilgore grew up in San Rafael, north of the Golden Gate, where his father ran a lumber company. During this period, he became part of the "jock revolution'" and corresponded with its "guru," Jack Scott, in Berkeley.[8] Both students were radicalized by campus events and antiwar demonstrations. Soliah fell in love with Kilgore and moved into his apartment. They transferred to the University of California, Berkeley in 1971, where they believed the heart of the revolution still beat. There, they stayed with Jack and Micki Scott for a few weeks before they moved into a house on Shattuck Avenue near the campus.

During this period, Soliah met Angela Atwood, then a young actress, and they auditioned for roles together. They had some success, once playing in Henrik Ibsen's *Hedda Gabler*. Meanwhile, they cowrote and costarred in a one-act play entitled *Edward the Dyke*; Soliah played the lesbian, while Atwood played the psychiatrist who tried to save her.[9] They also worked together as waitresses at the Great Electric Underground, located in the basement of Bank of America's world headquarters in downtown San Francisco. Soliah and Atwood spoke up for workers' rights and once attempted to unionize the restaurant's staff. When management insisted that their waitresses wear revealing costumes, both quit and walked away. They seemed inseparable until January 1974, when Atwood and her SLA comrades went underground following the arrests of Joe Remiro and Russell Little. Through Atwood, Soliah had been introduced to the SLA, but the collective had refused to accept her, believing that she was "too flaky" to be a serious revolutionary.[10]

While the SLA remained underground during the early months of 1974, Soliah and Kilgore became more heavily involved in the revolutionary movement. They organized the Bay Area Research Collective (BARC) to promote SLA literature and propaganda. BARC never had many members at any one time, and it was always in need of money to publish its literature. Apparently, Kilgore and Soliah believed BARC could be a propaganda arm for the SLA.[11] BARC also helped to organize the Ho Chi Minh Park rally.

Then, in June 1974 there stood Kathy Soliah, wearing sunglasses and a turtleneck sweater, taking over the microphone and dramatically declaring, "I am a soldier of the SLA." She praised Atwood ("Gelina") as a "truly revolutionary woman," claiming that "Gelina and her comrades fought until the last minute." She continued: "And though I would like to have her be here with me right now, I know that she lived and died happy. . . . SLA soldiers, although I know it is not necessary to say, keep fighting, I'm with you. And we are with you."[12]

No matter what their attitude toward Soliah had been prior to May 17, the Harrises knew they had to contact her. Emily vaguely recollected that Soliah had an apartment in Berkeley. Posing as an older woman and a friend of Soliah's mother, Harris learned that Soliah worked at a bookstore near the Berkeley campus. She walked into the bookstore and saw Soliah almost immediately. She then wrote a note, asking Soliah to meet her at the church around the corner from the store.

Soliah responded by calling Jim Kilgore and asking for money to give to the SLA. Kilgore rushed over and gave her what he could and left—he did not want to meet Emily Harris. Soliah then met Harris at the church door, gave her the money, and indicated that she could get more from her sister's savings account.

Emily Harris later said that what impressed her the most in meeting Soliah was that she seemed genuinely moved and excited when she met Harris at the church, and she really seemed to want to help the SLA. Soliah persuaded her sister, Jo, to empty her savings account to help the fugitives.

When the Eulogy Tape was completed, Soliah and Kilgore agreed to ensure it was released to a radical radio station. A friend from their Santa Barbara days, attorney Richard Allen Frishman, intended to return to his San Diego home and agreed to perform the deed. Soliah and Kilgore met Frishman near Lake Merritt in Oakland, where they handed the tape over to him. On June 7, Frishman dropped the tape off in a mattress around the corner from KPFA radio in Los Angeles.[13]

Meanwhile, Soliah's enthusiasm and financial assistance established her credentials with the SLA guerrillas. Emily promptly set up another meeting at an Oakland drive-in theatre, and Patricia Hearst and Jim Kilgore joined the meeting as well. Soliah and Kilgore told the SLA that they had been living in an apartment on Berkeley's Northside and invited them to move in. It belonged to a friend of Kilgore's who was sympathetic to the radical movement. Kilgore had been house-sitting the apartment and taking care of tropical turtles while his friend and girlfriend went on vacation.[14] The Harrises agreed to accept the invitation.

JACK SCOTT

The Oakland drive-in meeting lasted "several hours."[15] What interested the Harrises the most was learning that their comrades knew Jack Scott, who had been making waves nationally with his innovations in campus sports and politics. Soliah and Kilgore indicated that Scott might give them his support. The Harrises knew Scott by "reputation," and they knew about his Institute for the Study of Sports and Society (ISSS), which provided radical sports activists with an avenue for publishing their work.[16] Few names were more recognized as leaders of the "athletic revolution," a term coined by Scott himself, than Scott himself.

Scott seemed like a natural fit for the SLA. He came out of Scranton, Pennsylvania, where he excelled in track and football. In fact, he was so good that he attended Villanova and Stanford on athletic scholarships. Later, he married a writer and photographer,

Micki McGee, who would be of enormous help to him and his career. Politically, he supported Harry Edwards's campaign to boycott the 1968 Olympics in Mexico City, and he began to make a name for himself as a radical sports writer in a number of magazines. In 1971 the Free Press published his book *The Athletic Revolution,* which became the Bible for the "jock revolution." The book greatly influenced University of California, Los Angeles basketball center Bill Walton and a radical Berkeley student, Willie Brandt. Scott liked to play on the fringe of the revolution, and he became friendly with Brandt after meeting him at a local rally in support of radical student athletes.[17]

Scott had a way of making himself known. In 1970 he was hired to teach Education 191D, a course entitled "Intercollegiate Athletics and Education: A Socio-Psychological Evaluation." He came to class wearing gym shorts and track shoes, and he used a whistle to start the class. Along with writers and athletes such as Paul Hoch, Dave Meggsysey, Jay Weiner, and Lynda Huey, Scott launched a full-scale assault on the racism and sexism that was endemic in collegiate and professional sports. He sought to close the gap between the ideals of sports and its realities. "He wants to return to pure motives," wrote an admiring Huey, "to winning for the sake of excellence, not merely to fill the pockets of businessmen who own athletes."[18]

Scott denounced the dictatorial practices of coaches and athletic directors, and he sought to humanize and democratize sports by giving more power to athletes themselves. There was an "authenticity" to sports that attracted Scott all his life. "It's one area in life where there is no bull shit," he said. "You go out and do it, or you don't, and everybody can see."[19]

Jack and Micki Scott put his theories to the test when Robert Fuller, president of Oberlin College in Ohio, hired him to be the school's athletic director. Fuller had read Jack's book, and he wanted him to put the principles of the book into practice at Oberlin. Oberlin College had a radical tradition that went back into the mid-nineteenth century, but ultimately Scott's "Oberlin experiment" proved to be too much for many in Fuller's administration and in the athletic department.

At Oberlin, Scott was a whirlwind of activity. He hired Tommie Smith to be his assistant and track coach, Cass Jackson to coach football, and Pat Penn to handle the basketball program. Lynda Huey, a talented track star brought in to help with the women's program, later mused, "Oberlin's top coaching staff was an all-black triumvirate."[20] Scott ended admission charges to football games, and he allowed student athletes to have veto power over the hiring of coaches. He was the talk of the sports world. Well-known sports commentator and writer Howard Cosell visited Oberlin and left

Figure 23: Sports activist Jack Scott, 1975. (Associated Press)

impressed with Scott's work. And yet Scott found time to write a letter on Willie Brandt's behalf to lessen his prison sentence for bombings in and around the campus at University of California, Berkeley. By February 1974, however, Scott had been dismissed from his job and given a $40,000 severance package.[21] His enemies had begun to pile up, and Fuller, his protector, had been forced to resign as president. No Fuller, no Scott.

With the failure of the "Oberlin experiment" Jack Scott sank into a kind of depression. He returned to New York City, but he could not find much to do. He and Micki did manage to get ISSS up and running again, working with athletes and writers to get their work published. And he signed a contract with publisher William Morrow to write his autobiography, but he could not put anything down that made him happy. The fact was that he and Micki were bitter over the way he was forced to leave Oberlin. Writer Robert Lipsyte visited them a few months later and noted, "They seemed to have changed; they were more political, more international, more radical than reformist."[22] Lipsyte did not know the half of it.

In early February, as Scott doodled over his autobiography for William Morrow, he became fascinated with the kidnapping of Patricia Hearst. He attempted to get publishers to put money behind a book, but there were no takers. Then, he saw the televised shootout in Compton in which two-thirds of the SLA was wiped out, or, as Jack would angrily put it, "executed without trial."[23] By June, when Kathy Soliah gave her eulogy on the SLA martyrs, Scott was back in Berkeley and making contacts to get his book project on track. Soliah and Kilgore were both well known to Scott. What they knew about Scott—but few others did—was that he liked to play on the edge of revolutionary politics.

JACK SCOTT AND THE SLA

In 1972 a small group of guerrillas headed by Berkeley student Willie Brandt, had organized themselves into the Revolutionary Army and conducted a bombing campaign against symbols of capitalist and militarist oppression in America. Among its members were Paul Rubenstein, a former SDS member who roomed with Kilgore and Soliah; Mike Bortin from Lowell High School in San Francisco and a Berkeley activist, and Wendy Yoshimura, an artist and Brandt's lover. Many of these people would later play significant roles in the SLA's "lost year."

Yoshimura came to Berkeley in 1969 from Fresno. She was born during World War II at the Manzanar internment camp where her family had been incarcerated. Her parents moved to Japan after the war, returning to Fresno a decade later. Although Yoshimura attended local schools, she fell behind and felt out of place. She eventually moved to the Bay Area and attended the California School of Arts and Crafts in Oakland. It was there that she fell in love with Willie Brandt in 1969. He introduced her to Marxist-Leninist ideology and brought her into his revolution. When Brandt travelled to Cuba to harvest sugar cane, Yoshimura was happy to go along with him. And in 1970, when Brandt began his bombing campaign in the Bay Area, she did not hesitate to participate. Then, in late March 1972, Brandt was arrested, along with Mike Bortin and Paul Rubenstein.

Yoshimura knew that the police would soon be coming after her. Kathy Soliah moved quickly to aid Yoshimura, and she asked Jack and Micki Scott for help. Micki came over and scoured the apartment that Wendy shared with Willie to rid it of any evidence that would have aided the police. Jack drove Yoshimura to Los Angeles International Airport, bought her a huge stuffed rabbit, and flew with her to New York where she took care of Scott's property.[24] The question was, would Jack Scott do the same for the remaining members of the SLA?

This was Jack Scott's opportunity. He could help them escape and write an insider's account of the life and times of the Symbionese Liberation Army. He had most of his severance pay from Oberlin College to meet expenses, and the payoff for him could be enormous.

Scott was taken one night to 1675 Euclid Street in Berkeley where Kilgore and Soliah were housesitting for Kilgore's friend and his girlfriend, who had been involved in Brandt's bombing activities.[25] Patricia Hearst later described the scene when Scott arrived at the apartment. The SLA sat "cross-legged on the floor" in the back bedroom. "Teko [Bill Harris] had his submachine gun cradled in his lap; Yolanda [Emily] had her sawed-off shotgun across her knees, a bandolier full of shells across her chest. Both wore their gun belts with ammunition bags and holstered side arms. I had a .30 caliber rifle slung over my back. It was, in Teko's words, our show of strength."[26]

Jack Scott basically sold himself to the SLA. He was part of the revolution. He could talk the revolutionary jargon, and he seemed very knowledgeable about Carlos Marighella's *Mini-Manual of the Urban Guerrilla.* He compared himself to Harriet Tubman, the former slave who blazed an underground railroad to help other slaves escape into the free northern states prior to the Civil War. He invoked the Revolutionary Army, Wendy Yoshimura, and others whom "he had helped in the past."[27]

THE TRIP BACK EAST

Scott urged the SLA to think about leaving the Bay Area for the East Coast where they could rest and restore themselves in relative peace. They could continue their guerrilla training, read revolutionary tracts, and start the recruitment process for a new chapter of the SLA. Micki would seek out an isolated farmhouse in a rural area where they could reconstitute themselves. He suggested that his parents, John Joseph and Louise Scott, both over sixty years of age, could help drive Hearst to New York City in their Pontiac LTD. They would be happy to do it, and they had helped him before. He would arrange to have someone drive Emily and Bill Harris east as well. Scott volunteered to pay for the trip and accommodations. All he asked was that they follow his instructions and leave their weapons behind.[28]

Emily Harris was the first to go east, leaving with Scott's close friend and associate Phil Shinnick, an Olympic long jumper. Shinnick came to Berkeley from the University of Washington, and he achieved notoriety for the "Modesto Miracle"—a 27'4" jump that set a world record. (However, that jump was not official because no one had measured the wind factor in the jump.[29]) Shinnick spent the late sixties at Berkeley working on his doctorate in social psychology. There, he became Scott's protégé, and Scott served on his Ph.D. orals committee. Scott later hired him as an associate director of ISSS.

Patricia Hearst left two nights later, accompanied by Scott and his parents. They stayed on I-80 all the way into Pennsylvania, where Jack took over and drove Hearst to his New York City apartment on 92nd Street. It was a six-day trip. For Hearst, it seemed longer because she became tired of Jack Scott. He talked incessantly about himself and how he helped Wendy Yoshimura escape to New York. His parents talked from time to time about how proud they were of their son and his brother, Walter, who was a bit "crazy, but they loved him."[30]

Jack Scott would later recount a much different recollection of the trip. He said that shortly after they left the Euclid Street apartment they pulled over, and Scott turned to Hearst and said, "I want you to know that I'm willing to drive you anywhere you want to go." She moved away from him. Scott then repeated himself: "You can go anywhere you want." She replied, "I want to go where my friends are going."[31] Later, she loosened up and began to talk about personal things. Her mother, Catherine, she said, was a drunk and had problems with drugs, and she berated her mother for not refusing reappointment to the University of California Board of Regents as a gesture for the return of her daughter. She also remained angry with her father for not paying the ransom demanded.[32]

According to Scott, Hearst then gave him real dynamite for his book. Her kidnapping on February 4 had been bogus. In an interview with FBI agent Jennifer C. Burnett on October 6, 1999, while hospitalized and dying of throat cancer, Scott told his version of the cross-country trip and Hearst's shocking revelation.[33] She had planned it with Nancy Ling Perry at Fruity Rudy's orange stand near the Berkeley entrance—Perry provided the marijuana and other drugs used in Hearst and Weed's small apartment. Hearst had grown tired of living with Steven Weed because he would "snort cocaine and discuss philosophy in his living room with his friends." She told Perry that she wanted out; she did not want to marry Weed, but she also did not want to admit to her mother that she had been wrong about him. She believed that Weed "would not protect her" and that she "could use that as a reason to break up with him when she was later released."[34]

Nancy Ling Perry took their kidnapping plan to Cinque, who was building up the SLA at that time. Cinque liked it; it would "be great publicity," he thought. He did not want to let the other members of the collective in on it because it would be a good "test" for them.[35] Years later, Bill Harris, when asked about this account of the kidnapping, replied that he always thought it "very strange" that Hearst had shouted, "Take it fucking easy!" when she was shoved into the trunk of the car.[36] In 1976 both he and Emily Harris expressed doubt about the nature of the Hearst-Weed relationship.[37] Unfortunately, no evidence exists to confirm Jack Scott's recollection of his conversation with Hearst. Only the odd nature of Hearst's actions at Mel's Sporting Goods provides some possibility of this scenario being accurate.

When Hearst and Scott arrived at his New York apartment around midnight, they found Emily Harris talking with Micki Scott. Harris jumped out of her chair "with genuine emotion," Hearst later recalled. "She seemed truly happy to see me. I was home again and in her care. That's how dependent I had become."[38] Wendy Yoshimura visited them the next day and was introduced as Joan Shimada, but both Hearst and Harris knew who she really was. Hearst recalled that she found it hard at first to realize that Yoshimura was a true revolutionary. She seemed so "calm and friendly . . . with the nicest smile."[39] It turned out that Yoshimura would "babysit" them at the farmhouse Scott rented outside Honesdale, Pennsylvania, buy their groceries, and run their errands. For doing so, Jack Scott promised her a car and $600. Yoshimura may have agreed to this arrangement because she felt that she owed Jack Scott.[40]

Meanwhile, Bill Harris remained at 1675 Euclid Street in Berkeley. Jack Scott spent a lot of time on the telephone trying to find someone who would drive Harris to the farmhouse in Honesdale, but it was impossible. Consequently, Micki Scott escorted their guests to the farmhouse while Scott flew to the Bay Area to drive Harris to Pennsylvania himself.

When he arrived a week later, Bill Harris assumed total command of the guerrilla unit. He raged against the Scotts for the pathetic and dirty weapons they had provided; he screamed at his wife for not advancing the revolution and for having a "vacation"; and he tore into Wendy Yoshimura with special venom. He mocked her for hiding out in New York and New Jersey for the last two years; he criticized her for not reading George Jackson; and he said she was "lazy" and had wasted her potential for Third World leadership. "You could become their leader in this country," he said, "if you would only work at it."[41] Gratitude and grace were never Bill Harris's style.

Yoshimura was the only member of the group to fight back. When she became too angry or tired, she walked away, or she would stand her ground, "nose to nose." The truth was that Yoshimura did not see herself as a leader of any Third World movement. "Besides," she said, "all that crap about Third World leadership is racist in itself and based upon white guilt." In the end, Yoshimura concluded that Bill Harris was "a complete, all-around idiot."[42]

Despite Harris's temper, the SLA prepared itself for the revolution, physically, emotionally, and ideologically. Jack Scott recalled years later, "They exercised a lot, held drill camp-type maneuvers. Here were these adults crawling through the grass, hitting the dirt. Finally, we let them have a BB gun for target practice and they would sit for hours . . . bing, bing, bing. They were not exactly normal summer campers."[43] Harris said that despite all their differences on tactics and strategies, they must keep a united front before their enemies.[44]

The Scotts visited the farmhouse during June and July 1974, bringing sportswriter and friend Jay Weiner to spend some time with them. Weiner and Scott had been friends since their Oberlin College days when Weiner was a student worker. Scott persuaded Weiner to keep up a correspondence with Willie Brandt, who was then serving a ten-year sentence in Soledad Prison.[45] Scott never identified the residents as SLA fighters, but Weiner had no illusions about who they were. Scott hoped to persuade him to be used as an emergency contact, but Weiner preferred to keep his distance.

In late July 1974, Jack and Micki Scott informed the SLA that it had to move immediately to another safe house. The new location was outside Jeffersonville, New York, in the Catskill Mountains. Micki had rented the Honesdale farmhouse in her own name, and the Scotts were now afraid that the police were on to them. The Scotts had not kept a low profile in support of the SLA. They had taken a group of black athletes to Cuba to inspect its sports facilities and programs, and they believed the FBI was investigating them. They needed the SLA out of Honesdale—that night, if possible.

While the SLA was training at the Jeffersonville farmhouse, Kilgore and Soliah had continued to send it money earned from their house painting business. Kilgore also sent boxes of books on economics and political philosophy for the SLA to study. Once the group relocated to New York, Bill Harris singled out Hearst, making her read certain books and prepare herself to discuss them. Apparently, the favorite publication was *Prairie Fire*, a book put together by the Weather Underground. Harris wanted Hearst to get used to revolutionary jargon to give her credibility within the movement. For Hearst, life in the Catskills seemed easier than at Honesdale. They took some time off from training and visited the nearby community. She got closer to Yoshimura and found her to be "a quiet and wise woman. . . . She opened my mind to horizons somewhat broader than those of the SLA."[46]

It was in Jeffersonville that Patricia Hearst experienced a moment of "profound effect upon me and my own thinking, which I managed to hide from all the others." It came during another Harris–Yoshimura faceoff after she flatly refused to participate in physical drills, rejecting Harris's order to disguise herself as a white woman. Harris demanded to know what Yoshimura would do if the "pigs" surrounded the farmhouse. "So what are you going to do then? Huh? What are you going to do?" Yoshimura replied, "I know what I am going to do. I'm going to walk out of the house with my hands up!"

Hearst saw that the Harrises were shocked by Yoshimura's response. Bill Harris shouted that the "pigs" will "shoot you down like a dog." Emily Harris tried to use reason: "It's really better to die for the people, sister, than to be locked up in prison. It's too demoralizing for the people to see their freedom fighters go to prison." Yoshimura responded quietly that her beloved Willie Brandt "is in prison and he's going to get out. . . . You really can't do the revolution any good at all if you're killed. And, I don't intend to get killed, not if I can help it."[47]

Hearst could hardly believe what she had heard. She later wrote,

"[I] sat there, saying nothing, hardly noticed, but I was so relieved" to hear those words spoken aloud. She continued, "I wanted to stay alive; I did not want to have to die for the revolution or anything else. I told myself . . . if the police came here, I too would surrender. No matter what they did to me, I would walk out with my hands up. This was the first thought of opposition to the SLA Codes of War that I allowed myself to harbor."[48]

Scott's work on his SLA book slowed in July and August 1974, but he was determined to put down the basic elements of the story. To achieve that, he brought Paul Hoch, a professor at Dawson College in Montreal, to the farm. Hoch was in his mid-thirties, he was overweight, and he looked like a hippie. Like Jay Weiner and Phil Shinnick who later visited the safe house, Hoch was someone Scott could trust with the SLA. Hoch was an avowed Marxist and a leader in "the athletic revolution." His book, *Rip Off the Big Game*, provided a significant Marxist critique of modern athletics, and Scott hired him to teach a course in physical education at Oberlin College. Hoch participated in antiwar demonstrations in London, leading to his arrest for "shitting on a picture of the Queen."[49]

The purpose of Hoch's visit was to put the SLA book together so that Scott's ISSS could publish it. Patricia clearly did not like the man, but he seemed sympathetic to her plight, even shocked by some of the treatment meted out to her by SLA members since her kidnapping. He brought a tape recorder to record SLA statements. At the end of each session, Hoch insisted that the tapes be transcribed and then destroyed. His voice was on the tapes, and he wanted no negative repercussions from authorities should the tapes come into their possession. Bill Harris had no problem with that. He had listened to Patricia Hearst's voice and thought she "sounded drugged or under duress."[50]

Over the summer months, relations between the Scotts and the Harrises became increasingly strained. The Harrises sought to indoctrinate the Scotts into their cause. But the Scotts did not believe that murder and bombings were the way to go, and so the Harrises began to think of them as phonies who could mouth revolutionary slogans but were fundamentally bourgeois. A prime example of the growing tension occurred on the Fourth of July when Jack and Micki Scott put together a barbecue with beef and wine. It cost about $20. Harris later called Scott out on that. "The fact that you didn't spend five dollars for hamburger shows where you're at. You're part of the bourgeoisie." Stung by Harris' ingratitude, Scott furiously replied, "You're the ones with fucked up values. We've never had a single thank you for the things we've done for you. And you have the gall to try to guilt-trip us."[51]

It came to a head in late August. Bill Harris had taken control of Scott's book, seizing his tapes and transcripts. Meanwhile, the Harrises longed to return to the Bay Area, and the reports they received from Kathy Soliah and Jim Kilgore encouraged them even more. They asked Scott for help, but he was reluctant. He had spent about half of his Oberlin severance pay in their behalf, and the rent was due in a few days on the New York farmhouse. Emily Harris suggested that they return to Honesdale, but the Scotts remained fearful because the rental was in Micki's name. Micki told the Harrises that the Honesdale farmhouse had been sold, but they did not believe her. They later confirmed that Micki had lied, and they confronted her.

Ultimately, the Scotts agreed to let the SLA return to Honesdale for a few weeks, and they agreed to provide funding for their trip back to the Bay Area.[52] Because the book had been sabotaged by Bill Harris's censure, Jack Scott had already moved on, and he was anxious to get away from the SLA. He was shutting down his New York apartment, and he and Micki planned to move to Portland, Oregon, and live in the home of Portland Trail Blazer center Bill Walton. Walton was having a miserable year in Portland, and Jack would be his public relations "guru," physical trainer, and adviser.

14

COMING HOME

THE SLA'S RETURN TO CALIFORNIA REQUIRED a great deal of careful planning. Instead of heading back to San Francisco, the SLA set up safe houses in Sacramento, which, despite its outwardly conservative appearance, had its own local radical component. The Black Panthers had an active unit in the capital city, and the last holdouts of Charlie Manson's family lived near downtown. Sacramento was about a ninety-minute drive from the East Bay, and so it was relatively easy for Kathy, Steve, and Jo Soliah, Jim Kilgore, Mike Bortin, and their associates to drive up to Sacramento to participate in study sessions and operational planning. Living anywhere in the Bay Area at that time could have restricted their activities.

Preparations for the move were completed in mid-September 1974. Jack and Micki Scott had rented a Ryder truck loaded with furniture from their New York apartment. Patricia Hearst went with them, posing as a pregnant woman for the entire trip. Along the way, they dropped Micki off at the Cleveland airport so that she could visit Tommie Smith at Oberlin College and then fly to southern California to help Lynda Huey finish her book. Scott and Hearst then continued west on I-80 toward Las Vegas, where his parents lived in an apartment complex. They had a scare in Indiana when a highway patrolman stopped them for a traffic violation, and faced another setback when the rental truck broke down near Cheyenne, Wyoming, and needed repairs. Bill and Emily Harris headed to New York City and then took a train to Sacramento, spending a week in Chicago, where Emily Harris could visit friends and see her childhood haunts. Wendy Yoshimura remained in New York for about a month before she boarded a "hippie bus" to San Francisco, where she stayed with a friend who had regular contact with Willie Brandt in Soledad Prison.[1]

At noon on September 25, 1974, Scott and Hearst arrived at his parents' apartment complex. Micki was floating in the swimming pool at the time of their arrival, His parents, however, were a bit flustered because they had just received word that Jack's older brother, Walter, was coming for a visit. Walter Scott had worked for the federal government all of his adult life. He had just completed an assignment in Libya, and he then traveled to London in preparation for his return to the United States. Walter was an alcoholic, and he was emotionally and psychologically unstable. No one, not even Scott, knew what Walter might do or say when he found out how his brother had involved their aging parents in the SLA saga.

It was imperative to transfer Hearst to Sacramento before Walter's arrival. Kathy Soliah called Jack Scott to set up a line of communication with Kilgore. Hearst was given a code and told to make a telephone call from a public booth to someone named "Jerry." Jerry turned out to be Richard Allen Frishman, who had delivered the Eulogy Tape to a Los Angeles radio station months earlier. Hearst called Frishman's number in Santa Barbara and said, "I am Mrs. Erickson and I am calling about my divorce." Frishman replied, "The lawyer isn't here now, he'll be at this number in a couple of minutes."[2] When Hearst called the number, Kilgore answered the telephone.

Patricia Hearst stayed with Jack and his parents that night, but Micki rented a room for herself off the strip in downtown Las Vegas. Kilgore flew to Las Vegas on the second day. It had been decided that he would accompany Hearst to California, and that he would carry a .38 caliber pistol because he was one of the best shots in the SLA.[3] Meanwhile, Jo Soliah had established a safe house for them in a low-income neighborhood on 1721 W Street in Sacramento, across from a movie theater. She also had stocked the house with food from neighborhood grocery stores. Soliah selected the house because it formed part of "a transient neighborhood where nobody knew the neighbors too well."[4] The anonymity would allow the SLA to come and go without any undue attention from neighbors.

With the safe house established, Jack Scott and Patricia Hearst hugged each other and parted ways. Scott flew to Portland to stay with Bill Walton, and on September 27 Kilgore and Hearst took an overnight Greyhound bus from Las Vegas to Sacramento. Kathy and Steve Soliah met them at the downtown bus station. That would be the last time Jack Scott and Patricia Hearst would see each other. And this farewell happened just in time; Walter Scott flew into Las Vegas the very day Hearst left for Sacramento. Walter was drunk and mean, and he arrived suspecting that something was up. He intimidated his parents verbally and physically, and he learned just enough to know that they had played host to Patricia Hearst.[5]

The Harrises arrived in Sacramento by train from Chicago about two weeks later. With their leadership in place, the SLA located two other safe houses. By early 1975, the SLA had established one safe house at 914 T Street and another at 2728 Capitol Street. Hearst lived on Capitol Street with Kathy Soliah during most of their stay in Sacramento. They moved from safe house to safe house with relative ease. They kept to themselves, and they survived off donations from the Bay Area, shoplifting, and identify theft. The W Street safe house was their central location. There, Bill Harris held his study and tactical planning sessions.

Often, Kilgore, the Soliahs, Yoshimura, and Bortin drove up from the Bay Area to attend these sessions. Bortin sometimes brought his girlfriend, Pat Jean McCarthy, from Berkeley. McCarthy was not a good fit for the collective. Although she had helped the SLA in the past, possessed a real understanding of revolutionary issues, and, in Patricia Hearst's words, was "a 'master shoplifter,'" she was also "schizoid" and "really nutty," and she was careless in her handling of weapons at gun ranges.[6] For her part, McCarthy was careful to not get too close to them. She preferred to work aboveground with community groups.

LEADERSHIP TENSIONS

Bill Harris wanted to start the revolution by spearheading attacks, such as bombings and bank robberies, on the system. The SLA had to make a statement—we're back! As in Honesdale and Jeffersonville, Harris ruled the group in Sacramento using emotional and physical intimidation. Balling his fists, he screamed and cursed, demanding that they get in shape through calisthenics and running. Patricia Hearst ran four miles daily through the streets of Sacramento and at a nearby high school athletic field. Bill singled out the new members—Bortin, the Soliahs, and Kilgore—claiming they were not doing enough, they were not bringing in enough money, and they preferred to talk theory rather than act.

Part of Harris's problem was that the new members were not dependent on him or the group. They thought for themselves, and they could leave any time they wanted. In fact, they stood up for themselves. Jim Kilgore, for example, was much steadier and more thoughtful than Harris. He believed the SLA needed to read more, study the revolutionary literature that was then newly available, and attempt to make broader appeals for popular support. To be part of a revolutionary vanguard without popular support seemed suicidal. Kathy Soliah backed him up, but both Emily and Bill Harris mocked and ridiculed that critique in favor of action, any kind of action. Yoshimura and Harris continued to bicker, and after one of Harris's blow-ups she returned to San Francisco, vowing not to return until the group became serious about its future.

Mike Bortin was in favor of violent action as a political statement. He discussed killing prominent establishment leaders, such as former CIA director John J. McCone and California attorney general Evelle J. Younger. There was a lot of bully in the man, and he intimidated Patricia Hearst.[7] Stephen Schwartz, who loathed Bortin since their days at Lowell High School in San Francisco, recalled him as being "an unappetizing smartass of no intellectual distinction."[8] Bortin, however, did not see himself that way. He had been radicalized by Sen. Robert F. Kennedy's murder in June 1968. He had then lost hope in the system and instead involved himself in Berkeley student demonstrations.[9] He supported anything that required action and violence, but something else irked him.

Bortin lost respect for Harris because Harris insisted he was the leader of the SLA and could not be challenged or criticized. Bortin did not like Harris's leadership style, and he was prepared to criticize it whenever the moment called for it. He brought Bridget, a leftist intellectual and organizer for the Trotskyite Socialist Workers Party (SWP), to one of the study sessions to see what she thought about the SLA's leader. Bridget remained about a week or so and left. She "condemned the SLA for having no discipline, no structure, no organization."[10] The collective was disorganized and chaotic, as she deemed it, with no short-or long-term strategy to overthrow the system.

Bridget had a point. The SLA had been planning for months to spring Joe Remiro and Russell Little from the Alameda County Courthouse, but its plans were ill conceived. It had been in contact with Remiro and Little, and so it had some knowledge of how the courthouse staff worked, as well as the layout of the building. Little's girlfriend, Sally—who was also Remiro's cousin—provided more detail. However, when she learned how the operation would work, she was appalled and thought that the SLA under Bill Harris's leadership had devised a plan that would surely get everyone killed. An assault team would crash into the building and commandeer elevators to the second floor where they would free their comrades.

Poorly conceived, the plan demonstrated Harris's leadership incompetence, and it would mean the complete and utter destruction of the SLA.[11] Even so, Sally was desperate. Kilgore resisted the plan; he thought that it had no chance of succeeding. However, Kathy Soliah supported the plan and worked with Sally to help move it to reality.

Bill Harris pleaded with the SLA. He believed that something had to be done for its brothers in revolution; they expected nothing less. Bortin had shifted to Kilgore's position. He thought that the odds for success were "one chance in a million." When the Harrises continued to press their case, Kilgore shut them down stating, "No, it's not our duty to sacrifice ourselves to free them." Later, after Remiro and Little received the news, they responded with a curt "Fuck you."[12]

A RETURN TO BANK LOAN ROBBERIES

Defeated, the Harrises began planning a bank robbery, which would satisfy their appetite for violence and destruction. Early in 1975, Emily Harris spotted the Guild Savings and Loan Association at 4375 Arden Way, in Sacramento's Arden Plaza. She thought it was "a perfect bank."[13] It was in a small shopping center, and included a sidewalk that went through an underpass to a residential neighborhood. If they placed their getaway car just outside the underpass they could escape easily. Bill Harris argued that the getaway car would be too far away from the assault team. Regardless, Harris eagerly agreed to the operation.

Bill Harris believed that this bank robbery was the perfect opportunity for the SLA's new crew to test their discipline when conducting larger projects. He also believed that by involving them in the Guild Savings and Loan assault, "the group could gain confidence."[14] That remark was aimed at the Soliahs, Bortin, McCarthy, and Kilgore, and he urged them to drive over to Arden Plaza and take a good look at the physical layout of the site. The team of Harrises and Hearst put the plans together and revealed them at a later meeting. One person was missing—Wendy Yoshimura. She had returned to her San Francisco apartment and had not yet returned. Harris asked Bortin to make sure Yoshimura made it to Sacramento for the meeting, and he took her absence as a personal rebuke. Harris said he was not surprised by Yoshimura's attitude, and Bortin could not help but agree, saying that this was "not a good attitude for someone involved in the collective." McCarthy, who had driven up with Bortin, vigorously defended her friend. If her sister, she said, "did not want any part of it, that was her business," though Yoshimura would return to the group about a month later.[15]

Kilgore and Bortin would be the inside men of the operation, whereas Harris reserved for himself the role of backup in case of police interference. Kathy Soliah, eager to be part of the assault, suggested that she go to Arden Plaza and keep a lookout for the police so she could time their response "for future operations." Harris thought that would be good to know and agreed. Steve Soliah would park the getaway car, a Chevrolet Impala, in the nearby residential area. Kilgore and Bortin opposed the idea of Harris as backup. They thought "that there was no reason for it," and that it would bring more people into the operation than was necessary. Kathy Soliah supported Harris, but Kilgore and Bortin could not be budged. Ultimately, there would be no backup for the assault.[16]

On the evening of February 24, 1975, the assault team rented a motel room near McKinley Park. The next day, Soliah drove to Arden Plaza and took her position in a greeting card shop where she could see the savings and loan building. She observed Bortin, wearing a white coat and hiding a .45 caliber revolver and a "Big Apple" cap, and Kilgore, sporting a blue-grey raincoat under which he held a shotgun, walking toward the door of the savings and loan. Kilgore noticed several customers inside the building, and they decided to walk around until the people inside dispersed. A few minutes elapsed before they opened the door and walked in.

Bortin took the lead and walked quickly to one of the tellers. "Good morning," he said pleasantly and pulled out his pistol. He announced that the Guild Savings and Loan was being robbed. He ordered the teller to open the safe, and he grabbed two bags of money, several rolled coins, and $7,500 in money orders. He ordered the staff to lie down and be quiet and walked past Kilgore, who turned and followed him back out into the plaza.[17]

The men hurried down the walkway toward the Chevrolet Impala. They got in, and Soliah drove to the switch car parked on L Street near Sutter General Hospital. It was a clean getaway.

From her position, Kathy Soliah saw Bortin and Kilgore leave the savings and loan and head down the sidewalk to the residential area nearby. She left the shop and walked into a coffee shop. A woman of Asian descent, whom Soliah assumed to be the office manager of the robbed bank, entered and told one of the baristas, "They took everything." Within five minutes, the police arrived in front of the savings and loan. Soliah then entered a telephone booth and called a company to tow away the parked Chevrolet Impala on L Street.[18] According to plan, Emily Harris and Patricia Hearst took a bus to McKinley Park. Within a few minutes, Steve Soliah drove up in the switch car, meeting them there. Kilgore and Bortin handed the women a straw bag filled with their weapons, clothes, and money. Soliah then drove away with the two men. The women walked to a bus stop, traveled to 24th Street, and then walked to the W Street safe house. Emily counted the money. The take was $3,700 in cash.[19]

Although Harris was upset with Soliah for going to the coffee shop, he was proud of the smoothness of the operation. Everything had gone pretty much to plan. As he had hoped, the success of the robbery increased the SLA's confidence. As far as it could tell, law enforcement did not connect the robbery to the SLA, and the press seemed silent as well.

A couple of weeks after the robbery, Wendy Yoshimura returned to the collective and seemed willing to help put together another—and bigger—operation. Mike Bortin, always on the lookout for big jobs, patrolled Fair Oaks Boulevard on a bicycle casing banks. A couple of weeks after that, on a weekend, Pat Jean McCarthy drove Bortin and Emily Harris through Sacramento's suburbs to look at fifteen or so banks.

ANOTHER BANK ROBBERY AND A MURDER

Whether one of the banks cased on that weekend was the Crocker National Bank at 5746 Marconi Street in Carmichael, a Sacramento suburb, is unknown. But at some point this bank piqued the SLA's interest. Located a mile from Arden Plaza, the bank formed part of the Hillside Shopping Center, which had seen better days. The SLA liked the fact that the bank was in the jurisdiction of the sheriff's department, not the Sacramento police. The area surrounding the bank was residential, which made for "an easy getaway." The bank had front and rear parking lots, three entrances, and a drive-up window, all of which had to be covered. Although Emily Harris worried that a mirror "placed in a peculiar manner" might be hiding a camera,[20] the rear parking lot abutted a cyclone fence that had a hole in it large enough for a man to pass through, making the bank all the more appealing.

Planning for the operation took place in the T Street safe house with Hearst, the Harrises, Kilgore, Bortin, Steve and Kathy Soliah, and Yoshimura in attendance. As usual in these meetings, almost all had something to say about the plan. Emily Harris demanded that she be placed on the inside team and be given command of the operation. This infuriated Bortin. Bill Harris insisted that he and Steve Soliah be in the backup vehicle. However, Soliah was not ready to join the assault since he was still feeling pain from the five broken ribs he had suffered in an accident in San Jose five weeks earlier, and Kilgore opposed the backup plan because it meant that too many people would be involved in the operation. He preferred to operate lean, with just enough force to get the job done without unnecessary violence. Kilgore also worried that the plan might enable authorities and the local press to connect the bank job to the SLA. But Bill Harris had been denied a backup role in the Guild Savings and Loan heist, and he insisted that he be backup in the Crocker National Bank robbery.

When the SLA finally reached an agreement, it was decided that Emily Harris would be the leader, with Kilgore, Bortin, and Kathy Soliah in support. Steve Soliah would drive the backup vehicle, a stolen blue-grey Mustang, and Bill Harris would accompany him.

Soliah would park the vehicle across the street from the bank. That would allow them to cover the inside team and provide suppressive fire should the sheriff's deputies come roaring in. This was proper, Bill Harris assured the team, because he and Soliah were the best shots in the SLA.[21] A follow-up meeting a week later confirmed that Wendy Yoshimura would drive one of the switch vehicles, and Patricia Hearst would drive the other. The escape routes were not revealed until April 20, the night before the scheduled robbery.

The operation began at nine o'clock in the morning of April 21, when Hearst and Kathy Soliah walked from their Capitol Street apartment to a rendezvous point in Winn Park. Hearst wore a pink flower blouse, slacks, sunglasses, and a brown wig, while Soliah wore a Mexican top, a turtleneck sweater, presumably pants, and hiking boots. She carried a straw bag in which she hid a Browning automatic pistol and a carbine. A few minutes later, Kilgore drove up in a rented Volkswagen van with Bortin and Emily Harris as passengers. Emily Harris wore khaki pants, a cap, sunglasses, and a heavy coat, under which she held a hair-triggered shotgun.

Hearst and Soliah boarded the van, and Kilgore drove to a rented garage at 28th and D Streets. Bortin and Soliah got out and drove away in a stolen Pontiac Firebird that had been stored at the garage for the robbery. Bortin carried weapons in a straw basket.[22]

Bortin and Soliah drove the Firebird to McKinley Park, and Kilgore followed in the Volkswagen van. As they waited in their parked vehicles, Steve Soliah drove by in the Mustang with Bill Harris sitting next to him. Wendy Yoshimura passed by in a Ford Pinto. She wore a dark wig. Hearst, now driving the van, pulled out and followed the Firebird to a grocery store parking lot. Kilgore and Emily Harris got out of the van and into the Firebird. That vehicle now carried the inside team: Bortin, Kilgore, Kathy Soliah, and Emily Harris. The Firebird headed straight to the Crocker National Bank. Hearst followed, parking in a funeral home parking lot. All she had to do was wait for the Firebird to return. The wait would be five minutes.[23]

The Pontiac Firebird entered the residential area behind the Crocker bank and parked near the cyclone fence. The four members of the inside team, wearing ski masks, jumped out, hurried through the hole in the fence, and began to walk toward the bank's rear door. Steve Soliah parked the Mustang on Marconi Avenue where he and Bill had a good view of the bank and nearby stores. Soliah slouched down behind the steering wheel, but Harris, looking "fidgety and nervous," got out and walked slowly down the sidewalk, keeping his eyes on the bank and stopping next to a light pole.[24]

As the inside team proceeded across the rear parking lot, Myrna Opsahl got out of her vehicle, carrying a small adding machine, and headed toward the rear door. She was forty-two years old, the mother of four, the wife of a surgeon, and an active member of her Seventh Day Adventist Church. Opsahl, like her friends who joined her in the parking lot, had come to count the church's Sunday donations and deposit them in the bank, just as she did every Monday morning. She opened the rear door, but Kilgore was there already, and he held it open for her and her friends so they could enter the bank.[25]

Myrna Opsahl was twelve feet inside the bank when the rest of the SLA stormed inside. Emily Harris shouted, "You motherfuckers, get down, put your nose on the ground and don't move."[26] Employees and customers dropped, but Myrna Opsahl, perhaps in shock, froze. Harris moved toward her, raising her shotgun, and it fired, hitting the woman fully in the abdomen. Opsahl slid slowly to the floor, hardly making a sound, and began to bleed out. Harris backed away and began to count, "One minute, two minutes. . . ."[27]

The robbery team seemed disorganized and confused. They cursed and kicked the tellers; they dropped money on the floor; and, more important, they left three .9 mm cartridges on the floor. No one attended to Myrna Opsahl, who lay dying on the floor, not even one of her closest friends who was next to her. Finally, Harris brought the ordeal to an end. She stopped counting. "We're running out of time," she shouted. "Let's get out of here. Time's up."[28] The SLA squad then exited through the rear door and ran "in a confused fashion" across the parking lot to their getaway car.

By now, authorities had been alerted of the Crocker National Bank robbery. Myrna Opsahl was taken by ambulance to the American River Hospital, where she died within an hour. Her husband, Trygve Opsahl, was the attending surgeon, and he could do absolutely nothing as he watched his wife slip away. His children were taken out of school and transported to the hospital. Later in the day, it was reported that Opsahl and his children sat in their car, in shock and disbelief, staring at the sandwiches Myrna had prepared for them.[29]

Once near the getaway vehicle, one SLA member looked back to see if the backup was still available. They pulled off their outer clothes and threw them into the trunk of the Firebird and drove away with "a very loud muffler."[30] They passed the shopping center and turned onto Fair Oaks Boulevard. As soon as he saw the Firebird leave the area, Bill Harris returned to the Mustang, and Steve Soliah drove slowly past the Lucky grocery store and away. About a mile from the bank, Soliah parked the Mustang at the Continental Gardens Apartment complex on Mensch Circle, and the two men walked through the complex to Yoshimura's Ford Pinto. Yoshimura moved over, and Soliah got behind the wheel and drove them away.

The Firebird roared past Hearst parked in the Volkswagen van, and she followed it to the corner of La France and Foothill. Those in the Firebird climbed into the van, one of them shouting, "Go, go, go!"[31] Hearst proceeded to Winn Park. Inside the van, there was a sense of excitement and fear. Myrna Opsahl was on their mind. Kathy Soliah said "a woman teller" had been shot, and Hearst wanted to know who did it. Emily Harris looked at her: "I did it, let's not talk about it." Soliah hoped the woman might live, but Kilgore thought not. "No," he said. "I looked at her."[32]

At Winn Park, Hearst and Kathy Soliah left the Volkswagen van and walked back to their Capitol Street apartment. Over the next two hours, many members of the assault team came by to discuss what had just occurred. The first was Jim Kilgore. He was very anxious about Myrna Opsahl and recounted how she had lost her life. He blamed Emily Harris; she had been nervous and was "careless with the gun." He said that if Opsahl had not been directly in front of him, he would have been the one who was dead, killed by one of his own comrades.[33] Emily Harris was the second to come to the door. She confirmed that Opsahl was indeed dead. Emily Harris's disregard for Opsahl's life masked her guilt. It "didn't really matter because the woman was a 'bourgeous [sic] pig' whose husband was a doctor."[34] She did not blame the hair trigger. Rather, she believed that the safety on the shotgun must have slipped and that Opsahl did not move fast enough to comply with her orders.

Myrna Opsahl's murder ratcheted up the media attention. The SLA was now "hot" and had to be very careful. Emily Harris told her comrades that a radio had reported that a pregnant teller was kicked during the robbery. Kathy Soliah confessed she had done that.[35] Bill Harris showed them the brass part of a shotgun shell and said, "This is the murder round." Myrna Opsahl was on his mind as well. He knew that his wife had murdered her, and to ease the tension he tried to make a small joke out of it. "If it hadn't been for good old [Opsahl] . . . ," he said, "one of our comrades would have been dead. She got all the buckshot."[36] He buried the brass under a tree in McKinley Park.

At Bill Harris's direction, the SLA met at the T Street safe house to evaluate the Crocker National Bank job. The SLA had left the bank with $15,257,[37] but Bill Harris and other members of the SLA were not happy with how the robbery was conducted. This would be a tough and brutal session. Before the Harrises came into the room, Bortin expressed his feelings that the assault team seemed out of control inside the bank following Opsahl's murder. Her killing had been unnecessary. He aimed his fire at Emily Harris, whom he called "nervous and incompetent." Bill Harris deflected attention from his wife by criticizing Steve Soliah for not bringing a weapon to the job. Harris said he "did not know what Soliah would have done if the 'pigs' would have come up." But, in the end, Harris conceded to Bortin's larger point—the bank robbery had been "a sloppy job."[38]

Bill Harris also pointed out that they all now faced murder charges, including Patricia Hearst, and they could all go to the gas chamber. He returned to the same rhetoric that he used against Yoshimura in the Jeffersonville farmhouse: "All revolutionaries die eventually in one way or another." In the larger scheme of things, he said, Myrna Opsahl was a minor tragedy. He then delivered a lengthy paean to the revolution and the struggle for the people. Hearst could barely conceal her contempt. "I loathed the Harrises more than ever before," she wrote. "They were violent, evil, unpredictable, incompetent people."[39]

MOVING BACK TO THE BAY AREA

The impact of the Crocker National Bank robbery and the Opsahl murder accelerated the plan to move back to the Bay Area. As the SLA members had feared, authorities and the local press began to speculate that the action at the bank had all the characteristics of an SLA military operation.[40] In fact, local authorities did list the SLA as a possible suspect, but they believed that it was more likely a group called Tribal Thumb, an anarchist cell emerging from the East Bay in 1972. They had used "a similar modus operandi" in a November 1973 bank job in Berkeley.[41]

And so the SLA moved back to the Bay Area. Kathy Soliah and Jim Kilgore found an apartment at 1246 Geneva Street in San Francisco near the Mission District. The move took place shortly after they celebrated Cinco de Mayo in Sacramento. Kathy Soliah drove Hearst into San Francisco in a rented truck. Within weeks, the SLA had established safe houses at 401 Irvington Street in Daly City, another on Lyon Street near the Haight Ashbury District, and one each at 288 Precita Street and 625 Morse Street, both also in San Francisco. These safe houses were interchangeable in terms of living arrangements, largely because of Bill Harris's bad temper. By late August, the Harrises were staying at the Precita house. Hearst, Yoshimura, and Steve Soliah moved into the Morse Street house in early September.

The SLA continued its revolutionary rhetoric, but began to associate itself with the New World Liberation Front (NWLF), which had been involved in a bombing campaign along the Pacific Coast for the last two years. It was a shadowy group, and law enforcement agencies seemed to have no success in trying to find out what it was. The SLA's bombing campaign became very active during the summer of

1975. The Geneva Street apartment resembled a bomb factory, and Bill Harris became a self-taught bomb maker. The group failed to touch off bombs in the Mission and Sunset District police stations in San Francisco; they dropped pipe bombs under police cars in Emeryville, California, and in Marin County; and in August 1975, Jim Kilgore, Bill Harris, and Kathy Soliah attempted to bomb police cars in Los Angeles. Two days later, the SLA touched off bombs at the Marin County Civic Center.[42] On the planning board for future targets were the Law Enforcement Assistance Administration (LEAA), San Mateo Resident Agency for the FBI, Levi Strauss, Standard Oil properties, and the Health, Education, and Welfare offices in San Francisco. Except for the failed attack on the San Francisco police stations, Patricia Hearst claimed that she did not participate in the bombing campaign. She opposed the bombings and any talk of developing a police assassination program.[43] The facts have revealed, however, that Hearst played an active role in SLA activities—particularly as a lookout in the Marin County Civic Center bombing in late August 1975.

Mike Bortin proved to be one of the strongest advocates of the bombing campaign, and he sought materials from as far north as southern Oregon. Kilgore and Kathy Soliah favored "small actions" or symbolic bombings against corporate and public institutional sites, whereas Bortin and the Harrises sought to make a big splash in the public's consciousness. But, unlike the Harrises, Bortin believed in spontaneous action, and he was tired of the study groups and planning sessions that the Harrises thrived on. Throughout their San Francisco days, Bortin persistently advocated "killing pigs . . . not by bombing them, but by shooting them." One memorable incident occurred during a study session when Bortin drew a diagram of Miz Brown's Feed Bag, a popular police haunt. Bortin claimed he had eaten there at least forty times. All it would take, he said, was for a couple of SLA soldiers to walk in "and kill four or five police officers."[44] Bill Harris rejected this plan. But Bortin continued to argue that what the SLA was doing with its bombing campaign "was not big enough" for him.[45] Interminable debates over Marighellist tactics and strategies took the SLA nowhere. When Bill Harris threw Bortin's girlfriend, Pat Jean McCarthy, out of the collective, Bortin was enraged. He was now fed up with Harris's leadership.

In addition to the bombing campaign, the SLA had become preoccupied with strategizing about how it would break Willie Brandt out of Soledad Prison. Just as the Remiro-Little matter in their Sacramento days, members spent much of their time planning a spectacular prison break. Their designs may have been inspired by the Ron Beaty escape from Chino in October 1972, led by a Venceremos cadre from Palo Alto. Emily Harris had been involved in the defense committee on behalf of the defendants. If Venceremos could successfully spring Beaty from Chino, with one guard killed, then the SLA with its experienced crew should be able to do the same or better for Willie Brandt.

Moreover, the SLA had already established a go-between. Richard Allen Frishman from Santa Barbara, remained in contact with Jim Kilgore, and they often went shooting together at the Coyote Point Pistol Range in San Mateo. The SLA relied on Frishman to deliver messages from Brandt (Frishman was Brandt's attorney) to the SLA so that it could plan a successful mission. Even Patricia Hearst was involved in securing information and planning the operation. At one point, Kilgore drove her to Soledad City to meet with Frishman.[46] In July 1975, Frishman flew to San Francisco and spent the day at the Geneva Street safe house. He brought news that Brandt had a court date in Salinas. This gave the SLA hope that it could rescue him outside of Soledad Prison. Emily Harris proposed that they apply the Venceremos tactics used to free Ron Beaty, but Frishman declared the Beaty and Brandt situations not comparable, which infuriated Emily Harris. The meeting degenerated into a shouting match.

Kilgore and Hearst stepped outside the apartment to escape the arguing. Frishman left later in the evening and gave Kilgore $60 to help defray expenses.[47] He knew that the SLA was incapable of doing anything significant to help Willie Brandt.

JACK SCOTT REEMERGES

Meanwhile, Jack and Micki Scott emerged from hiding. Scott's "guru" job for Bill Walton in Portland, Oregon, had proved disappointing. The 1974-75 season had been one of the worst years in Walton's career as he careened from injury to injury. In addition, the FBI had apparently zeroed in on the Scotts for allegedly aiding the SLA, and that attention strained their relationship with Walton. In late February 1975, they disappeared, met with several radical lawyers, and reemerged in April 1975 before television cameras in San Francisco at Rev. Cecil Williams's Glide Memorial Church with Bill Walton at their side.[48] Jack Scott denied he had done anything wrong. He claimed the FBI was harassing him and his family.

Randolph Hearst contacted Jack Scott to set up a meeting. Scott insisted that as a precondition for the meeting Hearst publish a statement saying that he supported Scott's actions regarding his daughter. Hearst agreed, and while the subsequent meeting with Scott led to no tangible results, somehow Hearst's spirits were lifted. For the first time, he felt his daughter "was safe."[49] The meeting led to a series of other meetings and telephone calls between the two men during the summer of 1975. However, Jack Scott, to his detriment, seemed to do most of the talking. On July 18, after a dinner at Senor Pico's in Ghiardelli Square, Hearst told Catherine that Jack Scott "had talked too much and that guy was going to get into trouble."[50]

Randolph Hearst worried that Scott might be attempting to extort money from him. Scott clearly wanted to write a book on Patricia Hearst and the SLA, and he hinted about his expenses. However, he also wanted to maintain his credibility within the radical community. Over time, Randolph Hearst became convinced that Scott knew the location of his daughter.

In mid-July 1975, Rev. Cecil Williams set up an extraordinary meeting in the Fairmont Hotel between Hearst and Jack and Micki Scott, Jack Scott's parents, and his older brother, Walter. Jack and Walter Scott had been drinking, and Walter, Hearst noted, was already "bombed." Jack Scott demanded that Hearst fly to New York City, meet with his attorney, William Kunstler, and "bad mouth the FBI." He worried that his parents could be in trouble with the authorities. Randolph Hearst refused. By the time the meeting had come to an end, Scott was ready "to belt" Hearst, but Walter restrained him, and both "rolled down a flight of stairs."[51]

Walter Scott was forty-one years old, twice divorced, emotionally disturbed, and an alcoholic. His father barely talked to him, but Jack loved him. Back in their days in Scranton, Pennsylvania, Walter had been a protective and nurturing brother, and Jack never forgot it. Walter worked for the government as a computer technician, but Walter claimed he had killed people for U.S. intelligence agencies. In fact, when he called his father in Las Vegas in September 1974—while Scott was transporting Hearst to California—he was on his way home, fired from his job because he had killed three people in Libya without proper authority.[52] At least, that is what Walter had claimed. Walter also informed his family that he needed money. Jack wrote him a check for $3,000 immediately since Walter had to at that point kept Patricia Hearst a secret. But that quickly changed. The two brothers went out for drinks, and Jack, who could not help himself because he wanted to impress Walter, gave Walter intimate details about his travels with Patricia Hearst. Indeed, Jack bragged, "The cops were chasing [us] all over the country and all the time she was with me. Would you believe it?"[53]

It was not important that Walter believed him; it was important that he used it against Jack. By December 1974, Walter had run out of money again. In January 1975, when raging drunk, he made anonymous telephone calls to the Washington, D.C., police and the FBI. He told them about Jack had Patricia Hearst, but he hung up the phone before giving his own name. The FBI followed through on the tips, even interviewing Jack and Micki Scott in Bill Walton's home outside Portland. The Scotts no doubt suspected why the FBI had begun to focus on them.

Then, on January 31, 1975, Walter, while intoxicated, told the Scranton, Pennsylvania police chief, "I know where Patty Hearst is."[54] The police cleaned him up and turned him over to the FBI. For money and the promise of a good-paying job in the federal government, Walter gave them all the information he could, and then flew to England and Ireland. It took the FBI little time to locate the Honesdale farmhouse and give the house a thorough search. They found Patricia Hearst's scent in a mattress and discovered Wendy Yoshimura's fingerprints. It was their first solid lead since the Compton shootout, but it was five months old. The FBI still had a long way to go to find Patricia Hearst.[55]

THE FBI—FINALLY CLOSING IN

The fact remained that the FBI, for most of the time, did not know the whereabouts of the Symbionese Liberation Army. FBI agents always seemed to be more than a step behind. Some of it was bad luck, such as when Camilla Hall slipped through their net when she went underground in early 1974. Some of it was shoddy work. But the real problem was the lack of public support from the radical community in the East Bay and the nation.[56] Clarence Kelley, who became director of the FBI in 1974, wrote, "The absence of even one solid lead was almost unbelievable in a case like this. When the SLA went underground, none of our informants could—or would—give us any information concerning their whereabouts."[57]

Lack of informants within the radical East Bay community certainly hindered the investigation, but there were other factors as well. The Hearst investigation cost taxpayers $5 million, and agents sifted through over 27,000 leads.[58] For Clarence Kelly, the Hearst kidnapping was "unique." He called it "a political kidnapping . . . no casebooks could be followed; no precedents had been set." He was baffled that Patricia Hearst chose not to escape from her captors. This decision "paralyzed the investigation" and "dealt a severe psychological blow to us all."[59]

Interestingly, the FBI's discovery of Wendy Yoshimura's fingerprints at the Honesdale farmhouse was the turning point in their long and exhausting investigation of Patricia Hearst's whereabouts. Until then, FBI agents did not know that Yoshimura had been part of the second team of the SLA.[60] The FBI connected Yoshimura to her lover, Willie Brandt, who remained in prison. And the FBI had learned that Jack Scott knew Brandt. They had participated in a 1970 Berkeley demonstration together, and Scott had written a letter to Brandt's probation officer urging that Brandt receive a shorter sentence for his bombing conviction. Following their lead on Brandt, the FBI researched Brandt's visitor records at Soledad. They discovered that Kathy Soliah had visited him six times. When agents looked into her last working address at a restaurant in the Sir Francis Drake Hotel, they found that Soliah had not been seen for some time.[61]

Temporarily stymied, FBI agents contacted Soliah's parents, Martin and Elsie Soliah, in Palmdale, California. It was hard for the Soliahs to believe that their children might be involved in terrorist activities, but they agreed to assist the FBI in any way they could. They informed the agents that they corresponded by mail, but the FBI quickly discovered that the San Francisco address was simply a drop box where Kathy Soliah picked up her mail. At the agents' request, Martin Soliah flew to San Francisco and placed a letter in Soliah's drop box asking to meet with her. On August 29, Kathy Soliah met with her father on the steps of the downtown Federal Building, and along with siblings Steve and Jo, they had dinner together. Martin Soliah urged his children to cooperate with the authorities before it was too late, but Kathy remained adamant: "I don't have anything to hide. I don't trust the FBI."[62]

LEADERSHIP ISSUES

As the FBI closed in on the SLA in San Francisco, the collective had already cracked wide open over personality, strategy, and leadership issues. The assault on the Marin County Civic Center in San Rafael and on the Los Angeles Police Department on August 20 represented a pivotal point in the SLA's cohesion. In fact, looking back on these events in which she played a significant role, Patricia Hearst wrote, "Everything pretty much spiraled out of control after that."[63] Bill Harris gave his wife command of the Marin County Civic Center operation, while he led Jim Kilgore and Kathy Soliah south to Los Angeles to bomb the police.

He constructed the bombs for both operations—bombs that were much larger and more lethal than earlier ones. In fact, these bombs, he said, were "anti-personnel," meaning they were intended to kill and maim people, not just to destroy property.[64] While Harris and his co-conspirators drove south to Los Angeles, Emily divided the cell into two teams for the Marin County Civic Center operation: one composed of Jo Soliah and Bonnie Jean Wilder, a radical and a friend of Kathy Soliah's, and the other composed of Steve Soliah and

Patricia Hearst. She told the teams that the bombs were to detonate at the Civic Center twenty minutes apart in order to inflict as many casualties as possible.

When Wendy Yoshimura learned of this, she was appalled. It was not that she opposed bombings in principle; after all, she had joined Willie Brandt's Revolutionary Army a few years earlier, and she had helped to plant a bomb at a San Francisco police station a few weeks earlier. For Yoshimura, bombs were curious things. They were impersonal; they inflicted death, pain, and destruction without any accounting of guilt or responsibility. When Emily Harris told them that one bomb was to be placed near the door to the Law Library, Yoshimura protested that it would hurt not only "pigs" but also innocent civilians. This did not faze Harris in any way. She responded with her husband's stock revolutionary speech, which he had unleashed after Myrna Opsahl's murder in the Crocker National Bank. Revolutions can be messy, she said, and there are times when innocent people die. And yet the students using the Law Library were not innocent victims, she declared: "Those law students are studying to be lawyers and they'll go to work for some big, piggy corporation, and so they are pigs too." In any event, Yoshimura gave up the fight, and, according to Hearst, "Wendy refused to have anything to do with us during this operation."[65]

The Marin County Civic Center operation began in the evening of August 20, 1975, as the two teams approached the complex. Steve Soliah, who seemed almost serene as he drove Hearst to the center, parked near a small lake. He then retrieved his backpack and bicycle from the car and headed toward the parking lot in front of the sheriff's office. He returned within five minutes, and the two then slowly left. Meanwhile, Jo Soliah and Bonnie Jean Wilder were placing their bomb near the Law Library. Both bombs did explode, but for some reason Steve Soliah's bomb failed to detonate as planned. It exploded right after his older sister's bomb instead of twenty minutes later, leaving no casualties in its wake. Later, Soliah and Wilder left a communiqué near a radical radio station crediting the New World Liberation Front for the bombing.

The Los Angeles strike proved typical of Bill Harris's leadership. Los Angeles was toxic to the cell's existence. Cinque led the founding members to their destruction in Compton because he did not know the lay of the land as well as he thought he did. Similarly, Harris, Kilgore, and Kathy Soliah arrived in the city and did not know what to do. It was a debacle, not quite as debilitating as the Compton shootout over a year earlier, but the SLA never fully recovered from it. Harris had no real plan, no real targets in mind, and no real exit strategy. It seemed that all he wanted to do was drop the bombs and run. The consequences were predictable. It brought out the worst in all three of the bombers.

The utter, complete frustration with the situation brought to the surface all of the hurt feelings, sexual resentments, and political differences that had begun to emerge after the group moved back to San Francisco. In Los Angeles, they found a Veterans of Foreign Wars convention under way. With Soliah waiting in the car, Kilgore and Harris entered the convention with the bomb, but when a security official gave them a hard look, they lost their nerve and hurried back to their car. Then it all spilled out. Harris and Kilgore began screaming at each other in the streets, and Soliah stuck up for Harris and mocked Kilgore's sexual prowess. At a red light, Kilgore lost it and hit Soliah in the face, leading to a fight with Harris. They sobered up immediately when the light changed, and cars began to honk at them. Finally, in the evening Kilgore and Soliah placed a bomb under a police car at the Hollenbeck police station and another under a police car parked nearby at an International House of Pancakes restaurant. However, both failed to detonate, adding to Harris's frustration, and the group returned to San Francisco completely dejected.[66]

Hearst describes vividly in her memoir the internal deterioration in the aftermath of these assaults. Even if the Marin County Civic Complex bombing had been flawed in its execution, it nonetheless counted as a strike against the police, unlike the Los Angeles venture, much to Bill Harris's detriment. The Harrises strove hard to contain the anger and resentment of the cell membership. Yoshimura had already shown her independence, and Mike Bortin had long called the bombing campaign ineffective and yearned for more immediate and bloody direct action. Kilgore was out for blood after the humiliation in Los Angeles, and Kathy Soliah had now seemed to shift against the Harrises' leadership.

In a desperate move to keep the cell relevant to the revolution, the Harrises declared that they would seek out recently paroled James H. "Doc" Holiday, a Los Angeles-based murderer, to take over leadership of the SLA. Holiday had led the Black Guerrilla Family and had supported the SLA while in prison. This move was a throwback to the days in which the old SLA crew rallied behind a black leader, but the new SLA wanted nothing to do with it. Kilgore delivered the coup de grâce: "What did the old SLA ever accomplish? You killed a black man, kidnapped a little teenaged girl and robbed a bank. What the hell did that amount to?" [67] Bill and Emily Harris contacted Doc Holiday during a political rally in Golden State Park. They then met again a couple of days later to hear Holiday reject their offer of being the new SLA leader.[68] As it turned out, the SLA had just days remaining to serve the revolution.

THE FINALE

On September 7, Hearst and Yoshimura moved into a $180 a month apartment at 625 Morse Street in San Francisco They had in fact been living together since June, developing a closer, more respectful relationship. For one thing, they had become more adult and more serious, and they had begun to put their experiences into perspective. Indeed, they analyzed their experiences from a more feminist point of view, and critiqued Bill Harris's oppressive chauvinism. Yoshimura slowly "persuaded Patty to move away from the domicile and domination of the Harrises."[69] They put their thoughts down in a letter to Bill Harris. In it, they criticized his macho style of leadership, which was endemic in many New Left leaders. As expected, Harris went ballistic and could not be restrained. When Yoshimura had enough of his abuse, she enlisted Kathy Soliah, whom she considered to be a feminist, to act as a mediator between the two women and Bill Harris. Soliah obliged, and she began to drive regularly back and forth between the two safe houses at 625 Morse and 288 Precita Streets—a major tactical error on her part.[70]

On September 15, FBI special agent Ray Campos drove to an apartment house in Daly City looking for Mike Bortin. While there, he discovered Kathy and Jo Soliah doing some house painting. He delivered this information to the FBI office and returned covertly with another agent in the afternoon. Shortly thereafter, the Soliahs left the apartment complex with Jim Kilgore and drove to 625 Morse Street. The next day, Ray Campos saw Steve Soliah taking off in a car and driving to 288 Precita Street. The FBI observed the apartment for some thirty hours. As agents watched, a man resembling Bill Harris exited the apartment and walked to a nearby laundromat. An agent followed to get a closer look at him. The agent confirmed that it was indeed Bill Harris.

On September 18, FBI agents were ready to move against the SLA leaders. They acted on the assumption that Patricia Hearst was at the Precita address. Just a little after noon, Bill and Emily Harris left their apartment for a run. The agents let them go, thinking they would be less likely to retaliate when apprehended if they were exhausted by exercise. Around 1:30 p.m., the Harrises returned. The FBI closed in and arrested them. Bill Harris stopped dead in his tracks, but Emily Harris resisted and cursed the officers. The arresting agents then discovered that Patricia Hearst was not in the Harris apartment. Knowing the arrests would be flashed on local news stations, agents Tom Padden and Jason Moulton rushed over to 625 Morse Street accompanied by two San Francisco police detectives, Timothy F. Casey and Larry Pasero. Moulton was new to the FBI, but Padden had been an agent for years and was very well

Figure 24: Steven Soliah is taken to Sacramento County Jail by U.S. Marshals after his arraignment on bank robbery charges. Sacramento, California, October 30, 1975. (Walter J. Zeboski/Associated Press)

respected. The four men walked onto the property and found landlord Jerry Brill working in his plumbing shop on the ground floor. They showed him photographs of Bill and Emily Harris, Patricia Hearst, and Wendy Yoshimura. Brill did not recognize Hearst or Yoshimura, but he thought that Emily Harris had been around. He said that two female tenants were on the top floor.

Padden and Casey headed up the back stairs, while Moulton and Pasero went up the interior stairs. When Padden and Casey reached the apartment, they looked in and saw the fugitives sitting at a table talking. Padden went to the Dutch door and shouted, "FBI! Freeze!" Patricia Hearst made a move toward her purse lying nearby, but Padden stopped her by shouting, "I'm going to blow her [Yoshimura's] head off." Yoshimura then opened the Dutch door, and Casey quickly handcuffed Patricia Hearst. "She looked very pale," Casey said. He asked her why she was there. To which, Hearst replied, "I'd rather not tell you about it."[71] Before they left the apartment, Patricia Hearst requested permission to change her underwear. She had soiled them.

At the time of her arrest, Wendy Yoshimura had just put the finishing touches to a letter intended for her "Dearest Brother," Willie Brandt. In it, she provided a detailed analysis of the failure of the SLA to accomplish any meaningful act for the people. In fact, she wrote, the SLA had "ceased to be a group," and she tried to account for that. The absolute and unyielding demand for security was "a big factor," but equally significant was the way in which the media almost deified the leadership. Yoshimura conceded that the events over the past summer had revealed leadership failures.[72]

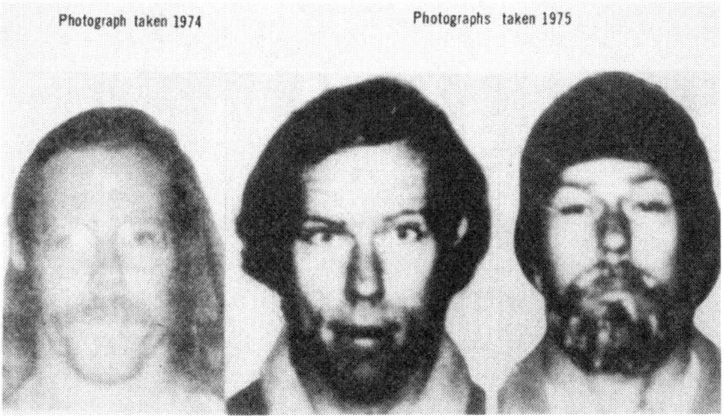

Figure 25: James Kilgore is arrested in South Africa after being on the run for over 25 years. San Francisco, California, November 8, 2002. (Jakub Mosur/Associated Press)

She went on to point out that, while she "did not much like them [the Harrises]," they nonetheless possessed a "fierce dedication" to the movement, and I was under their spell." Yoshimura then delivered an eviscerating critique of the Harrises' leadership style. She saw them as people with "weak egos lacking very much in sense of themselves. . . . They are doctrinaire Marighellists. These people are totally unable to check out the objective situation and deal with it. They simply do not know how to take a theory and apply it to the situation that exists." At their core, she wrote, Emily and Bill Harris were riddled with guilt because they were born white. They put persons of color on a pedestal. More than that, Bill Harris's guilt stemmed from his responsibility for the deaths of his comrades in the Compton shootout. Yoshimura did not hold back. Bill Harris had "fucked up" at Mel's Sporting Goods.[73]

The second team of the SLA disintegrated and fractured over the summer of 1975. Each member had his or her own agenda and refused to compromise. Mike Bortin simply quit after Bill Harris attempted to discipline him and other members. Yoshimura explained in her letter to Brandt that the new additions to the SLA wanted to go their "own way." Bill and Emily Harris had no clear understanding of the meaning of "third world leadership" as a product of "white guilt," and they could not separate the political from the personal. Moreover, they possessed a "very shallow understanding" of the women's movement; they had no real insights into "the importance of the international perspective"; and they had a stubborn insistence that "only armed struggle . . . is valid and that anything

Figure 26: Left to right, Emily Harris; Patricia Hearst; and Wendy Yoshimura as they leave San Francisco's Federal Building after their arraignment. September 18, 1975, San Francisco, California. (Bettmann/Contributer/Getty)

else (aboveground, etc.) is irrelevant."[74]

Finally, Yoshimura told Brandt that she was going to make a major decision in her life "within a week or so." She was either going to head east again or stay in the Bay Area and work with other like-minded individuals. She assured Brandt that she was in a good place and optimistic about the future. She had learned a lot about herself, and for that alone, she wrote, "I would not exchange it for anything! I think most of us came out of this ahead." Especially Patricia Hearst. "She is incredible!" Yoshimura continued. "She amazes me! I swear only the toughest could have come out of it as she did. What an ordeal she went through! What an ordeal all of us went through! I can write a book about it."[75]

Wendy Yoshimura was processed at the Alameda County Court House in Oakland. Bill and Emily Harris, as well as Patricia Hearst, were driven to the Federal Building in San Francisco. Patricia Hearst was later driven to the San Mateo County Jail. Steve Soliah was arrested near Patricia Hearst's apartment when he tried to warn her. The remaining SLA crew heard of their arrests on the radio and promptly disappeared. At the San Mateo facility, Patricia Hearst was asked what her occupation was. Harnessing Tania, she replied, "Urban guerrilla."[76]

15 END OF AN ERA

IN CONCENTRATING THEIR ACTIVITIES AROUND THE Berkeley area, the SLA had hoped to recapture the excitement and passion of the protest movements of the 1960s. But it failed. The world had changed dramatically since 1970, and the SLA had not noticed. Marcus Foster's murder alienated the SLA from the public and New Left sympathizers alike. Patricia Hearst's kidnapping further discredited the SLA. Under the leadership of escaped convict Donald Defreeze (Cinque Mtume) and then Vietnam veteran Bill Harris, the SLA had spiraled out of control. Its methods of violence and extortion were broadcast widely. The world watched in horror and amazement as the SLA outmaneuvered the FBI time and time again.

WHAT HAPPENED?

Many questions revolving around the kidnapping of Patricia Hearst and her involvement in the SLA remain unanswered. However, Hearst's actions suggests she became a willing participant in the SLA after her kidnapping. Her transformation into "Tania," the urban guerilla, left the country in shock. Despite her many opportunities, not once since the shootout more than a year before her arrest had she attempted to contact friends or family. The excitement she experienced in the SLA outweighed the potential consequences of her actions. She both admired and feared the SLA's dedication and growing obsession with death. The SLA was willing to die for what it believed to be the start of a revolution. Hearst's voluntary participation in several bank robbery operations suggests that she herself possessed that same dedication and willingness to die.

Throughout its short existence, the SLA managed to elude the FBI's massive manhunt while continuing to produce communiqués, extorting a food program from Patricia Hearst's father, and robbing banks. Unlike any group before or after, the SLA had unlimited access to the media. As professor of psychology Murray Miron observed, "The world was pulled through the titillation of the kidnapping of one of its more distinguished citizens, dumb-founded by the childish and vague extravagance of the ransom demands, disconcerted by the helplessness of the authorities, chagrined by the debasement demanded by the threats, incredulous over the victim herself becoming a criminal in concert with her abductors, and, finally emotionally drained into ennui after an incredible public display of fiery self-immolation."[1]

The Harrises had done their best to rekindle the SLA after the Compton shootout, but ultimately they had failed. The activities of this "second team" consisted mainly of political bombings, stealing cars, and robbing banks to support their lifestyle underground. The former SLA revolutionaries had become common criminals. On September 18, 1975, after the FBI captured Bill and Emily Harris, Patricia Hearst, Wendy Yoshimura, and Steven Soliah, in a tape-recorded conversation with her close friend Trish Tobin, Patricia Hearst would voice her dissatisfaction with her arrest and acknowledge she had changed tremendously over the last eighteen and a half months. Hearst would go on to serve just over two years in prison following her conviction for her role in the Hibernia Bank robbery.

For 102 days, the SLA had eluded the FBI, controlled the media, and incited fear among Bay Area residents because of their use of violence. The many individuals and organizations affiliated with progressive causes and generally associated with the New Left suffered tremendously because of the SLA's actions. In their attempt to locate the SLA after Patricia Hearst's abduction, law enforcement agencies placed people and organizations with ties to SLA members under surveillance. The FBI tried to interview some of these individuals, but with mixed results. Within progressive circles, Cinque Mtume became increasingly viewed as an agent provocateur because the actions of the SLA led directly to police actions against those involved in progressive causes.

Upon the incarceration of the Harrises and Patricia Hearst, FBI director Clarence Kelly reflected on the performance of his agency in the investigation. In spite of all its efforts and funding, the FBI had made few inroads into securing intelligence about the SLA's whereabouts and agenda. "There were no informants," Kelly recalled. "Absolutely no leads reached the Bureau from those fringe elements in our society who knew, really knew, where the various SLA hideouts were located. None."[2] By the mid-seventies, New Left paranoia and distrust of the FBI had precluded any real effort to develop a relationship with the agency on the HEARNAP case, and because of other events, such as COINTELPRO, the Vietnam conflict, the Kent

State killings, and the Watergate scandal, the distrust filtered down to the public at large. As a result, Kelly swung the agency away from political surveillance of extremist groups. The political intelligence the FBI obtained in the future came largely out of criminal investigations. This new focus was to have profound implications for its activities in the 1990s and after the terrorist attacks on the United States on September 11, 2001.[3]

The SLA's violence raised questions and concerns among political activists across the political spectrum. As noted, David Horowitz, the editor of the leftist magazine *Ramparts,* wrote an editorial in 1974 that was critical of the revolutionary group's violent proclivities. The violence of the SLA, coupled with the New Left's inability to find a new cause to rally around in the aftermath of Vietnam, doomed the movement.

With the demise of the New Left in U.S. politics and on college campuses across the nation came the rise of conservative politics led by Ronald Reagan. The excesses of the student protest movement helped to elect Reagan governor of California in 1966. The student protest movement embodied by the Free Speech Movement and its successors in the sixties had occurred during the second term of California governor Edmund G. "Pat" Brown, who was a liberal Democrat. His inability to control the protests, which had played out with alarming frequency, and the outbreak of violence in Watts in 1965 convinced voters that Reagan's response to the students to "observe the rules or get out" was the right way to deal with the growing anarchy throughout California.[4]

This attitude toward the college protesters paid dividends for Governor Reagan. Never fearful of antagonizing the left, much like he did with his botulism comment referring to the SLA and the PIN food program, Reagan had many popular quips attributed to him denigrating hippies and protesters. In one instance, Reagan responded to a hippie holding a sign reading "Make love not war" by saying the sign holder did not look capable of either. In another confrontation with protesters, Reagan mentioned that a hippie's hair was cut like Tarzan's, he acted like Jane, and he smelled like Cheetah. These comments putting down student protesters and hippies endeared Reagan to a growing number of Americans who were antagonized by these protest movements and referred to themselves as "conservative" politically. These voters became the vanguard of the "Reagan Republicans" and "Reagan Democrats" who fueled the Reagan Revolution in 1980.

It was the presidential primaries of 1976, however, that introduced Reagan as a national candidate. These primaries began during the trial of Patricia Hearst for the Hibernia Bank robbery and provided the nation with a reminder of the generational divide that defined the late 1960s and first few years of the 1970s. In this atmosphere, Reagan challenged an incumbent Republican president, Gerald R. Ford, for the Republican nomination. Reagan came extremely close to defeating President Ford. Following his defeat at the Republican National Convention in Kansas City, the prevailing opinion was that Reagan's chance to run for president had come and gone. He would be 69 years old in 1980, far too old to be seriously considered for the Republican nomination. However, in 1980 Reagan once again demonstrated his political power, and his election became a political watershed in U.S. history.

The political theater of the SLA—the communiqués, the food program, the announcement that Patricia Hearst had joined the revolution—provided fuel for the machine that became the Reagan Revolution. Events such as the Hibernia Bank robbery sold newspapers and kept the SLA in the news, but it failed to win converts or the "hearts and minds" of the American people. Instead, the SLA became an oddity, never able to shrug off its inexplicable decision to assassinate Marcus Foster in 1973. Instead of anarchy and guerrilla theater, Americans craved law and order, Reagan-style.

In the aftermath of the Vietnam War, Watergate, and the Iranian hostage crisis, Americans wanted peace and prosperity. In fact, they wanted a champion that made them feel good about being an American and their role in the world—someone who had a plan to restore the economy and reassert the nation's role as the leader of the free world. Reagan became this man—this champion who had faced down protesters at Berkeley and proclaimed his disdain for various elements of the New Left.

Reagan provided a platform for many Americans who were disgusted by what they perceived to be the patronizing of the "youth of America." In the ever-shifting sands of American politics, 1980 became the year of revolution, but not the one the SLA had hoped for as the country shifted away from the liberal politics of the Great Society.

Today, the SLA continues to serve as a reminder of the anarchy of the 1960s. It attempted to bring back an era in 1974 that the majority of Americans looked back on not with revolutionary passion but with sadness because of the political assassinations, the war in Vietnam, and the violence that accompanied the South's difficult process of desegregation. The political kidnapping of Patricia Hearst brought back painful memories of the lawlessness of the previous decade. By the time Patricia Hearst and Bill and Emily Harris were arrested, the nation had undergone fundamental changes. On August 9, 1974, Richard Nixon had succumbed to the pressures of the Watergate investigation and resigned as president of the United States, and the substantially less polarizing Gerald R.

Ford had ascended to the presidency. In April 1975, fighting in the Vietnam War came to a halt as the North Vietnamese army rolled into Saigon. Now, the sixties were over, and the nation had moved on. However, the kidnapping of Patricia Hearst and her willing participation in the SLA were extremely significant. A rebel who had turned against her parents in favor of the SLA, Hearst came to represent a generation of rebellious teens and college students who, like her, had also forsaken their parents.

THE TRIAL AND ITS AFTERMATH

On February 5, 1976, the trial of Patricia Hearst began in the U.S. District Court in San Francisco. F. Lee Bailey tried to convince the jury that his client, Patricia Hearst, had been coerced into joining the SLA and robbing the Hibernia Bank. The opposing U.S. attorney brought evidence before the court, which, in his opinion, proved that Hearst had been a willing and active member of the SLA. The prosecuting attorney outlined three events that the defense could not successfully rebut. First, when arrested, Hearst no longer lived with her former captors and had ample opportunity to call her family and walk away to end her ordeal. The same could be said during the time of her cross-country trip to New York. Second, during Bill and Emily Harris's altercation at Mel's Sporting Goods, Hearst had fired in the direction of the store employees as they attempted to handcuff Bill Harris. And, third, Hearst proved unable to explain why she kept a little Olmec monkey that Willie Wolfe had given her. In the last SLA tape, she mentioned how much she loved him and how "the pigs probably have the little Olmec monkey that Cujo (Wolfe) wore around his neck. He gave me the little stone face one night."[5] When Hearst was arrested, she had the Olmec monkey in her purse. Had she truly hated Wolfe, it is hard to believe she would have kept that trinket with her for over a year of cross-country trips and ever-changing safe houses. Ultimately, the jury found Hearst guilty of participating in the Hibernia Bank robbery and of joining the SLA willingly.

On January 20, 2001, Patricia Hearst was one of 140 persons to receive a last-minute pardon from President Bill Clinton on his last day in office. Bill Harris served time in jail from 1975 through 1983 for the kidnapping of Patricia Hearst. In 2002 Harris pled guilty for his role in the Crocker National Bank robbery, which included the murder of Myrna Opsahl, and he was released from prison in September 2006, after serving half his sentence. Emily Harris, now known as Emily Harris Montague, also served jail time for her role in the kidnapping of Patricia Hearst, the Crocker National

Bank robbery, and the murder of Myrna Opsahl. Because Emily Harris Montague was the shooter in Opsahl's death, she remained in prison until February 2007. For the murder of Marcus Foster, Joe Remiro received a life sentence and currently resides in Pelican Bay State Prison. Little, although sentenced to life in prison for the Foster murder as well, had his conviction overturned on appeal on February 27, 1979. He was acquitted in retrial on June 5, 1981. A look back at these events reads like fiction, and in the end, although the SLA had been dismissed as an aberration in U.S. history, it is a true account that marks the critical pivotal point at which an entire nation changed face.

NOTES

INTRODUCTION | SETTING THE STAGE

1. Jean Kinney, *An American Journey: The Short Life of Willy Wolfe* (New York: Simon and Shuster, 1979), 256; David Horowitz, *Radical Son: A Generational Odyssey* (New York: Touchstone, 1997), 237.
2. W. J. Rorabaugh, *Berkeley at War: The 1960's* (New York: Oxford University Press, 1989), 19–24.
3. Terry Anderson, *The Movement and the Sixties: Protest in America from Greensboro to Wounded Knee* (New York: Oxford University Press, 1995), 87.
4. Mario Savio, speech on the steps of Sproul Hall, Berkeley, California, December 2, 1964.
5. Anderson, *Movement and the Sixties*, 77.
6. Rorabaugh, *Berkeley at War*, 38–39, 44.
7. Todd Gitlin, *The Sixties: Years of Hope, Days of Rage* (New York: Bantam Books, 1993), 385–90.
8. McLellan and Avery, *Voices of Guns,* 58–59fn.
9. Ibid., 58.
10. Venceremos ("We shall overcome") was a Marxist-Leninist-Maoist organization that formed at Stanford University in 1971. It identified itself as a part of a Third World struggle against U.S. imperialism. Thus the SLA's emphasis on Third World leadership came directly from Venceremos. Eventually, the group splintered. One faction advocated an armed struggle against the U.S. government, and another faction wanted to establish a grassroots political organization to challenge the status quo. The internal struggle was nullified by the October 6, 1972, ambush of prison guards (one of whom was killed) during the escape of Venceremos convict organizer Ronald Beaty. On December 12, Beaty was captured. He then told police

everything he knew about Venceremos, thereby hastening an end to this revolutionary group. See also McLellan and Avery, *Voices of Guns;* and Les Payne, Tim Findley, and Carolyn Craven, *The Life and Death of the SLA* (New York: Ballantine Books, 1976).

11. SLA members Camilla Hall and Patricia Soltysik lived together for a time on Channing Way. Soltysik was particularly affected by the growing politicization of Channing Way.
12. McLellan and Avery, *Voices of Guns,* 132. They describe a newspaper account of a Nazi leaflet that was distributed at an Oakland shopping center. The leaflet mentioned the targeting of "satanic Jews and all their lackeys who are stirring up the niggers against us." It also said that "there might be shotgun blasts into the guts of mixmaster principals and superintendents."
13. Ronald Kessler, *The Bureau: The Secret History of the FBI* (New York: St. Martin's Paperbacks, 2003), 174; Rhodri Jeffreys-Jones, *The FBI: A History* (New Haven, CT: Yale University Press, 2007), 169–73, 177. See also Athan Theoharis, ed., *The FBI: A Comprehensive Reference Guide* (Phoenix, AZ: Oryx Press, 1999), 126–27, 374.

CHAPTER 1 | THE BERKELEY "PATRIOTS"

1. The term *radical New Left* was used widely during the 1960s and 1970s by members of the New Left. They wanted to differentiate themselves from the "Old Left" of the previous generation.
2. McLellan and Avery, *Voices of Guns*, 178.
3. Ibid., 186. See also John Bryan, *This Soldier Still at War* (New York: Harcourt Brace Jovanovich, 1975), 99.
4. Bryan, *This Soldier Still at War*, 110–12.
5. Fred Soltysik. *In Search of a Sister* (New York: Bantam Books, 1976.) Fred Soltysik, the older brother of Patricia, described the dysfunctional Soltysik home life and its effect on his sister.
6. McLellan and Avery, *Voices of Guns*, 90, 93.
7. Payne, Findley, and Craven, *Life and Death of the SLA*, 91. The authors also briefly analyze why Hall became a lesbian, demonstrating how views toward homosexuality have changed dramatically since the book was published in 1976.
8. McLellan and Avery, *Voices of Guns*, 116.
9. Ibid., 116.
10. Kinney, *An American Journey*, 106–12, 137.
11. Ibid., 114.
12. *Guerrilla: The Taking of Patty Hearst,* directed by Robert Stone (2004; New Video, 2005), DVD.
13. Kinney, *An American Journey*, 144.
14. Bryan, *This Soldier Still at War*, 135.

15. Ibid., 136.
16. Ibid.
17. Bryan, *This Soldier Still at War,* 136–37. See also Payne, Findley, and Craven, *Life and Death of the SLA,* 100.
18. Susan Lyne and Robert Scheer, "The Story of the SLA: How and Why the Group Kidnapped Patty Hearst and Came to Be Urban Guerrillas." *New Times,* April 16, 1976," 28. The Peking Man House received its name not from the political beliefs of its inhabitants, but from the name of a food stand operated by David Gunnell and his girlfriend, Jean Wah Chan.
19. Payne, Findley, and Craven, *Life and Death of the SLA,* 102–3.
20. McLellan and Avery, *Voices of Guns,* 81.
21. Payne, Findley, and Craven, *Life and Death of the SLA,* 104.
22. McLellan and Avery, *Voices of Guns,*82-84.
23. Ibid., 70.
24. Ibid., 79–80.
25. Payne, Findley, and Craven, *Life and Death of the SLA,* 102.
26. Bill Harris, interview by Greg Cumming, April 7, 2009. Interviews were largely conducted by email.
27. Lyne and Scheer, "Story of the SLA," 26.
28. *Guerrilla: The Taking of Patty Hearst,* DVD.

CHAPTER 2 | CINQUE MTUME

1. David Boulton, *The Making of Tania Hearst* (London: New English Library, 1975), 45. See also Marilyn Baker and Susan Brompton, *Exclusive! The Inside Story of Patricia Hearst and the SLA* (New York: MacMillan Publishing, 1974), 87.
2. Payne, Findley, and Craven, *Life and Death of the SLA,* 10–11. See also McLellan and Avery, *Voices of Guns,* 309.
3. McLellan and Avery, *Voices of Guns*, 311, 312.
4. *Guerrilla: The Taking of Patty Hearst,* DVD.
5. McLellan and Avery, *Voices of Guns,* 314.
6. Ibid., 316–17.
7. Ibid., 317–18.
8. Ibid., 319.
9. Ibid., 319.
10. Ibid., 61, 62.
11. Ibid., 63.
12. Mayfield would eventually play a key role in Cinque's escape from Soledad Prison and his arrival in the Bay Area. In return for Mayfield's assistance, DeFreeze intended to confer on him the rank of captain in the SLA although there is no new evidence that Mayfield accepted and played any other role in the development of the SLA. Payne,

Findley, and Craven, *Life and Death of the SLA,* 8. See also McLellan and Avery, *Voices of Guns*, 63, 88; and National Archives, FBI interview of Patricia Hearst, April 13, 1976, 14. In *The Life and Death of the SLA*, Jim Mayfield is referred to as "Sherman." Mayfield's role in the escape of DeFreeze is also mentioned in *The Voices of Guns* as the driver who picked up DeFreeze in Gonzales and brought him to the Bay Area. Patricia Hearst confirmed the role of Mayfield in the escape in the April 13 interview with the FBI.

13. Ibid., 58, 63. On page 58, Westbrook refers to Russell Little as the "sneakiest little son of a bitch." Wolfe gets off easier. Westbrook thought of Wolfe as "just an immature little kid." Both Wolfe and Little will play an instrumental role in the development of the SLA.
14. McLellan and Avery, *Voices of Guns,* 87–90. See also Payne, Findley, and Craven, *Life and Death of the SLA,* 1–2.
15. McLellan and Avery, *Voices of Guns,* 88; Payne, Findley, and Craven, *Life and Death of the SLA,* 2. Both versions of the DeFreeze escape state that DeFreeze hitchhiked to Gonzales despite the fact that he was still wearing his prison uniform. Apparently, the family that gave DeFreeze food and shelter for the night was unaware of the significance of his attire.
16. Payne, Findley, and Craven, *Life and Death of the SLA,* 3. Kinney, in *An American Journey,* states that Willie Wolfe picked up DeFreeze at the home of the Mexican American family (p. 201). However, most sources claim that Mayfield served as point man for the pickup.
17. Payne, Findley, and Craven, *Life and Death of the SLA,* 6–8; McLellan and Avery, *Voices of Guns,* 88.
18. Payne, Findley, and Craven, *Life and Death of the SLA,* 7.
19. George L. Jackson, *Soledad Brother: The Prison Letters of George Jackson* (Chicago: Lawrence Hill Books, 1994), 27.
20. George L. Jackson, *Blood in My Eye* (Baltimore: Black Classic Press, 1990), 39.
21. Ibid., 14.
22. Ibid., 12.
23. Patricia Campbell Hearst and Alvin Moscow, *Patty Hearst: Her Own Story* (New York: Avon Books, 1988), 89.
24. Ibid., 93.
25. Eric Cummins, *Radical: The Rise and Fall of California's Prison Reform Movement* (Stanford, CA: Stanford University Press, 1994), 153 and 224.

CHAPTER 3 | THE LAUNCH

1. McLellan and Avery, *Voices of Guns*, 89–90. Thompson, proprietor of a food stand known as Harlem on My Mind, reportedly was a member of

the Black Panther Party, at one time siding with the Eldridge Cleaver faction when he resided in New York. Thompson seemed to constantly hang around the periphery of the SLA without being a member.

2. McLellan and Avery, *Voices of Guns*, 90. See also Payne, Findlay, Craven, *Life and Death of the SLA*, 96–97.
3. Soltysik, *In Search of a Sister*, 63.
4. Dan Berger, *Outlaws of America: The Weather Underground and the Politics of Solidarity* (Oakland, CA: AK Press, 2006), 46.
5. McLellan and Avery, *Voices of Guns*, 92.
6. Ibid., 93–94.
7. The original ten members of the SLA were Cinque, Russell Little, Patricia Soltysik, Nancy Ling Perry, Willie Wolfe, Joe Remiro, Angela Atwood, Camilla Hall, and Bill and Emily Harris.
8. McLellan and Avery, *Voices of Guns, 93.*
9. Ibid., 99–104. The revolutionary group to which Wolfe, Little, and Remiro were linked was known as the Partisans Vanguard Party or Vanguard for short. It was one of a large number of such leftist groups that formed during this time period. Like most of them, the Vanguard had no impact.
10. McLellan and Avery, *Voices of Guns*, 94; Kinney, *An American Journey*, 164–65. Both versions provide an account of Wolfe as the primary recruiter for Cinque's new organization. Kinney, in particular believes that Wolfe's affability played a key role in his bringing everyone together. Although Wolfe may have known everyone who joined the SLA before the founding of the revolutionary group, Wolfe never served in anything remotely close to a leadership position.
11. Baker and Brompton, *Exclusive!* 91.
12. Ibid., 120.
13. Ibid., 119.
14. Payne, Findley, and Craven, *Life and Death of the SLA*, 119; McLellan and Avery, *Voices of Guns*, 94.
15. Payne, Findley, and Craven, *Life and Death of the SLA*, 121–23; McLellan and Avery, *Voices of Guns*, 94.
16. Payne, Findley, and Craven, *Life and Death of the SLA*, 113, 121, 124; McLellan and Avery, *Voices of Guns*, 94.
17. Payne, Findley, and Craven, *Life and Death of the SLA*, 125.

CHAPTER 4 | THERO WHEELER

1. Ibid., 125, 126, 141–42
2. There are many different versions of the leadership of the SLA. According to Marilyn Baker in *Exclusive!* the women were the leaders. In fact, Baker calls Patricia Soltysik the "brains of the SLA" (p. 87). In an email exchange with Greg Cumming on February 2, 2009, former

SLA member Bill Harris had a much different take on the structure of the group: "Everything was a group decision. We functioned as a collective and a true democracy."

3. Payne, Findley, and Craven, *Life and Death of the SLA,* 126.
4. Ibid., 127; McLellan and Avery, *Voices of Guns,* 195.
5. Boulton, *The Making of Tania Hearst,* 7–9.
6. McLellan and Avery, *Voices of Guns,* 95, 96.
7. Payne, Findley, and Craver, *Life and Death of the SLA,* 133.
8. Ibid., 136.
9. After the death and wounding of the prison guards, Venceremos became a primary target for police and other law enforcement agencies, and Venceremos leaders and members were placed under surveillance. The police arrested Beaty a few months later. Beaty then quickly turned informant, providing law enforcement with the names of the group's leadership and members, among other details. Beaty's arrest and quick conversion created an atmosphere of distrust and paranoia throughout Venceremos, which accelerated the organization's breakup.
10. Ibid., 96.
11. Payne, Findley, and Craven, *Life and Death of the SLA,* 141.
12. McLellan and Avery, *Voices of Guns,* 147–48. Wheeler said that only Cinque and Soltysik came to the apartment. Every other account, including one from Mary Alice Seim, includes Perry as one of the visitors.
13. Payne, Findley, and Craven, *Life and Death of the SLA,* 142–44.
14. McLellan and Avery, *Voices of Guns,* 147.
15. Ibid., 105, 123, 179.
16. Ibid., 105.
17. Payne, Findley, and Craven, *Life and Death of the SLA,* 136.
18. Ibid., 320–21. Wheeler's comments on the level of support for the SLA from former Venceremos leaders vary greatly. In fact, because Wheeler had mentioned that his friends from Venceremos did not at all support the SLA, It is difficult to fully trust him as a source on this issue.
19. Payne, Findley, and Craven, *Life and Death of the SLA,* 134–35.
20. Bryan, *This Soldier Still at War,* 183.

CHAPTER 5 | THE ASSASSINATION

1. The Editors, "The Symbionese Liberation Army: Terrorism and the New Left," *Ramparts* 12 (1974): 21.
2. McLellan and Avery, *Voices of Guns,* 137; Payne, Findley, and Craven, *Life and Death of the SLA,* 149–54.
3. Payne, Findley, and Craven, *Life and Death of the SLA,* 156.
4. Robert Blackburn, phone interview by Greg Cumming, August 27, 2009.
5. Ibid.

6. Payne, Findley, and Craven, *Life and Death of the SLA,* 164.
7. Kinney, *An American Journey,* 215.
8. Blackburn interview, August 27, 2009.
9. Payne, Findley, and Craven, *Life and Death of the SLA,* 158.
10. Ibid, 158–62.
11. McLellan and Avery, *Voices of Guns,* 147.
12. Ibid., 142–43.
13. Ibid.; Blackburn interview, August 27, 2009.
14. McLellan and Avery, *Voices of Guns,* 142–43.
15. Ibid.
16. McLellan and Avery, *Voices of Guns,* 142. Save our Schools had been established by radical white former Venceremos members.
17. Blackburn interview, August 27, 2009.
18. Ibid.
19. Ibid. See also Kinney, *An American Journey,* 215; and Payne, Findley, and Craven, *Life and Death of the SLA,* 162.
20. In the interview with Greg Cumming on August 27, 2009, Blackburn referred to Vera Silverman on more than one occasion as a community gadfly who did not have a strong following within the Oakland community.
21. Soon after the assassination of Foster and the Bay Area's outpouring of grief in support of the slain educator, Wolfe left the Bay Area and spent Christmas and New Year's with his family. The story commonly told is that the trip by Wolfe involved obtaining much-needed money from his father. However, it is possible that another reason for the trip back east was Wolfe's crisis of confidence. He had misread the tone of the October 9 school board meeting, and his report led to the targeting of Foster, which surviving members of the SLA now consider a huge mistake.
22. Lyne and Scheer, "Story of the SLA," 31.
23. John Palmer Spencer, *Caught in the Crossfire: Marcus Foster and America's Urban Education Crisis, 1941–1973* (New York: New York University Press, 2002), 404.
24. McLellan and Avery, *Voices of Guns,* 128.
25. Robert Blackburn interview by Greg Cumming, September 2, 2009.
26. Ibid.
27. McLellan and Avery, *Voices of Guns,* 128.
28. Ibid., 128–29; Blackburn interview, September 2, 2009.
29. McLellan and Avery, *Voices of Guns,* 130–31.
30. Ibid., 131.
31. Ibid., 132–33. The mention of the cyanide bullets in the communiqué was not clear to those outside of the investigation. The SLA never went into detail about their unique bullets.
32. Payne, Findley, and Craven, *Life and Death of the SLA,* 172.
33. McLellan and Avery, *Voices of Guns,* 132; Payne, Findley, and Craven,

Life and Death of the SLA, 172.

34. McLellan and Avery, *Voices of Guns,* 132; Payne, Findley, and Craven, *Life and Death of the SLA,* 173. McLellan and Avery mention a newspaper account of Nazi leaflets being distributed at an Oakland shopping center with a warning that "there might be shotgun blasts into the guts of mixmaster principals and superintendents."
35. McLellan and Avery, *Voices of Guns,* 146–48.
36. *Berkeley Barb*, February 22–28, 1974. 2.
37. Ibid.

CHAPTER 6 | TRIUMPH TO TURMOIL

1. Payne, Findley, and Craven, *Life and Death of the SLA,* 176.
2. Lyne and Scheer, "Story of the SLA," 32.
3. Kinney, *An American Journey,* 219.
4. Ibid., 57, 59–60.
5. Ibid., 67–69.
6. McLellan and Avery, *Voices of Guns,* 159–60; Payne, Findley, and Craven, *Life and Death of the SLA,* 189–90.
7. McLellan and Avery, *Voices of Guns,* 160. See also National Archives, Pacific Regional Branch Office, RG 118, U.S. Attorney's Files, FBI interview of Patricia Hearst, April 23, 1976. In the interview, Hearst described the process by which the Third World Liberation Front obtained fictitious identifications. The SLA used a similar process.
8. The Concord safe house had been rented under the name DeVoto, but for some reason that name did not show up in the police search. In all likelihood, the search was conducted using a phone directory, and either the SLA did not install a phone line or a phone line had been installed recently and so did not appear in the directory.
9. McLellan and Avery, *Voices of Guns,* 159–64; Payne, Findley, and Craven, *Life and Death of the SLA,* 189–92. Remiro and Duge accused each other of firing the first shot and instigating the violence.
10. McLellan and Avery, *Voices of Guns,* 163–64.
11. Bryan, *This Soldier Still at War,* 202.
12. Prior to the arrest of Little and Remiro, the SLA had contemplated splitting its organization into two distinct groups; one above ground—it would provide a steady flow of information from the local communities, money, and other necessary support—and one underground—it would serve as a combat unit. The SLA ultimately decided to establish two combat units, one of which (Remiro, Little, Atwood, and the Harrises) would move to San Jose (Lyne and Scheer, "Story of the SLA," 32). However, this plan fell to the wayside with the arrests.
13. Federal Bureau of Investigation, HEARNAP Files, 2920, Washington, DC, 1 [hereafter FBI, HEARNAP Files].

14. McLellan and Avery, *Voices of Guns,* 164–65.
15. Baker and Brompton, *Exclusive!* 51.
16. McLellan and Avery, *Voices of Guns,* 168.
17. Ibid., 171, 172.
18. Leonard Garment, *Crazy Rhythm: From Brooklyn and Jazz to Nixon's White House and Watergate and Beyond* (Cambridge, MA: Da Capo Press, 2001), 167. According to Garment, one of President Richard Nixon's advisers, the American Film Institute was showing the movie *State of Seige* at the Kennedy Center in Washington, D.C. When Garment pointed out to the American Film Institute's director, George Stevens, that the film glorified political assassinations, Stevens quickly cancelled the movie because the Kennedy Center's namesake had been the victim of such an assassination.
19. This letter was printed in the February 1–7, 1974, edition of the *Berkeley Barb.*
20. McLellan and Avery, *Voices of Guns,* 513.
21. Ironically, Cinque and his comrades missed the opportunity to link their movement to the Founders by failing to invoke Thomas Jefferson's famous admonition in a letter to William S. Smith in 1787, "What country can preserve the liberties if their rulers are not warned from time to time that their people preserve the spirit of resistance?" Jefferson continued on this theme and wrote, "The tree of liberty must be refreshed from time to time with the blood of tyrants. It is its natural manure." Fawn M. Brodie, *Thomas Jefferson: An Intimate History* (New York: W. W. Norton, 1974), 241.
22. McLellan and Avery, *Voices of Guns,* 516.
23. *Berkeley Barb*, February 1–7, 1974, 2.
24. National Archives, FBI interview of Patricia Hearst, April 12 and 13, 1976, 14. "Arco's design modification of the M-1 carbine intrigued the FBI because of its simplicity and its extremely high cyclic rate of fire. The Los Angeles Police Department, in its official report on SLA activities in the city, referred to Joe Remiro as the group's armorer. However, this was a false assertion. Remiro was mechanically inclined, but he had no experience as a gunsmith.
25. FBI, HEARNAP Files, document 2826, 2. The owner of the property identified Soltysik and Harris as the persons who had rented the house.
26. FBI, HEARNAP Files, document 2730, 4.
27. FBI, HEARNAP Files, document 2823, 3, 4.
28. FBI, HEARNAP Files, document 2826, 1.
29. FBI, HEARNAP Files, document 2730, 2, 4.
30. Ibid.

CHAPTER 7 | THE KIDNAPPING

1. Notes relating to Patricia Hearst and her activities at Berkeley were found in Nancy Ling Perry's spiral notebook at the Concord safe house. Also, in phone interviews with Greg Cumming, Bill Harris mentioned that the SLA had kept Hearst under surveillance for quite a while.
2. Payne, Findley, and Craven, *Life and Death of the SLA,* 199.
3. Roger Rapoport, "Hearst Abductor Tells Inside Story," *Oakland Tribune*, October 16, 1988, A2
4. McLellan and Avery, *Voices of Guns,* 195--96.
5. Ibid., 194.
6. Hearst and Moscow, *Patty Hearst*, 33. In her account of the kidnapping, Hearst derisively quotes Weed as crying out to Cinque, Harris, and Atwood, "Take my wallet. That's all we have. Take anything you want . . . anything you want." Taking Weed up on his offer, they did—they took his bride-to-be.
7. McLellan and Avery, *Voices of Guns,* 189–92.
8. Roger Rapoport, *Oakland Tribune*, October 16, 1988, A2.
9. Ibid. See Lyne and Scheer, "Twenty Months with Patty/Tania," *New Times,* March 5, 1976, 18. A few firsthand accounts (FBI, HEARNAP Files, document 562) report Hearst screaming for help, but not all. In fact, the majority of the firsthand accounts do not recall Hearst screaming at all. McLellan and Avery (*Voices of Guns,* 191) portray Hearst as screaming hysterically while trying to break free. In the process, Hearst's robe fell off, exposing her upper body, and her screams became sobs as she begged to be released.
10. FBI, HEARNAP Files, unnumbered document, 2.
11. Susan Darby Hendry, *Soliah: The Sara Jane Story* (Bloomington, IN: Cable Publishing, 2002), 90–91. Hendry continues to perpetuate the myth that a second African American male had taken part in the kidnapping of Patricia Hearst. Hearst emphatically stated in her autobiography that Cinque, Bill Harris, and Angela Atwood were the only members of the SLA to enter the apartment.
12. The search also led to the discovery of over a pound of marijuana in the master bedroom closet.
13. McLellan and Avery, *Voices of Guns,* 199–200.
14. Payne, Findley, and Craven, *Life and Death of the SLA*, 211; McLellan and Avery, *Voices of the Guns,* 204.
15. FBI, HEARNAP Files, document 56, 2–3.
16. The cost of the food giveaway was estimated in 1974 based on the value of the dollar at that time.
17. Hearst and Moscow, *Patty Hearst,* 53–53; Harris interview, February 2, 2009.
18. McLellan and Avery, *Voices of Guns,* 208.
19. Ibid., 209.

20. Payne, Findley, and Craven, *Life and Death of the SLA*, 213.
21. McLellan and Avery, *Voices of Guns,* 251. Governor Reagan had mentioned that very few people "would accept food that was ransom for a kidnap victim." He would later mention, in response to the PIN program, that "it's just too bad that we can't have an epidemic of botulism."
22. Ibid., 212.
23. Payne, Findley, and Craven, *Life and Death of the SLA*, 213–14.
24. The best example of the wariness of the New left toward the SLA was an anonymous editorial, "The Symbionese Liberation Army: Terrorism and the New Left," in the May 1974 edition of *Ramparts* magazine (pp. 21–27). The editorial was actually written by David Horowitz, who feared retribution from the SLA because of his scathing condemnation of their violence, focusing heavily on the Foster assassination.
25. Payne, Findley, and Craven, *Life and Death of the SLA*, 215.
26. McLellan and Avery, *Voices of Guns*, 241.
27. Payne, Findley, and Craven, *Life and Death of the SLA*, 216.
28. McLellan and Avery, *Voices of Guns*, 245.
29. Ibid. Arnold Townsend of WAPAC became the PIN coalition leader. The relationship between Townsend and Ludlow Kramer was strained at best.
30. McLellan and Avery, *Voices of Guns,* 242.
31. Payne, Findley, and Craven, *Life and Death of the SLA*, 224.
32. McLellan and Avery, *Voices of Guns,* 243.
33. Ibid.
34. Ibid., 247.
35. Ibid.
36. Sara Jane Moore was recently paroled from prison and has freely discussed her past, including in a television appearance. She has spoken about her involvement with the FBI and radical movements in the Bay Area.
37. McLellan and Avery, *Voices of Guns,* 244.
38. Ibid., 250.
39. Ibid., 251.
40. Ibid., 252. The dollar values reflect 1974 prices.
41. FBI, HEARNAP Files, document 999, 1.
42. The FBI transcripts referred to Atwood as "Dalina."
43. Quotes taken directly from the FBI's transcript of the fourth SLA communiqué.
44. This is referring specifically to the anonymous editorial in the May 1974 edition of *Ramparts,* a leading journal of the New Left. David Horowitz, the author of the anonymous editorial, wrote in *Radical Son: A Generational Odyssey* that "fearful of reprisals that the SLA might take on my family, I had not signed the editorial. Looking back, I realize that this was the first time in my life I had been afraid of the left." As

an interesting side note of history, it is possible that the SLA played an important role in converting Horowitz from his New Left beliefs into a neoconservative.

45. Patricia Hearst maintains that she never had a relationship with Wolfe. She contends that Wolfe raped her while she was a captive. In a January 9, 2009, email, former SLA member Bill Harris explained that Patricia was never abused: "there were 5 women and 3 men who would not have tolerated any form of prisoner abuse. Any sexual abuse would have been punished severely. At all times PH was treated with respect and dignity because our intention was to eventually release her and we knew she would be asked about and would reveal how she was treated. Once freed she would be our best propaganda." During her trial for her part in the Hibernia Bank robbery, Patricia told the prosecutor that she had been raped by Wolfe and that she could not stand him. However, when arrested, she had in her possession an "Olmec Monkey" figurine given to her by Wolfe.
46. McLellan and Avery, *Voices of Guns,* 254.
47. Hearst and Moscow, *Patty Hearst*, 80.

CHAPTER 8 | THE MEDIA

1. Payne, Findley, and Craven, *Life and Death of the SLA*, 206.
2. It is important to keep in mind that three members of the SLA—Bill and Emily Harris and Angela Atwood—had a background in the theater. Atwood seemed to have a flair for the dramatic as well as a talent for makeup and costume.
3. John A. Lester, *Girl in a Box: The Untold Story of the Patricia Hearst Kidnap* (San Jose, CA: Shoestring Publications, 2004), 26, 32.
4. McLellan and Avery, *Voices of Guns,* 200.
5. Hearst and Moscow, *Patty Hearst*, 162–63.
6. The Editors, "The Symbionese Liberation Army."
7. Lester, *Girl in a Box*, 22–23.

CHAPTER 9 | THE FBI

1. Ibid.
2. Steven Weed and Scott Swanton, *My Search for Patty Hearst* (New York: Warner Books, 1976), 65.
3. Ibid., 50.
4. Kessler, *Bureau*, 174.
5. Ibid.
6. Boulton, *Making of Tania Hearst,* 8–9, 32–36.
7. Mark Felt and John O'Connor, *A G-Man's Life* (New York: Public Affairs,

2006), 223. L. Patrick Gray was the immediate successor to J. Edgar Hoover as director of the FBI. However, he had the interim title because he had not been confirmed by the Senate. Gray had been a Nixon loyalist since the 1960 presidential campaign.

8. Bob Woodward, *The Secret Man: The Story of Watergate's Deep Throat.* New York: Simon and Shuster, 2005.
9 J. Anthony Lukas, *Nightmare: The Underside of the Nixon Years* (Athens: Ohio University Press, 1999) 287.
10. FBI, HEARNAP Files, document 23, 1. See also Weed and Swanton, *My Search for Patty Hearst*, 62. During the early weeks of the investigation, the FBI thought Weed might have had some involvement in the abduction.
11. FBI, HEARNAP Files, document 257.
12. FBI, HEARNAP Files, document 58.
13. Ibid. The names of the other suspected members have been redacted by the FBI.
14. FBI, HEARNAP Files, document 988.
15. Hearst and Moscow, *Patty Hearst,* 79.
16. McLellan and Avery, *Voices of Guns,* 219.
17. Ibid.
18. FBI, HEARNAP Files, document 1195; McLellan and Avery, *Voices of Guns,* 219.
19. McLellan and Avery, *Voices of Guns,* 218–219.
20. FBI, HEARNAP Files, unnumbered document, March 25, 1974, Wannall to Miller regarding electronic surveillance for intelligence purposes on the Symbionese Liberation Army (SLA) on the Patricia Hearst case, 1.
21 James Bamford, *The Puzzle Palace* (New York: Penguin Books, 1983), 370–71.
22. FBI, HEARNAP Files, unnumbered document, March 25, 1974, 3.
23. FBI, HEARNAP Files, document 1124, 1.
24. Ronald Kessler, *The FBI* (New York: Pocket Books, 1993), 246.
25. FBI, HEARNAP Files, document 1271, 2.
26. Ibid.
27. Ibid.
28. FBI, HEARNAP Files, document 1301, 1.
29. Harris interview, February 2, 2009.
30. FBI, HEARNAP Files, document 1301, 2.
31. Ibid.
32. The term *Keystone Cops*, often spelled *Keystone Kops*, refers to fictional incompetent policemen who were featured in silent film comedies in the early twentieth century.
33. FBI, HEARNAP Files, document 1698.
34. Kessler, *FBI*, 49. Oliver "Buck" Revell, a pilot and FBI agent, would track Soviet spies on the weekend via plane. Revell did this on his own time because he knew his boss, J. Edgar Hoover, would not approve.

According to Revell, Hoover was adamant about the FBI not having an "air force." Therefore, he did not want his agents using planes or helicopters.

35. Hearst and Moscow, *Patty Hearst,* 193.
36. Ibid.
37. McLellan and Avery, *Voices of Guns*, 437.
38. FBI, HEARNAP Files, document 1711, 1.

CHAPTER 10 | THE SLA: FROM CAPTORS TO COMRADES

1. FBI, HEARNAP Files, document 1663, 2.
2. McLellan and Avery, *Voices of Guns,* 213.
3. Lyne and Scheer, "Twenty Months with Patty/Tania," 22.
4. Hearst and Moscow, *Patty Hearst*, 38–39.
5. Ibid., 38. Emory student Barbara Jean Mackle was kidnapped on December 17, 1968, in Georgia and buried alive in a coffin with food and water. A ransom was paid, and Mackle was found on December 20 based on the approximate directions given to police by the kidnappers.
6. Carolyn Anspacher and Jack Lucey, *The Trial of Patty Hearst* (San Francisco: Great Fidelity Press, 1976), 154.
7. Hearst and Moscow, *Patty Hearst,* 112.
8. Anspacher and Lucey, *Trial of Patty* Hearst, 211.
9. Ibid., 121.
10. Ibid., 224–25.
11. Harris interview, February 2, 2009.
12. Ibid.
13. Anspacher and Lucey, *Trial of Patty Hearst,* 432–33.
14. Ibid., 433.
15. Ibid.
16. Harris interview, February 2, 2009.
17. Ibid., 258.
18. Ibid., 261.
19. Hearst and Moscow, *Patty Hearst,* 100.
20. When Patricia had been desperate to leave the boarding school at Santa Catalina, she turned to her father to help her out. He also served as the conduit for communications between Patricia and her mother.
21. Hearst and Moscow, *Patty Hearst*, 26–30.
22. Ibid.
23. Ibid., 22–30.
24. Ibid., 91. Hearst provided some insight into Cinque's state of mind when she wrote that during meetings, he insisted that the television be turned toward the wall to prevent the government from using it to spy on those in the house.

CHAPTER 11 | TANIA, QUEEN OF THE REVOLUTION

1. Anspacher and Lucey, *Trial of Patty Hearst,* 437.
2. McLellan and Avery, *Voices of Guns,* 205–6.
3. Hearst and Moscow, *Patty Hearst,* 217.
4. Ibid., 103–5, 107.
5 Ibid., 105.
6. Lyne and Scheer, "Twenty Months with Patty/Tania," 27–28.
7. Ibid., 24–26.
8. James Browning, interview by Greg Cumming, November 5, 2008.
9. Lyne and Scheer, "Twenty Months with Patty/Tania," 27: See also Hearst and Moscow, *Patty Hearst,* 90. Hearst mentioned that she truly feared law enforcement and that Cinque reinforced this fear by telling her over and over again that the FBI would come storming in at some point to kill the SLA and its prisoner.
10. Hearst and Moscow, *Patty Hearst,* 55.
11. McLellan and Avery, *Voices of Guns,* 235.
12. Bryan, *This Soldier Still at War,* 251; McLellan and Avery, *Voices of the Guns,* 296–97.
13. McLellan and Avery, *Voices of Guns,* 284–85.
14. Ibid., 294–96.
15. Hearst and Moscow, *Patty Hearst,* 125.
16. Bryan, *This Soldier Still at War,* 250.
17. Lester, *Girl in a Box*, 82–84.
18. FBI, HEARNAP Files, document 1227, 1.
19. Anspacher and Lucey, *Trial of Patty Hearst,* 201.
20. Hearst and Moscow, *Patty Hearst,* 114–15.
21. Ibid., 215.
22. FBI, HEARNAP Files, document 1227, 1.
23. Ibid.
24. Hearst and Moscow, *Patty Hearst,* 133.
25. Lyne and Scheer, "Story of the SLA,"34.
26. Ibid.
27. Ibid.
28. Ibid.
29. Hearst and Moscow, *Patty Hearst,* 124.
30. *Berkeley Barb,* April 5–11, 1974, 4.
31. McLellan and Avery, *Voices of Guns,* 222–25.
32. Lyne and Scheer, "Twenty Months with Patty/Tania," 28.
33. Ibid.
34. Hearst and Moscow, *Patty Hearst,* 137.
35. FBI, HEARNAP Files, document 1640, 157–201.
36. Hearst and Moscow, *Patty Hearst,* 160.
37. Ibid. Eyewitness accounts taken by the FBI have Cinque yelling out, "This is the SLA" and "Get down," without the colorful language

provided by Patricia Hearst.

38. McLellan and Avery, *Voices of Guns,* 323.
39. Hearst and Moscow, *Patty Hearst,* 161. Even though she wrote that she knew the gun was inoperable, the film footage showed Hearst pointing her weapon at two men who tried to enter the bank during the robbery.
40. Ibid. Eyewitness accounts taken by the FBI (HEARNAP Files, document 1640) corroborate this portion of Patricia Hearst's version of the bank robbery.
41. FBI, HEARNAP Files, document 1640, 233.
42. Ibid., 6. In their April 24, 1974 communiqué, the SLA claimed to have taken $10,660.02 in the robbery.
43. Ibid., 171.

CHAPTER 12 | ROAD TO PURGATORY

1. FBI, HEARNAP Files, document 1398, 1.
2. James Browning, interview by Greg Cumming, October 14, 2008.
3. FBI, HEARNAP Files, document 1482, 1.
4. McLellan and Avery, *Voices of Guns,* 334.
5. Ibid., 327.
6. Hearst and Moscow, *Patty Hearst,* 168–69. Hearst quoted Cinque in the aftermath of the robbery as saying that the reason for it was to ensure that Hearst's ties to the SLA were more than mere words.
7. McLellan and Avery, *Voices of Guns,* 334.
8. Hearst and Moscow, *Patty Hearst,* 173.
9. James Lubinskas "Remembering the Zebra Killings," August 30, 2001, http://97.74.65.51/readArticle.aspx?ARTID=21980.
10. Clark Howard, *Zebra: The True Account of the 179 days of Terror in San Francisco* (New York: Richard Marek Publishers, 1979), 341–48.
11. Hearst and Moscow, *Patty Hearst,* 173–74.
12. Ibid., 174.
13. Ibid.
14. Payne, Findley, and Craven, *Life and Death of the SLA,* 253. Support for this theory of the SLA's recruitment of new members is found in the FBI's HEARNAP Files, document 2055. The FBI found three nurse uniforms in the hideout at 833 West 84th Street.
15. Hearst and Moscow, *Patty Hearst,* 174–75. Hearst mentions that not everyone contacted by the SLA had been eager to join in the revolution. In hindsight, it is amazing that no one contacted the police to inform them of the recruitment efforts of the SLA.
16. Ibid., 178.
17. The remnants of the SLA—Bill and Emily Harris, along with Patricia Hearst—issued a communiqué in June responding to the shootout that claimed their six comrades. The communiqué resembled an obituary;

it eulogized not only their friends, but also the SLA itself.
18. FBI, HEARNAP Files, document 1640, 254.
19. Lyne and Scheer, "Twenty Months with Patty/Tania," 29. The Harrises mentioned that they had to tone down many of Patricia's statements because of their vicious attacks against her parents.
20. FBI, HEARNAP Files, document 1640, 259.
21. McLellan and Avery, *Voices of Guns,* 339.
22. Hearst and Moscow, *Patty Hearst,* 185.
23. Ibid., 188. The last part of the statement, "Happy Hunting Charles" was meant for FBI Special Agency in Charge Charles Bates, who was leading the search for the SLA.
24. FBI, HEARNAP Files, document 2233, 89–90. See also McLellan and Avery, *Voices of Guns,* 338. It provides a slightly different story, stating that Lolabelle Evans, who lived in the apartment directly below the SLA, complained about a cockroach infestation in her apartment, and the manager believed they were coming from the apartment above. When he entered apartment 6, he discovered the writings and debris left behind by the SLA and then called the police.
25. Hearst and Moscow, *Patty Hearst,* 183 and 201.
26. Ibid.
27. Ibid., 204.
28. Ibid,. The FBI and other law enforcement agencies, however, were no closer to the SLA than at any other time during their investigation.
29. Ibid., 198.
30. Ibid., 206.
31. Ibid., 207.
32. FBI, HEARNAP Files, document 1725, 2.
33. Hearst and Moscow, *Patty Hearst,* 209. Emily Harris in an interview with *New Times* (Lyne and Scheer, "Twenty Months with Patty/Tania," 18–36) stated that they all met at a shopping center in South Central Los Angeles. However, that is not very likely because the group would have stood out in this mostly African American neighborhood.
34. Hearst and Moscow, *Patty Hearst,* 211–12.
35. Lyne and Scheer, "Twenty Months with Patty/Tania," 29.
36. Hearst and Moscow, *Patty Hearst,* 213.
37. National Archives, Pacific Regional Branch Office, San Francisco/San Bruno, Record Group 118, Patricia Hearst interviews by FBI, April 12–13, 1976, 7–8 [hereafter National Archives, Hearst interviews]. See also Hearst and Moscow, *Patty Hearst,* 211.
38. Hearst and Moscow, *Patty Hearst,* 213.
39. Ibid., 202. See also Lyne and Scheer, "Twenty Months with Patty/Tania," 29.
40. Hearst and Moscow, *Patty Hearst,* 202.
41. Ibid., 218. Empty bottles of Akadema plum wine were always present in the SLA hideouts discovered by law enforcement agencies.

42. Ibid.
43. University of California, Los Angeles (UCLA), UCLA Special Collections, Young Research Library, Collection 293, Mayor Tom Bradley Administrative Papers, 1973–1993, draft report prepared by Los Angeles Police Department (LAPD), "The Symbionese Liberation Army in Los Angeles," July 19, 1974, 22. See also FBI, HEARNAP Files, document 1843, 1. According to the initial FBI report, Bill and Emily Harris entered the store at 4:40 p.m.
44. FBI, HEARNAP Files, document 1845, 8.
45. Later that day, Harris would tell Thomas Dean Matthews, the owner of the Ford van the three fugitives had "borrowed," that he had shoplifted a bandolier, not socks. FBI, HEARNAP Files, document 1627, 10.
46. McLellan and Avery, *Voices of Guns,* 341; UCLA, Young Research Library, draft report prepared by LAPD, 22.
47. Shana Alexander, *Anyone's Daughter: The Times and Trials of Patty Hearst* (New York: Viking Press, 1979), 102.
48. UCLA, Young Research Library, draft report prepared by LAPD, 22. See also McLellan and Avery, *Voices of Guns,* 342; and Anspacher and Lucey, *Trial of Patty Hearst*, 81.
49. Anspacher and Lucey, *Trial of Patty Hearst*, 230.
50. Hearst and Moscow, *Patty Hearst*, 224.
51. Ibid., 226–27.
52. UCLA, Young Research Library, draft report prepared by LAPD, 23.
53. McLellan and Avery, *Voices of Guns,* 342.
54. Ibid., 343.
55. UCLA, Young Research Library, draft report prepared by LAPD, 24
56. Ibid, 24. See also FBI, HEARNAP Files, document 1627, 9; and Hearst and Moscow, *Patty Hearst*, 231.
57. Hearst and Moscow, *Patty Hearst*, 231–32.
58. FBI, HEARNAP Files, document 1627, 8–11.
59. Hearst and Moscow, *Patty Hearst,* 234.
60. UCLA, Young Research Library, draft report prepared by LAPD, 26–27.
61. Ibid., 29–30.
62. Ibid., 30.
63. McLellan and Avery, *Voices of Guns*, 349. See also Payne, Findley, and Craven, *Life and Death of the SLA*, 275.
64. Payne, Findley, and Craven, *Life and Death of the SLA*, 235–36. See also McLellan and Avery, *Voices of Guns,* 345.
65. Hearst and Moscow, *Patty Hearst,* 241–42.
66. UCLA, Young Research Library, draft report prepared by LAPD, 39.
67. Daryl F. Gates and Diane K. Shah, *Chief: My Life in the LAPD* (New York: Bantam Books, 1992), 132.
68. Ibid.
69. UCLA, Young Research Library, draft report prepared by LAPD, 41.
70. Ibid., 41–42. See also McLellan and Avery, *Voices of Guns,* 356–57; and

Payne, Findley, and Craven, *Life and Death of the SLA*, 285.
71. UCLA, Young Research Library, draft report prepared by LAPD, 42.
72. Gates and Shah, *Chief*, 118–23.
73. Bryan, *This Soldier Still at War*, 285–86.
74. UCLA, Young Research Library, draft report prepared by LAPD, 42.
75. Ibid., 45.
76. Ibid., 46.
77. Ibid., 47
78. Ibid., 57.
79. Ibid., 59.
80. Ibid., 61.
81. Ibid., 61–63.
82. Ibid., 65.
83. Ibid., 65.
84. FBI, HEARNAP Files, document 1301, 2.
85. Ibid., 80, 84–85. Soltysik is listed as dying from multiple gunshot wounds and smoke inhalation and burns.
86. Ibid., 80–83.

CHAPTER 13 | HEADING EAST

1. Hearst and Moscow, *Patty Hearst,* 226.
2. Ibid., 232.
3. Ibid., 235
4. Ibid., 236.
5. Ibid., 250.
6. Jerry Belcher and Don West, *Patty/Tania* (New York: Pyramid Books, 1975), 192; Payne, Findley, and Craven, *Life and Death of the SLA*, 365–69.
7. National Archives, Hearst interviews, April 12–13, 1976.
8. Hendry, *Soliah,* 35. A year later, Moore gained lasting notoriety with her assassination attempt on President Gerald R. Ford in San Francisco.
9. Ibid., 61; McLellan and Avery, *Voices of Guns,* 381.
10. Hearst and Moscow, *Patty Hearst,* 243.
11. Hendry, *Soliah,* 115.
12. Ibid., 116.
13. National Archives, Hearst interviews, April 12–13, 1976, 9; July 21, 1976, 1; September 2, 1976, 1–2; Belcher and West, *Patty/Tania,* 291.
14. National Archives, Hearst interviews, August 27, 1976, 1.
15. Ibid.
16. Ibid., 1–2.
17. Payne, Findley, and Craven, *Life and Death,* 303–04.
18. Lynda Huey, *A Running Start: An Athlete, A Woman* (New York: Quadrangle/ New York Times Book Co., 1976), 165.

19. Robert Lipsyte, *SportsWorld: An American Dreamland* (New York: Quadrangle/New York Times Book Co., 1975), 269; David W. Zang, *SportsWars: Athletes in the Age of Aquarius* (Fayetteville: University of Arkansas Press, 2001), x; Mark Dyerson and J. A. Mangan, eds., *Sport and American Society: Exceptionalism, Insularity and Imperialism* (New York: Routledge, 2007); and Tim Elcombe, "Reform America: The Oberlin Experiment—The Limits of Jack Scott's 'Athletic Revolution' in Post-1960s America," *International Journal of the History of Sport* 22, no. 6 (2005): 1060–85.
20. Huey, *A Running Start,* 166.
21. Payne, Findley, and Craven *Life and Death,* 303; Howard Kohn and David Weir, "Tania's World: An Insider's Account of Patty Hearst on the Run," *Rolling Stone,* October 23, 1975, 41.
22. Lipsyte, *SportsWorld,* 269–70.
23. Robert Love, ed., *The Best of Rolling Stone: 25 Years of Journalism on the Edge* (New York: Doubleday, 1975), 41.
24. Hendry, *Soliah,* 47–51; Hearst and Moscow, *Patty Hearst,* 280–81; David Wellman and Robert Fitzgerald, "The Appearance of Justice and the Advantages of State: The Process of *Voir Dire* in Political Trials," *Contemporary Crises* 2 (1978): 373.
25. National Archives, Hearst interviews, August 27, 1976, 1.
26. Hearst and Moscow, *Patty Hearst,* 262.
27. Ibid., 263.
28. Ibid., 264; Love, *Best of Rolling Stone*, 179–80.
29. David Eskinazi, "Wayback Machine: Dr. Phil's Push for Justice," June 25, 2013, http://www.sportspressnw.com.
30. National Archives, Hearst interviews, April 12–13, 1976, 11.
31. Love, *Best of Rolling Stone,* 181.
32. National Archives, Hearst Pardon.
33. Jack Scott's testimony came as a result of the Kathleen Soliah/Sara Jane Olson trial. His testimony was meant to damage the credibility of Patricia Hearst if she testified for the prosecution.
34. Ibid. According to David Boulton, a British journalist, Nancy Ling Perry sold orange juice and pot from Fruity Rudy's. Weed had "no recollection of her, [but] she seems to have been acquainted with him since his name and telephone number were listed in her diary." Boulton, *Making of Tania Hearst*, 18–19.
35. National Archives, Hearst Pardon.
36. Ibid.
37. Lyne and Scheer, "Twenty Months with Patty/Tania," 26–27. For her part, Patricia Hearst has always denied complicity in her kidnapping by the SLA. For example, during the "lost year," she met Oakland attorney Dan Siegel, who advised the SLA on publishing a book about their movement. Siegel knew members of the SLA through Jack Scott and Pat Jean McCarthy (Mike Bortin's girlfriend), the latter through their

membership in the October League, a Marxist-Leninist outfit formed in the background of the 1969 split of the Students for Democratic Society. Siegel asked Hearst if she had cooperated in her own kidnapping, and Hearst replied with a firm negative answer. In fact, she asked Siegel if he had any news about her parents and family. Siegel did not. National Archives, Hearst interviews, April 23, 1976, 5.

38. Hearst and Moscow, *Patty Hearst,* 272.
39. Ibid., 275.
40. Ibid.
41. Ibid., 277.
42. Ibid., 277–78.
43. Phoebe Hoban, "Citizen Patty," *New York*, August 8, 1988, 35–36.
44. Hearst and Moscow, *Patty Hearst,* 280.
45. National Archives, Hearst interviews, April 12–13, 1976, 12; August 11, 1977, 5–6; Payne, Findley, and Craven, *Life and Death,* 303–4.
46. Hearst and Moscow, *Patty Hearst,* 286.
47. Ibid., 287.
48. Ibid.
49. Ibid., 288.
50. National Archives, Hearst interviews, April 12–13, 1976, 12–13; August 11, 1977, 7; Hearst and Moscow, *Patty Hearst,* 289.
51. Love, *Best of Rolling Stone,* 76.
52. Hearst and Moscow, *Patty Hearst,* 291–97.

CHAPTER 14 | COMING HOME

1. National Archives, Hearst interviews, April 12–13, 1976, 14; August 11, 1976, 8.
2. National Archives, Hearst interviews, August 27, 1976, 5–6.
3. Ibid., 6.
4. Jess Bravin, *Squeaky: The Life and Times of Lynette Alice Fromme* (New York: St. Martin's Press, 1997), 178.
5. Payne, Findley, and Craven, *Life and Death of the SLA,* 310.
6. National Archives, Hearst interviews, April 26, 1976, 1–2.
7. National Archives, Hearst interviews, April 19, 1976, 1; Hearst and Moscow, *Patty Hearst,* 303.
8. Steven Schwartz, "Thursday, February 20, 2003." http://www.frontpage.com.
9. "Michael Bortin," December 25, 2010, http://www.DiscovertheNetwork.com.
10. Hearst and Moscow, *Patty Hearst,* 304; Bridget's real name was Stephanie Lee Jones. National Archives, Hearst interviews, April 23, 1976, 1.
11. National Archives, Hearst interviews, April 26, 1976, 2–4.

12. Hearst and Moscow, *Patty Hearst,* 312–14. On March 1, 1975, a week after the Guild Savings and Loan Association robbery, Remiro and Little made a desperate attempt to escape the Alameda County jail. They were subdued after a brief but brutal fight. Ibid., 319–20; McLellan and Avery, *Voices of Guns,* 438–39.
13. National Archives, Hearst interviews, April 5, 1976, 1.
14. Ibid.
15. Ibid., 2.
16. Ibid.
17. Ibid., 4.
18. Ibid.
19. Ibid., 5; Hearst and Moscow, *Patty Hearst*, 318.
20. National Archives, Hearst interviews, April 13 and 15, 1976, 2.
21. Gary Delsohn, *The Prosecutors: A Year in the Life of a District Attorney's Office* (New York: Dutton, 2003), 33–34.
22. National Archives, Hearst interviews, April 12–13, 1976, 3.
23. Hearst and Moscow, *Patty Hearst*, 331.
24. Federal Bureau of Investigation (FBI), Bureau File No. 91-56075, Field Office File No. 91-7670, Sacramento, CA, May 14, 1975, 78 [hereafter FBI report].
25. Ibid., 68; Delsohn, *Prosecutors,* 33; Cosmo Garvin, "Obstruction of Justice," *Sacramento News and Review,* January 20, 2002, hhttp://www.newsreview.com.
26. FBI report, 83.
27. Ibid., 12, 74.
28. Ibid., 20.
29. Garvin, "Obstruction of Justice"; Delsohn, *Prosecutors,* 34.
30. FBI report, 85, 124.
31. National Archives, Hearst interviews, April 12–13, 1976, 4.
32. Ibid.
33. Hearst and Moscow, *Patty Hearst,* 332–33; National Archives, Hearst interviews, April 12–13, 1976, 5.
34. Hearst and Moscow, *Patty Hearst*, 333; National Archives, Hearst interviews, August 27, 1976, 8.
35. National Archives, Hearst interviews, April 12–13, 1976, 5.
36. Ibid.
37. Ibid., 6.
38. Ibid., 7; Hearst and Moscow, *Patty Hearst*, 335.
39. Hearst and Moscow, *Patty Hearst*, 335.
40. National Archives, Hearst interviews, April 12–13, 1976, 5.
41. FBI report, 155; Payne, Findley, and Craven, *Life and Death,* 312.
42. National Archives, Hearst interviews, April 23, 1976, 11–17.
43. Ibid., 18.
44. National Archives, Hearst interviews, April 12–13, 1976, 1.
45. National Archives, Hearst interviews, April 23, 1976, 10.

46. National Archives, Hearst interviews, August 27, 1976, 4.
47. National Archives, Hearst interviews, May 14, 1976.
48. Annie Nocenti and Ruth Baldwin, eds., *The High Times Reader* (New York: Nation Books, 2004), 49–51; Jack Scott, *Bill Walton: On the Road with the Portland Trail Blazers* (New York: Thomas Y. Crowell Publishers, 1976), xv–xviii; Michael Drosnan, "The Victims of the Hearst Hunt," *New Times,* May 2, 1975, 22.
49. National Archives, Randolph Hearst interview, File No. SF 7-855, October 11, 1977, 2.
50. Ibid., 2.
51. Ibid., 4.
52. Love, *Best of Rolling Stone.*
53. Ibid.
54. Ibid.; Richards Gid Powers, *Broken: The Troubled Past and Uncertain Future of the FBI* (New York: Free Press, 2004), 332; Payne, Findley, and Craven, *Life and Death of the SLA,* 313–14.
55. Love, *Best of Rolling Stone.*
56. Powers, *Broken,* 330.
57. Clarence M. Kelley and James Kirkpatrick Davis, *Kelley: The Story of an FBI Director* (Kansas City: Andrews, McMeel Publishers, 1987), 200.
58. Powers, *Broken,* 332.
59. Kelley and Kirkpatrick, *Kelley,* 220–21.
60. The new SLA or second team of the SLA (as it is called in this book) under the leadership of Bill Harris never actually used the name Symbionese Liberation Army.
61. Powers, *Broken,* 332; Love, *Best of Rolling Stone.*
62. Hendry, *Soliah,* 155–56; McLellan and Avery, *Voices of Guns,* 475–78.
63. Hearst and Moscw, *Patty Hearst,* 354; Bryan Burrough, *Days of Rage: America's Radical Underground, the FBI, and the Forgotten Age of Revolutionary Violence* (New York: Penguin Press, 2015), 341.
64. Hearst and Moscow, *Patty Hearst,* 351.
65. Ibid.
66. Ibid., 353–54; National Archives, Hearst interviews, April 23, 1976, 18; Burrough, *Days of Rage,* 340–41.
67. Burrough, *Days of Rage,* 341.
68. Howard Kohn and David Weir, "The Lost Year of the SLA," *Rolling Stone,* April 22, 1976.
69. Alexander, *Anyone's Daughter,* 100–101.
70. Payne, Findley, and Craven, *Life and Death of the SLA,* 320.
71. Ibid.; Michael Taylor, "Timothy Casey—S.F. Officer Who Cuffed Fugitive Patricia Hearst," *SFGate,* December 6, 2005.
72. McLellan and Avery, *Voices of Guns,* 481.
73. Ibid., 482.
74. Ibid., 481–83.

75. Ibid., 483.
76. Hearst and Moscow, *Patty Hearst,* 365.

CHAPTER 15 | END OF AN ERA

1. FBI, HEARNAP Files, document 2866, 10.
2. Powers, *Broken*, 333.
3. Ibid.
4. Lou Cannon, *Governor Reagan: His Rise to Power* (New York: Public Affairs, 2003), 157.
5. McLellan and Avery, *Voices of Guns,* 367.

BIBLIOGRAPHY

ARCHIVAL COLLECTIONS

Federal Bureau of Investigation, Washington, D.C., HEARNAP Files.

National Archives, Pacific Regional Branch Office, San Francisco/San Bruno, Record

Group 118, U.S Attorney's Files, Case File 810766. Accession Number 118-90-0002, boxes 1–7.

University of California, Los Angeles, UCLA Special Collections, Young (Charles E.)

Research Library, Collection 293, Mayor Tom Bradley Administrative Papers, 1973–1993.

NEWSPAPERS

Berkeley Barb
Los Angeles Times
Oakland Tribune
Sacramento Bee
San Francisco Chronicle

INTERVIEWS

Bancroft, David
Blackburn, Robert
Browning, James
Hallinan, Terrence
Harris, William

BOOKS

Alexander, Shana. *Anyone's Daughter: The Times and Trials of Patty Hearst.* New York: Viking Press, 1979.

Anderson, Terry H. *The Movement and the Sixties: Protest in America from Greensboro to Wounded Knee.* New York: Oxford University Press, 1995.

Anspacher, Carolyn, and Jack Lucey. *The Trial of Patty Hearst.* San Francisco: Great Fidelity Press, 1976.

Aptheker, Bettina. *The Trial of Angela Davis.* Ithaca, NY: Cornell University Press, 1999.

Austin, Curtis J. *Up Against the Wall: Violence in the Making and Unmaking of the Black Panther Party.* Fayetteville: University of Arkansas Press, 2006.

Ayers, Bill. *Fugitive Days: Memoirs of an Antiwar Activist.* Boston: Beacon Press, 2001.

Baker, Marilyn, and Susan Brompton. *Exclusive! The Inside Story of Patricia Hearst and the SLA.* New York: Macmillan, 1974.

Bamford, James. *The Puzzle Palace: A Report on America's Most Secret Agency.* New York: Penguin Books, 1983.

Beal, M. F., and Friends. *Safehouse: A Casebook Study of Revolutionary Feminism in the 1970's.* Eugene, OR: Northwest Matrix, 1976.

Belcher, Jerry, and Don West. *Patty/Tania.* New York: Pyramid Books, 1975.

Berger, Dan. *Outlaws of America: The Weather Underground and the Politics of Solidarity.* Oakland, CA: AK Press, 2006.

Berkowitz, Edward D. *Something Happened: A Political and Cultural Overview of the Seventies.* New York: Columbia University Press, 2006.

Boulton, David. *The Making of Tania Hearst.* London: New English Library, 1975.

Bravin, Jess. *Squeaky: The Life and Times of Lynette Alice Fromme.* New York: St. Martin's Press, 1997.

Brodie, Fawn M. *Thomas Jefferson: An Intimate History.* New York: W.W. Norton, 1974.

Browder, Laura. *Her Best Shot: Women and Guns in America.* Chapel Hill: University of North Carolina Press, 2006.

Brown, Scot. *Fighting for US: Maulana Karenga, the US Organization and Black Cultural Nationalism.* New York: New York University Press, 2003.

Bryan, John. *This Soldier Still at War.* New York: Harcourt Brace Jovanovich, 1975.

Burrough, Bryan. *Days of Rage: America's Radical Underground, the FBI, and the Forgotten Age of Revolutionary Violence.* New York: Penguin Press, 2015.

Califano, Joseph. *The Student Revolution: A Global Confrontation.* New York: W. W. Norton, 1970.

Cannon, Lou. *Governor Reagan: His Rise to Power.* New York: Public Affairs, 2003.

Choi, Susan. *American Woman.* New York: Perennial, 2003.

Cohen, Robert. *Freedom's Orator: Mario Savio and the Radical Legacy of the 1960s.* New York: Oxford University Press, 2009.

Cummins, Eric. *Radical: The Rise and Fall of California's Prison Movement.* Stanford, CA: Stanford University Press, 1994.

Davis, Angela. *An Autobiography.* New York: International Publishers, 1988.

Davis, Brian Joseph. *I, Tania.* Toronto: ECW Press, 2007.

DeBray, Regis. *Revolution in the Revolution?* New York: Grove Press, 1967.

Delsohn, Gary. *The Prosecutors: A Year in the Life of a District Attorney's Office.* New York: Dutton, 2003.

Dershowitz, Alan M. *The Best Defense.* New York: Vintage Books, 1983.

Diggins, John Patrick: *The Rise and Fall of the American Left.* New York: W. W. Norton, 1992.

Downs, Donald Alexander. *Cornell '69: Liberalism and the Crisis of the American University.* Ithaca, NY: Cornell University Press, 1999.

Dyerson, Mark, and J. A. Mangan, eds. *Sport and American Society: Exceptionalism, Insularity and Imperialism.* New York: Routledge, 2007.

Farber, David. *The Age of Great Dreams: America in the 1960s.* New York: Hill and Wang, 1994.

______. *Chicago '68.* Chicago: University of Chicago Press, 1988.

Felt, Mark. *The FBI Pyramid: From the Inside.* New York: G. P. Putnam's Sons, 1979.

Felt, Mark, and John O'Connor. *A G-Man's Life.* New York: Public Affairs, 2006.

Garment, Leonard. *Crazy Rhythm: From Brooklyn and Jazz to Nixon's White House, Watergate, and Beyond.* Cambridge, MA: Da Capo Press, 2001.

Gates, Daryl F., and Diane K. Shah. *Chief: My Life in the LAPD.* New York: Bantam Books, 1992.

Gilio, Maria Esther. *The Tupamaro Guerillas: The Structure and Strategy of the Urban Guerrilla Movement.* New York: Saturday Review Press, 1972.

Gitlin, Todd. *The Sixties: Years of Hope, Days of Rage.* New York: Bantam Books, 1993.

______. *The Whole World Is Watching: Mass Media and the Unmaking of the New Left.* Berkeley: University of California Press, 2003.

Goines, David Lance. *The Free Speech Movement: Coming of Age in the 1960s.* Berkeley, CA: Ten Speed Press, 1993.

Graebner, William. *Patty's Got a Gun: Patricia Hearst in 1970s America.* Chicago: University of Chicago Press, 2008.

Gray, L. Patrick, III, and Ed Gray. *In Nixon's Web: A Year in the Crosshairs of Watergate.* New York: Times Books, 2008.

Guevara, Che. *Guerrilla Warfare.* Lincoln: University of Nebraska Press, 1998.

Hearst, Patricia Campbell, and Alvin Moscow. *Patty Hearst: Her Own Story.* New York: Avon Books, 1988.

Hendry, Sharon Darby. *Soliah: The Sara Jane Story.* Bloomington, IN: Cable Publishing, 2002.

Horowitz, David. *Radical Son: A Generational Odyssey.* New York: Touchstone, 1997.

Howard, Clark. *Zebra: The True Account of the 179 Days of Terror in San Francisco.* New York: Richard Marek Publishers, 1979.

Huey, Lynda. *A Running Start: An Athlete, A Woman.* New York: Quadrangle/New York Times Book Co., 1979.

Jackson, George L. *Blood in My Eye.* Baltimore: Black Classic Press, 1990.

______. *Soledad Brother: The Prison Letters of George Jackson.* Chicago: Lawrence Hill Books, 1994.

Jeffreys-Jones, Rhodri. *The FBI: A History.* New Haven, CT: Yale University Press, 2007.

Jenkins, Phillip. *Decade of Nightmares: The End of the Sixties and the Making of Eighties America.* New York: Oxford University Press, 2006.

Jimenez, Janey, and Ted Berkman. *My Prisoner.* Kansas City: Sheed, Andrews, and McMeel, 1977.

Joseph, Peniel E., ed. *The Black Power Movement: Rethinking the Civil Rights–Black Power Era.* New York: Routledge, 2006.

Kelley, Clarence M., and James Kirkpatrick Davis. *Kelley: The Story of an FBI Director.* Kansas City: Andrews McMeel Publishers, 1987.

Kessler, Ronald. *The Bureau: The Secret History of the FBI.* New York: St. Martin's Paperbacks, 2003.

______. *The FBI.* New York: Pocket Books, 1993.

Kinney, Jean. *An American Journey: The Short Life of Willy Wolfe.* New York: Simon and Schuster, 1979.

Krassner, Paul. *Patty Hearst & the Twinkie Murders: A Tale of Two Trials.* Oakland, CA: PM Press, 2014.

Lester, John A. *Girl in a Box: The Untold Story of the Patricia Hearst Kidnap.* San Jose, CA: Shoestring Publications, 2004.

Lipsyte, Robert. *SportsWorld: An American Dreamland.* New York: Quadrangle/New York Times Book Co., 1975.

Love, Robert, ed. *The Best of the Rolling Stone: 25 Years of Journalism on the Edge.* New York: Doubleday, 1975.

Lukas, J. Anthony. *Nightmare: The Underside of the Nixon Years.* Athens: Ohio University Press, 1999.

Lunde, Donald T. *Hearst to Hughes: Memoir of a Forensic Psychiatrist.* Bloomington, IN: Authorhouse, 2007.

Magowan, Robin. *Looking for Binoculars: A Chronicle.* Santa Cruz, CA: Kayak, 1976.

Malcomson, Scott. *One Drop of Blood: The American Misadventure of Race.*

New York: Farrar, Straus and Giroux, 2000.
Marighella, Carlos. *Minimanual of the Urban Guerrilla.* St. Petersburg, FL: Red and Black Publishers, 2008.
McLellan, Vin, and Paul Avery. *The Voices of Guns.* New York: G. P. Putnam's Sons, 1977.
Nocenti, Annie, and Ruth Baldwin, eds. *The High Times Reader.* New York: Nation Books, 2004.
Ogbar, Jeffrey O. G. *Black Power: Radical Politics and African American Identity.* Baltimore: Johns Hopkins University Press, 2005.
Payne, Les, Tim Findley, and Carolyn Craven. *The Life and Death of the SLA.* New York: Ballantine Books, 1976.
Poveda, Tony G. *Lawlessness & Reform: The FBI in Transition.* Pacific Grove, CA: Brook/Cole Publishing, 1990.
Powers, Richard Gid. *Broken: The Troubled Past and Uncertain Future of the FBI.* New York: Free Press, 2004.
Rorabaugh, W. J. *Berkeley at War: The 1960s.* New York: Oxford University Press, 1989.
Sanders, Prentice Earl, and Bennett Cohen. *The Zebra Murders: A Season of Killing, Racial Madness, and Civil Rights.* New York: Arcade Publishing, 2006.
Schreiber, Brad. *Revolution's End: The Patty Hearst Kidnapping, Mind Control and the Secret History of Donald DeFreeze and the SLA.* New York: Skyhorse Publishing, 2016.
Schwartz, Steven. "Thursday, February 20, 2003." http://www.frontpage.com.
Scott, Jack. *The Athletic Revolution.* New York: Free Press, 1971.
______. *Bill Walton: On the Road with the Portland Trail Blazers.* New York: Thomas Y. Crowell Publishers, 1976.
Small, Melvin. *Antiwarriors: The Vietnam War and the Battle for America's Hearts and Minds.* Wilmington, DE: Scholarly Resources Inc., 2002.
Soltysik, Fred. *In Search of a Sister.* New York: Bantam Books, 1976.
Sorrentino, Christopher. *Trance.* New York: Farrar, Strauss and Giroux, 2005.
Spencer, John Palmer. *Caught in the Crossfire: Marcus Foster and America's Urban Education Crisis, 1941–1973.* New York: New York University Press, 2002.
Swanberg, W. A. *Citizen Hearst.* New York: Galahad Books, 1961.
Theoharis, Athan G., ed. *The FBI: A Comprehensive Reference Guide.* Phoenix: Oryx Press, 1999.
Thompson, Heather Ann, ed. *Speaking Out: Activism and Protest in the 1960s and 1970s.* Saddle River, NJ: Pearson Education, 2010.
Toobin, Jeffrey. *American Heiress: The Wild Saga of the Kidnapping, Crimes and Trial of Patty Hearst.* New York: Doubleday, 2016.
U.S. Congress. *The Symbionese Liberation Army.* Committee on Internal Security, 93rd Cong., 1974.

Varon, Jeremy. *Bringing the War Home. The Weather Underground, the Red Army Faction, and Revolutionary Violence in the Sixties and Seventies.* Berkeley: University of California Press, 2004.

Weed, Steven, and Scott Swanton. *My Search for Patty Hearst.* New York: Warner Books, 1976.

Welch, Neil, and David M. Marston. *Inside Hoover's FBI: The Top Field Chief Reports.* Garden City, NY: Doubleday, 1984.

Wilson, Major Carlos. *The Tupamaros: The Unmentionables.* Boston: Braden Press, 1974.

Zang, David W. *Sports Wars: Athletes in the Age of Aquarius.* Fayetteville: University of Arkansas Press, 2001.

ARTICLES

Deakin, Thomas J. "The Legacy of Carlos Maringhella." *FBI Law Enforcement Bulletin* 43 (October 1974): 19–25.

Drosnan, Michael. "The Victims of the Hearst Hunt." *New Times,* May 2, 1975, 14–23.

Elcombe, Tim. "Reform America: The Oberlin Experiment—The Limits of Jack Scott's Athletic Revolution in Post-1960s America." *International Journal of Sport* 22, no. 6 (2005): 1060–85.

Eskinazi, David. "Wayback Machine: Dr. Phil's Push for Justice." June 25, 2013. http://www.sportspressnw.com.

Garvin, Cosmo. "Obstruction of Justice." *Sacramento News and Review,* January 20, 2002. http://www.newsreview.com/sacramento.

Hoban, Phoebe. "Citizen Patty." *New York,* August 8, 1988, 29–36.

Isenberg, Nancy. "Not Anyone's Daughter: Patty Hearst and the Postmodern Legal Subject." *American Quarterly* 52 (December 2000): 639–81.

Kohn, Howard, and David Weir, "The Lost Year of the SLA." *Rolling Stone,* April 22, 1975. http://www.rollingstone.com.

______. "Tania's World: The Inside Story of the Patty Hearst Kidnapping, Part II: People in Need." *Rolling Stone,* November 20, 1975. http://www.rollingstone.com.

Lubinskas, James. "Remembering the Zebra Killings." August 30, 2001. http://97.74.65.51/readArticle.aspx?ARTID=21980.

Lunde, Donald T., and Thomas C. Wilson. "Brainwashing as a Defense to Criminal Liability." *Criminal Law Bulletin* 13 (September/October 1977): 341–82.

Lyne, Susan, and Robert Scheer. "Twenty Months with Patty/Tania." *New Times,* March 5, 1976, 18–36.

______. "The Story of the SLA: How and Why the Group Kidnapped Patty Hearst and Came to Be Urban Guerrillas." *New Times,* April 16, 1976, 26–36.

Morgan, Robin. "Why Should WE Care About Patty?" *MS,* March 1979,

60-61, 68, 73-75.

Taylor, Michael. “Timothy Casey—S.F. Officer Who Cuffed Fugitive Patricia Hearst.” *SF Gate,* December 6, 2005, http://www.sfgate.com.

Wellman, David, and Robert Fitzgerald. “The Appearance of Justice and the Advantages of State: The Process of Voir Dire in Political Trials.” *Contemporary Crises* 2 (1978): 373-405.

The Editors. “The Symbionese Liberation Army: Terrorism and the New Left.” *Ramparts* 12 (May 1974): 21-27.

DISSERTATION

Spencer, John Palmer. “Caught in the Crossfire: Marcus Foster and America’s Urban Education Crisis, 1941-1973.” PhD diss., New York University, 2002.

POLICE REPORT

Los Angeles Police Department. *The Symbionese Liberation Army in Los Angeles.* July 19, 1974.

FIGURES

Maggiora, Vincent. People’s Park confrontation. May 15, 1969. 2776px x 3423px. Polaris, 06162454, www.polarisimages.com.

Shames, Stephen. 1960s - demonstrations. 1970. 3021px x 2038px. Polaris, 04019568, www.polarisimages.com.

Press, Associated. Patty Hearst Case 1974. 1974. 3000px x 1652px. Associated Press, 687017236261, www.apimages.com.

Palmer, Jim. Sla Wheeler Tells his Story. December 31, 1975. 3300px x 2320px. Associated Press, 715409113816, www.apimages.com.

Press, Associated. Marcus Foster. April 1, 1970. 2140px x 3000 px. Associated Press, 7004010166, www.apimages.com.

Bettmann. Members of Symbionese Liberation Army in Handcuffs. March 13, 1974. 4255px x 2837px. Getty, 515112430, www.gettyimages.com.

Korody, Tony. Patty Hearst Kidnapping Case. 1974. 3543px x 5315px. Polaris, 05385228, www.polarisimages.com.

Bettmann. Family of Patty Hearst at News Conference. February 9, 1974. 3154px x 2920px. Getty, 515112396, www.gettyimages.com.

Albers, Clem. Patty Hearst Case. February 12, 1974. 1587px x 2391px. Polaris, 05786405, www.polarisimages.com.

Korody, Tony. Patty Hearst Kidnapping Case. February 25, 1974. 5116px x 3411px. Polaris, 05384627, www.polarisimages.com.

Press, Associated. Charles Bates, FBI. May 18, 1974. 3000px x 2433px. Associated Press, 7405180212, www.apimages.com.

Korody, Tony. Patty Hearst Kidnapping Case. April 1974. 3361px x 5008px. Polaris, 05384637, www.polarisimages.com.

Polaris. Patty Hearst Case. April 15, 1974. 1444px x 900px. Polaris, 05343509, www.polarisimages.com.

Korody, Tony. Patty Hearst Kidnapping Case. April 15, 1974. 3555px x 5339px. Polaris, 05385222, www.polarisimages.com.

Korody, Tony. Patty Hearst Kidnapping Case. May 17, 1974. 5392px x 3604px. Polaris, 05384885, www.polarisimages.com.

Rogers, Art. LA Police Raids SLA Hideout. May 17, 1974. 2863px x 1969px. Polaris, 05343537, www.polarisimages.com.

Press, Associated. May 19, 1974. 2593px x 2631px. Associated Press, 740519041, www.apimages.com.

Polaris. September 24, 1974. 1057px x 1544px. Polaris, 05343513, www.polarisimages.com.

Press, Associated. SLA Soliah. June 2, 1974. 1794px x 1992px. Associated Press, 7405010153, www.apimages.com

Press, Associated. Jack Scott. January 1, 1975. 2641px x 3000px. Associated Press, 77821031072, www.apimages.com.

Zeboski, Walter, J. Symbionese Army Arrests. October 30, 1975. 3300px x 2390px. Associated Press, 728986161835, www.apimages.com.

Mosur, Jakub. SLA Murder. November 8, 2002. 2200px x 1236px. Associated Press, 02110804414, www.apimages.com.

Bettmann. Patricia Hearst. September 18, 1975. 5528px x 3943px. Getty, 515403482, www.gettyimages.com.

INDEX